Management— The Essentials

Revised Printing

William E. Matthews
Christos M. Cotsakos College of Business
William Paterson University

KENDALL/HUNT PUBLISHING COMPANY
4050 Westmark Drive   Dubuque, Iowa 52002

WILLIAM E. MATTHEWS is an Associate Professor of Marketing and Management Sciences at the Christos M. Cotsakos College of Business at William Paterson University in Wayne, New Jersey. He teaches executive, graduate and undergraduate courses on management, project management, marketing management, and business, government and society. His research and consulting activities focus on strategic planning and the value (or otherwise) of widely taught management models. He received a B.Sc. in synthetic organic chemistry from King's College, University of Durham and his MBA and DBA from the Harvard University Graduate School of Business Administration.

Cover image from Digital Juice.

Copyright © 2005 by William E. Matthews

Revised Printing

ISBN 13: 978-0-7575-2402-8

Printed in the United States of America
10   9   8   7   6   5   4   3

CONTENTS

WORDS OF WISDOM ... OR OTHERWISE

OVERVIEW

Rather than beginning with a section entitled, "Introduction" (which, studies have shown, only one student in six and a half million actually reads), it makes more sense to begin by raising three questions:

- Where did the idea for this text come from?
- How should you use this text?
- What other insights do I have?

WHERE DID THE IDEA FOR THIS TEXT COME FROM?

To understand the genesis of this text, you have to go back and look at the typical management text and the interests of the three main parties (also known as stakeholders) with an interest in it, namely: the publisher, the instructor, and the students.

The Publisher

There are hundreds (if not thousands) of basic or fundamental management texts ... each with its own unique approach and characteristics. The vast majority consist of between sixteen and twenty chapters (to match the typical length of a semester) and are accompanied by a wide range of supplemental materials ranging from instructor's manual and student guides and test banks, experiential exercises, videos, team-building exercises, cases, and skills enhancement exercises to beautiful (if sometimes misleading) diagrams and charts dotted throughout the text to provide visual appeal and break up the monotony of the text.

The reason for this breath of offering (which is very impressive) is quite simple. Hard bound books are expensive to publish and substantial sales are not guaranteed. As a result, the publisher needs to put together a package of materials that will appeal to the widest audience. By providing as much supporting material as possible, they allow the instructor to "cherry pick" those aspects that he/she would like to emphasize.

The Instructor

From an instructor's viewpoint, this is great. If he/she likes to use videos then there are short videos on appropriate topics. If he/she believes that multiple choice questions actually measure anything of value, he/she can use those. These, and other components of a typical "package," certainly make the task of teaching the course much easier.

Invariably, at the end of the semester, the instructor tests the student's knowledge of the subject. What have they learned? Have they developed a meaningful understanding of the key

v

aspects of management? Can they use the basic tools and concepts to think through management issues? Are they prepared to move ahead to more specialized and complex areas of management?

The answer to these questions is often a depressing "no." A few will have developed a broad understanding but most will not have learned more than fragments of the whole. More frequently than one would wish, the instructor is forced to ask themselves a critical question: if I thought this point, concept or tool were important, why did less than ten percent of the class answer the question correctly on the final exam?

The Student

From the student's perspective, these texts pose problems because of the way the subject matter is presented. All the materials in a chapter appear to be of the same level of importance and the student is rarely in a position to judge whether they are critical or largely irrelevant. Furthermore, while some topics are reasonably easy to understand and can be understood with a superficial reading, others are quite complex and require in-depth investigation. Students are presented with the facts and left to their own ability to pull out the underlying ideas and concepts.

At the end of the course (irrespective of whether the student enjoyed it or felt they learned anything), the student often has little sense of the whole subject. Hopefully, they have learned a large number of facts.

HOW SHOULD YOU USE THIS TEXT?

The approach taken in this text is very different from that normally presented.

Each chapter begins with an *Overview* ... a statement of the topics that will be covered in the chapter. To simplify the process, I have made a decision as to what topics you should understand (within the broad framework of management) at the end of the course. Is my judgment correct? Not necessarily. Probably not. I'm sure that other instructors would make very different choices.

Wherever possible, I have de-emphasized the names of both individuals and models. Why? Because I suspect that, while they are very useful for creating multiple choice questions, memorizing them has little value. The ability to remember the title of Piggle and Wiggle's model is not overly useful if you can't remember what it was used for!!

Each chapter then consists of a series of topics ... and under each of these topics I have listed:

- A number of *Key Points* that you should know and understand.
- One or more *Examples* which, hopefully, will make the point more interesting and understandable.
- A series of short *Cases* with, at the end, a number of questions. The intent of these questions is to guide you to review the Key Points and see how you can apply them to the case.
- A brief *Summary* of the Chapter to refresh your understanding of the Key Points.
- Seven *Critical Thinking Questions* designed to get you to think outside the box. There are no right answers.
- A *Problem Case* (again with a series of questions) which attempts to bring together much of the material covered in the chapter.

The purpose of this text is not to dig deeply in any specific area. There are in-depth studies of all the topic areas covered by this introductory text. If, for example, you are specifically interested in the impact of technology or ethics and social responsibility, there are numerous volumes focusing on these subjects. The objective is to provide you with a baseline knowledge of the subject.

WHAT OTHER INSIGHTS DO I HAVE?

For your consideration, I have two additional insights:

- Management is a dynamic and fascinating subject.
- Successful managers can think and analyze!!

Management is a Dynamic and Fascinating Subject

Business is all around you. Even if you are an archaeologist or an astronomer (i.e., focused on history of the ancient world or the universe), you still live in a world that is driven by business. It doesn't matter if you are a business major (and plan to spend your life making your fortune) or a scientist (committed to discovering a cure for some rare disease), you will still be impacted throughout your life by business and what managers do within the framework of business.

Pick up any newspaper or magazine and you will see articles that relate to various aspects of the world around you. Leaf through any copy of *The New York Times, Business Week, The Wall Street Journal, Fortune, Forbes,* etc. and you will see article after article dealing with change or the threat of change. Virtually nothing stays the same for any long period of time. Companies come and go. Products come and go. Managers come and go. It is an ever changing world.

So, if management is a dynamic and fascinating subject, why do so many students reach the end of the basic management course with no greater enthusiasm than the fact they now have three more credits towards their degree. If you are an English major, this is unfortunate but not critical. If you are a business major with ten or twelve more management courses yet to complete, you are off to a bad start.

So, let's not screw it up!! The goal of this text is to get excited about the richness, diversity and the dynamic nature of the subject.

Successful Managers Can Think and Analyze!!

One of the problems with textbooks in general is that they ask a lot of questions but rarely give the reader any insights into how to answer them. For example, a question might ask:

> *Would you suggest that management introduce a Management by Objectives (MBO) program at this company?*

This question can be answered very simply with one of the following four responses.

- Yes.
- No.
- Don't know.
- Don't care.

Now, each of these certainly is an answer to the question. However, none of them is a particularly profound answer. They are better described as comments. They do not reflect any real management analysis. Certainly, nobody is going to pay you a great deal for this type of insight.

Let's look at the following pair of answers:

- Yes ... for the following four reasons.
- No ... for the following four reasons.

These are what can be called "supported conclusions." The individual answering the question has selected a conclusion and then supported their conclusion. This is better but it is still a comment not an analysis. So, let's go back to the question and see what, in fact, you are being asked:

> *What are the pros and cons of introducing a Management by Objectives (MBO) program at this company? And what would be your recommendation based on your analysis?*

This is what the person asking the question is looking for. The answer represents an analysis which demonstrates to him/her that you have looked at the question from a number of perspectives and that, based on this analysis, you have reached a specific conclusion or recommendation. Will the person who asked the question necessarily agree with your conclusion? No ... but they will be able to tell how you reached that conclusion (i.e., the steps in your decision making process).

And that, at the heart of things, is the nature of management. It is the study and analysis of multiple factors in a business environment and coming to a decision or recommendation that can be supported by your analysis.

MANAGERS: WHAT DO THEY DO?

OVERVIEW

Unfortunately, management (like parenthood) does not come with a well organized set of instructions. There is no book sitting on a shelf somewhere with the detailed answers to a manager's specific problems. It would be nice if there were ... but there isn't.

As a result, management is primarily a thought process. A first rate manager is not paid because he/she knows all the right answers. He/she is compensated for the ability to think through a situation, analyze it, and then propose and implement an optimal solution.

This chapter presents an overview of what managers do and why. You will become familiar with:

- The role of a manager.
- The four managerial functions.
- The various levels of management.
- The five managerial skills.

And, finally, we will look at:

- The evolution of management thought.

THE ROLE OF THE MANAGER

 Key Points:

1. There are a number of definitions of a manager. However, for the purpose of this text, let's define a manager as:

> *An individual who is responsible for the performance of the employees who report directly to him/her.*

The key elements in this definition are:

- Responsible ... they are the person who will be held to account if performance is unsatisfactory.
- Performance ... the quality of the activity required to satisfy a contract, promise, or obligation.
- Employees ... individuals compensated for their efforts to achieve the organization's goals.
- Report directly ... the relationship between the manager and his/her subordinates.

> **Example:** The president called me in to his office and charged me with getting the new warehouse ready for operations on May 31. However, I rapidly discovered that none of the people assigned to work on the warehouse actually reported directly to me. I had the responsibility of a manager but not the authority. So, I went back to the president and said, "if you want this warehouse ready by May 31, I need the following people." He looked at my list of requirements and said, "Fine. You're the manager."
>
> **Example:** "How's the wedding coming along, Mrs. Jones?" Almira Jones was talking with the cashier at the local supermarket about her daughter's upcoming wedding. "I'll be glad when she's on her honeymoon and I can go back to being a manager at G&H. I had forgotten how difficult it is to get something done when you don't have a secretary, an assistant, and a room full of staff. I took on the responsibility of organizing the wedding but I'm not managing it. I am just herding cats."

2. In even the simplest of organizations, there is a need for management. An organization will prosper only if somebody provides appropriate managerial and leadership skills. The key word is "appropriate." It has to be the right management at that point in time.

> **Example:** Brightwell Accounting consisted of Andrew Brightwell, two associates, and a secretary/receptionist/bookkeeper. While a competent accountant, Andrew's real skill lay in identifying and selling the firm's services. Having signed an engagement letter, he would pass the assignment on to his associates. Unfortunately, both his associates were newly minted CPAs and needed guidance and assistance. They received neither. And the lady who handled the secretarial/receptionist/bookkeeping role spent much of her time trying to track down Andrew to resolve problems. The firm was heading for disaster due to a lack of management.
>
> **Example:** Stephen Ascard, the president of Viscount Enterprises, was a first rate manager whose skill lay in keeping an operation moving smoothly. He was great at solving problems and resolving human resource issues. However, despite these skills, Viscount started to go steadily downhill. Eventually, the firm was acquired by another company which immediately replaced Ascard with a new president who was the exact opposite. He knew little or nothing about how to handle the day-to-day business but he was able to develop a vision for the company (i.e., where the company needed to be in five years time).

CASE 1.1

I AM HERE TO OBSERVE!!

"I always say to people that I have an 'open door' policy. I may not be in my office but the door is open. If people want to talk, I'm more than willing to listen."

Abe Falcone had been with Thomas Engineering for more than thirty years and was very rapidly approaching retirement. Having filled many senior positions in the organization, he was now the company's floating manager. "If they need a manager at the North Pole, I guess I'll be there," was his standard line. So, when the manufacturing plant in Roselle (Sydney, Australia) began to have serious quality control problems, management had Abe on the first flight out of San Francisco.

He spent the first few days meeting the people throughout the plant and becoming acquainted with the extent of the problems. He then held a series of meetings with the various departments and visited with the larger customers in the major cities.

After about ten days on the job, he was approached by two of the senior executives. "While we appreciate head office sending you out here, we still aren't too sure what your function or role is," they commented. "We have some serious problems and we need solutions ... and we need them soon. Are you here to evaluate the situation and make recommendations? If so, what are some of the recommendations you could make? Or do you have the authority to take whatever steps it takes to solve the problem?"

Abe sat silently for a moment. He was tempted to say that he was merely there to observe. After all, he was only supposed to be in Australia for a month or so. Then it would be back to San Francisco and retirement. However, he suddenly realized he was being asked a much more fundamental question.

Question: Is Abe functioning as a manager? If "yes" ... how? If "no" ... why not?

Question: What do you think the managers at the Roselle plant are looking for at this point in time?

Question: Can Abe be of any real assistance to the Roselle plant? Or should he cut short his visit and return to San Francisco?

THE FOUR MANAGERIAL FUNCTIONS

◎═→ Key Points:

1. Managers need to perform four (4) different functions, namely:

   - Planning ... determining the future directions and goals of the organization.
   - Organizing ... utilizing the human resources (i.e., the people) in the most efficient manner.
   - Leading ... motivating the personnel to achieve the organizations goals.
   - Controlling ... monitoring the actual performance of the organization (in terms of production, sales, profits, etc.) relative to the organization's goals and objectives.

> **Example:** "My typical day is more than full," Caroline Wehrmann explained. "Today, for example, I spent an hour or so working on a presentation to the board next month. They have asked me to evaluate whether we should sell one of our divisions. Then, I had interviews with a couple of applicants for a key position. Next, I had a meeting with my department heads to find out what they were doing. I need to know what is happening in their areas. It is more motivational than anything else. Then, I had a long meeting with both financial and manufacturing people to review where we actually stand compared to where we thought we would be. That meeting has just ended. Being a manager is a full time job."

2. *Planning* ... this is the function that answers three "do you know" questions:
Do you know:

   - Where you are now?
   - Where you are going?
   - How you are going to get there?

   If the answer to these questions is "no" then the chances of getting from here to there aren't very good!! A company needs to know where it is now, where it wants to be at some future point in time, and how it is going to get there.

> *Important note: This is equally true for an individual as it is for organizations.*

> **Example:** "Our long range plan calls for us to be number one in this business. So, I asked the group: what share of the market do we currently have? Nobody knew. So, I asked: what do you mean by being number one? 'Being larger than the company which everybody thought was number one' was as close as I got to an answer. I didn't bother to ask how we were going to get there!!"
>
> **Example:** "When I was in college in the 60s, I sat down and wrote out my goals and objectives. I wanted to work in the plastics industry. I set a goal of being wealthy and of traveling extensively. And I wanted to be married with at least three children. By writing things down, I provided myself with a road map. I'm retiring a wealthy man after years in the plastics industry and I've traveled to virtually every country in the world. And I have six great kids. Unfortunately, I have had to endure four wives and three divorces in the process.

3. *Organizing* ... this second function of a manger focuses on its human resources. Every organization has people resources. Here the key questions are:

- How do we make the most out of the existing personnel?
- How do we organize them to create the most favorable results?

> **Example:** The high school football coach was complaining to another teacher following the first full pre-season practice. "Each year, I am faced with the same problem. Runners who can't catch. Quarterbacks who can't move and blockers who can't block." "And each year, you have a winning season," his colleague replied. "You're the team manager. You make the most of what you've got. You assign them to positions where you think they can have the most impact."
>
> Rarely does an organization have a perfect team. It has people with strengths and weaknesses. So, the next question becomes:

- How do we add new people who will bring additional skills and capabilities to the organization?

> **Example:** "I've just come back from a visit to Salem Labs. and I must say their place seems much more alive and productive. We both have about twenty research chemists so why the difference? My gut feeling is that the difference lies in the leadership and the technology. I think we have to find some new people and invest in up-to-date equipment."

4. *Leading* ... a manager on his/her own cannot achieve the organization's goals. In most cases, they can only accomplish goals through others and thus they need to be able to influence others to achieve the selected goals and objectives. Here, the keys questions are:

- How do you lead somebody?
- How do you motivate them?

Or, in other words, how do you make them enthusiastic about the future of the organization and their role in it?

> **Example:** "When I took over this operation, the general atmosphere was functional but unenthusiastic. So, I went around and talked with the people. What I learned was that they didn't see the advantages of working any harder. My first step was to introduce a bonus program. Then, I set up a quarterly competition. Finally, I offered rewards for suggestions. Within a short period of time, the group was motivated and we were starting to develop some new and challenging goals and objectives."

5. *Controlling* ... the fourth critical role of a manager is to control his/her operation. This involves regularly monitoring where the company stands relative to where it should be in terms of three key areas:

- People.
- Accounting and financial data.
- Production volume and quality.

An effective manager needs to have (and use) the appropriate tools for controlling each of these aspects of the operation.

Example: "We have exactly the same number of people today as we did ten years ago. That's good since our volume has more than doubled. However, I conducted a survey recently and found that 45% of the workforce is planning to retire in the next three years. Also, we only have one person who is skilled using a laser cutter and he's out sick. It suddenly struck me that we've failed to keep track of our people resources."

Example: "Each week, I focus on three key pieces of information. First, how much did we sell (in terms of number of units and dollars)? Second, what was the gross margin (i.e., the profit after accounting for all direct costs associated with making and selling the product) on these sales? Finally, what is our current cash position? With good information on each of these items, I can feel comfortable that I know what is going on in this business."

Example: "This is a manufacturing business and, as far as I am concerned, the critical factor is: how many units did we produce per machine during the shift. If the number is on target, I'm happy. If it is more than the target, I start to worry about increased maintenance costs. And, if it is way below target, I go ballistic. However, I am also concerned about the quality of the product so I watch that like an eagle. If it starts to slip ... I pounce."

---

6. *Important note:* Not all managers perform all four roles to the same degree. Generally speaking, different functions are important at different points in time.

Example: When Max Bastin was appointed president of Kabel Industries, he found the situation very different from what he had expected. "I thought they'd hired me for my strategic planning skills and that was where I planned to start. However, I soon found out that the critical problem lay in the control area. So I spent about six months resolving those problems. Once I had that under control, I found myself spending most of my time leading and motivating the employees. No sooner did I feel comfortable with that, than I had to deal with an organizational problem that took up much of my time. In the end, I had been with Kabel for nearly two years before I got around to doing any planning at all."

CASE 1.2

PASCORE MANUFACTURING

> *"And to my nephew, Andrew Brown, I leave the stock and assets of Pascore Manufacturing. May he make a success of it."*

Since Andrew Brown hadn't expected to inherit anything from Uncle Bob [Pastore], his visit to the Pastore plant in downtown Cleveland was an enlightening experience.

After ringing the bell and waiting more than five minutes in the empty reception area, he went through the swinging doors into the plant. As he wandered around, a couple of people said "good morning" but nobody took much notice of him. So, knocking on the door of the first office that was occupied, he explained that he was Bob Pastore's nephew and the new owner. "Who has been in charge in Uncle Bob's absence?" he asked.

"I'm the production manager," Allan Scarfe replied. "It used to be our sales manager but he resigned a couple of months back. His assistant, Robin, has been keeping in touch with our customers and handling the materials purchasing. Michael Tomes handles the bookkeeping but he's only in on Thursday and Friday. And the manager of engineering retired last year and hasn't been replaced. Marion, Mr. Pastore's secretary, normally coordinates everything but she's having a hip replacement. So, I guess I'm in charge."

"We have some good people. They are getting a little old but they're very loyal and do a good job. And we are only running about a third of capacity. As soon as each shift ends, we pack the output and send it out. It's a very steady business. We have a very good reputation in terms of the parts we produce. Some of our customers get uptight when we send them a batch that doesn't meet specifications ... but we can handle that."

"I can't say if the company is profitable. Mr. Pastore and Mr. Tomes were the only people who saw the figures. We all get paid regularly and, each year, Mr. Pastore gave us each a substantial bonus. So, we'll certainly miss him."

Question: How would you describe Bob Pastore's apparent style of management?

Question: What do you see as the strengths and weaknesses of Pastore Manufacturing?

Question: In terms of the four functions of management, what would you do first if you were Andrew Brown?

THE VARIOUS LEVELS OF MANAGEMENT

Key Points:

1. Managers are generally divided into three main levels, namely:

   ■ First-level managers (e.g., supervisors, office managers, and crew chiefs).
   ■ Middle-level managers (e.g., branch managers, project leaders, and department heads).
   ■ Top-level managers (e.g., the chairman of the board, the president, and the senior vice presidents of the various functional areas).

   > **Example:** "I joined the company straight out of high school. My first job was digging a drainage ditch. Then, after a time, they made me the supervisor of a construction group. It was about then that I started going to college and, when I graduated, they moved me back East to take over as a branch manager. After that, I was in charge of a larger branch, then a network of five small branches. Then, they made me a regional manager. And, eventually, I took over as head of operations. There is talk of me moving up to the corner office next year. Not bad for a former ditch digger."

2. *First-level managers* ... these are individuals who oversee or supervise the activities of personnel such as assemblers, word processors, customer service representatives, etc.

   They are most often people who themselves started out as assemblers, word processors or customer service representatives who, because of their experience at doing the specific job, were promoted to a first level managerial or supervisor position. Their primary responsibility is to ensure the smooth day-to-day functioning of the personnel they supervise.

   > **Example:** "I used to operate one of the ten ton presses. It wasn't an exciting job but the pay was good. I spent three years doing that. Then, the boss asked if I would be the acting supervisor of the line. That involved walking up and down making sure that all presses were running smoothly, that the operators had everything they needed, etc."

3. *Middle-level managers* ... of the three levels of managers, middle-level managers are the most diverse since their role depends very much on the nature of the organization. As a result, they vary dramatically in terms of their responsibility.

   Some middle-level managers start out on the lowest rung of the organization, become first-level manager, and then move upwards to more senior middle-level management positions. Others enter middle-level management through a training program or as a result of their educational background.

Their responsibilities lie in between those of a first-level manager and a top-level manager in that they:

- Oversee the activities of the personnel who report to them.
- Provide direction and leadership to their specific area of responsibility.
- Act as an important linkage between the top-level management and the first-level managers.

Example: Paxton Industries had a policy that was strictly applied. If you wanted a career with the company, you had to start at the bottom. That meant that you had to work in the stockroom filling orders. You reached a middle level management position only after a number of years of steadily moving upwards. The belief was that only employees who had experience in every aspect of the business could be successful.

Example: Linwood & Sons followed exactly the opposite approach. While many mid-managers did come up from the ranks, they also looked outside the company and brought in highly skilled individuals with a reputation in the industry. Management believed that bringing in new blood was one way of maintaining the dynamic nature of the company.

Example: "One of the main changes I experienced when they made me department head was that I was now one level away from the front line people. I found it hard to get used to explaining to a manager or a supervisor what I wanted him/her to tell their people to do. I also discovered that I was now responsible for communicating with senior management and that they were relying on me for insights into what was happening at the lower levels of the organization."

---

4. *Top-level managers* ... these are the senior personnel within the organization and have most of the authority and power.

   Senior managers are either promoted from the ranks of middle-level managers based on their performance and expertise or are brought in from outside organizations because of past success at providing specific skills and capabilities.

   Their responsibility is to provide direction to the organization as a whole, to interface with other organizations, and coordinate the overall activities of the company. They do not normally become involved in day-to-day operations.

Example: "I used to pride myself on being able to operate every piece of equipment in the plant. Now, as president of this operation, I'd be hard pressed to find some of our plants. My role is to provide overall direction to the company. I have to rely on others for the handling of day-to-day operations."

Example: "When I was a supervisor and middle-level manager, I used to spend my days talking with people who I knew well. Most of my time involved being inside the organization. When I was appointed to a top level position with the organization, I found myself increasingly spending time outside the organization talking with customers, stock analysts, trade associations, etc. Last month, I only spent four days at home."

5. *Important note:* Many managers find it extremely difficult to adjust when promoted to a higher management level. In fact, they have a tendency to continue to do much of their previous job because they understand it and feel comfortable with it.

> **Example:** As a life insurance agent, Susan Cameron really enjoyed working with her clients. She knew them, their families, their financial situations, etc. Then, when she was promoted to department manager, her role changed dramatically. Her two main responsibilities were to accompany new agents on calls to potential clients and to review the paper work submitted by her agents. She hated both tasks and found them unrewarding. As a result, she maintained contacts with her own clients rather than handing them over to her agents. After six months of this, she resigned and went back to being an agent . . . a role she enjoyed.

CASE 1.3

MARKHAM PROPERTY SYSTEMS

According to Roger Hayes, only two things can kill you in business: failure and success. In his case it was the latter. He was just too good.

Roger joined RJP Properties as a property manager on the Wilson I Building. He looked after the tenants, maintained the building, and ensured that all the mechanical systems worked well. The tenants loved him and, within six months, he was made a senior property manager responsible for Wilson I and II. He did a great job.

Two years later, the manager of the department resigned and Roger was the logical choice to take over. He was no longer in charge of just the two buildings but seven property managers. He spent his days visiting each of the managers and ensuring that they did a good job. However, his primary interests were the buildings. And, when there was a fire at one building at 3:00 a.m., he was the one on-site working with the fire department.

A further three years on, the general manager left to take a position with one of the national chains, the director of property management took his position, and Roger moved up to the director role. Due to the rapid growth in the marketplace, the major function of the director was selling and promoting the company's services and interacting with the other four directors. Roger found himself essentially isolated from the practice of property management. He rarely visited any of the company's managed properties.

So, when a local property owner approached Roger with the opportunity to manage two high rise buildings in the Waterford Creek area, he jumped at it. He was back managing properties under the name Markham Property Systems. Again, he did a very good job. The same client asked him to take over two more buildings. Roger hired an associate. Eventually, Roger found himself responsible for twenty of the client's buildings and running a staff of eight property managers and ten administrative personnel. In fact, after a time, Roger had to hire an assistant general manager because he was spending so much of his time talking to potential clients about managing their properties.

Question: What happened to Roger Hayes? And why?

Question: What does Roger's experience say about the nature of the skills needed at different levels of an organization?

Question: Recognizing that different positions call for different skills, how would you handle the career of somebody like Roger who was an outstanding property manager?

THE FIVE MANAGERIAL SKILLS

🔑 Key Points:

1. The five (5) key managerial skills can be characterized as:

   - Technical skills ... the ability to do a specific task (e.g., write a report or handle a welding torch) particularly well.
   - Interpersonal skills ... an individual's ability to communicate and work with other people and develop an effective team.
   - Conceptual skills ... the ability to see the organization as a whole and visualize its future.
   - Diagnostic skills ... an individual's ability to look at a problem and develop a solution.
   - Political skills ... the ability to pull together allies and supporters to achieve the organization's goals.

   > **Example:** "I find myself having to wear so many hats as a manager. On the one hand, I need to be able to understand what the manufacturing people are talking about (technical skills). I also need to be able to get along well with everybody in the division (interpersonal skills). In addition, now that I am the head of this division, I need to be able to look at it as a total entity (conceptual skills) rather than at the marketing or manufacturing part alone. When we have problems, I need to step in, analyze the problem, and then come up with a solution (diagnostic skills). Finally, from time to time I find myself in a political struggle with other people—both within the division and throughout the company—and I have to be able to hang on to my power and not see it eroded by others (political skills). Being a manager is a tough job."

2. *Technical skills* ... these are the skills that relate to activities that involve methods, processes, procedures and techniques and they can range from a financial analysis to the development of a project schedule. It is the ability to do something specific particularly well.

   > **Example:** Martin Brocklehurst, a professor at a prestigious university, was asked how he managed to turn out so many articles that were published in the leading journals in his field. "Very simple. I do the research, which I enjoy and am good at. Then, I hand the material over to one of my colleagues, who isn't very motivated doing research but is extremely good at creating publishable articles. I do what I'm good at. He does what he's good at."

   > **Example:** The new equipment (an XVD multi-amplitude resostifier) was ready for its trial run and Stuart McNally, the line supervisor, pushed the button bringing the $2 million machine to life. Standing next to him, the manager of the department, Hale Scala, asked, "how does it work again?" "Well," Stuart explained. "The directed inflow manifold produces a consistent yet multi-directional stream of particles which interact with the guidance parameters to ..." Hale interrupted. "Never mind ... as long as one of us knows how it works, that's fine."

3. *Interpersonal skills* ... this is the individual's ability to communicate with and work with others to build a highly effective team.

   As we will see later in this text, this is an increasingly important skill as downsizing (i.e., the elimination of levels within the organization to cut costs) has resulted in fewer people available to handle tasks and thus the increased need for a number of individuals to work as groups.

Example: Wendy Tolbert, head of the advertising department, assigned Arlene and Katrina to work on an advertising campaign for Pure Brands. However, within weeks, it became clear that the relationship wasn't working. The client complained about both the lack of progress and the attitude of the two towards his personnel. While both Arlene and Katrina were very good at their job, they could be very aggressive. Wendy met with both women individually and held a joint meeting to discuss the problem. By highlighting the basic problems and addressing each woman's concerns, she was able to get them working together as a team ... to the satisfaction of the client.

Example: "Can you talk with the client? He's crazy and he's driving me nuts." Normally, Arthur tried to keep out of such disagreements between sales and their clients. However, in this case, the client was extremely important. So, after a full internal briefing, he called the client and set up an appointment. For the better part of an hour, the client ranted and raved. Eventually, he calmed down and Arthur expressed his understanding of the client's concerns and began laying out the details of the problem and the steps that could be taken to resolve them. A potentially serious situation had been defused.

---

4. *Conceptual skills* ... these are the skills that enable an individual to see and understand the organization as a whole and how the various elements depend on each other. The ability to recognize the relationship between the company and its external environment (i.e., its industry, its competitors, its customers, etc.).

   As an individual moves up the organization into senior management, this becomes an increasingly important skill for two reasons. First, top management are the ones most likely to be involved in terms of the external environment. Second, the environment changes so rapidly that failure to recognize and respond to these changes can be fatal.

Example: The sales person and his manager were adamant. "We need to increase the price to $1.45 per pound and make a good profit on this order and thus improve our overall profit margin for the year." As division head, Miles certainly understood their position. Profit margins were heading downwards and individual bonuses would be negatively affected. "While I understand your position, I have to take a rather broader perspective. Carter Chemicals has a new plant coming on stream next year and they are already looking for business. If we increase our price to $1.45, we may make a profit on this order and probably lose a major, long-term customer. We'd be giving them a reason to change horses. And I don't want to do that. In fact, it may well be in our best interest to reduce our price to $1.30 and sign a long-term contract."

Example: "We have an opportunity to hire Piet van Brogen. He'd be the ideal person to take over the Latin American operations when our current manager retires in two years time. The problem is that, while he's very good, he's also very expensive ... and we don't have a position for him now. If we bring him on board, it is going to cost us about $800,000 over the next two years having him waiting in the wings. On the other hand, long-term, we will have the right person for a very important area of expansion."

5. *Diagnostic skills* ... in all organizations, not everything goes according to plan so it is important to be able to analyze a situation and develop a plan of action to resolve the problem.

   This is an especially useful skill in a middle-level management position because it demonstrates an ability to identify, analyze, and resolve problems that, if unresolved, would have a serious impact on the success of the organization.

Example: "I have our dealer in Copenhagen on the line. They have just cracked the lens on their AV-5000. What shall we do?" Rose Lindsey looked up at the service manager. "What do you think we should do?" For the next fifteen minutes the service manager worked his way around to the conclusion that Rose had immediately determined, namely: take the lens off the AV-5000 in the showroom (a machine that was only demonstrated every week or so) and ship that to Copenhagen and ask headquarters to ship a replacement part to replace the one in the showroom. Problem solved.

Example: The heated discussion had been going on for nearly two hours and the group was no closer to a decision than it had been when it started. The manager stood up. "Look folks, we are going round in circles here. So, let me add some structure. We have three alternative courses of action: A, B, and C. I've listed the pros and cons of each on these three flip charts. So, which way do we go?" The provision of structure and analysis enabled the group to make a decision.

6. *Political skills* ... because of society's general distrust of politicians, the term has a rather negative connotation. The reality, however, is that an individual manager cannot achieve everything on their own. Managers need allies and supporters to reach the desired objec-

tives. So, political power is the ability to pull together individuals, groups and coalitions in a way that gives the manager the power to be effective.

Example: "Top management will never agree with you to shut down the Risdon plant. There is too much history tied up in that place. After all, that's where the company started." Corey Scott recognized the validity of that argument. Alone, she would never gain approval to close down that facility. So, she talked with the head of finance and got his agreement on the economic benefits of the move. She had lunch with the head of manufacturing and presented cost data on the long-term advantages of a new plant. She met with the head of human resources and developed a plan for the employment of personnel made redundant by the closure of the plant. By the time, she made her presentation to top management; she already had a majority of the members on her side.

Example: "When I proposed that we acquire Joss-Blythe, I discovered that there were three individuals in the company who were firmly against the acquisition and, if it went to a straight vote, I would be defeated. So, I met with each of them in turn to try to discover the specific reasons behind their opposition. One of them thought it would take the company in the wrong direction. Another felt it would overstretch our financial capabilities. And the third was concerned that the acquisition would threaten her long-term position with the company. So, I did my best to address these concerns. When the matter came up for a vote, I wasn't faced with strong opposition from any of them.

---

7. *Important note:* Different situations require a different mix of skills. Rarely does a manager have all five key managerial skills in equal amounts. Most tend to be very good at one or two and thus need to reinforce their position by others with complementary skills. It is also important, in an organizational sense, to determine which skills are required at a specific point in time. A short time later, the situation may well have changed and a different set of skills may be required.

Example: "My undergraduate degree was in engineering. So, I feel comfortable with issues that involve understanding processes and numbers (technical and analytical skills). I don't claim to be a "big picture guy" so I hired somebody who was ... and we worked together on that. Then, when it came to gaining acceptance of the game plan, I worked with another of my managers who was known for his interpersonal and political skills. I know where I am strong. However, I also know where I'm not so effective and need help and assistance."

Example: "When I took over this company, I spent a month going around and talking with people. What I was trying to do was understand the problems (using my analytical skills). Then, having that step, I worked on developing a long range strategy (using my conceptual skills). Then, I spent quite a bit of time selling this plan of action to the board (using my limited political skills). They bought into the plan ... and I was stuck with making it work (which required extensive use of my interpersonal skills). My technical skill ... I still don't have any."

CASE 1.4

JOSIAH BARTLEY & SONS

Josiah Bartley & Sons was a downtown Chicago retail menswear store. Founded in the early part of the 20th century, it had a reputation for high quality, high priced products. Over the years, competition became increasingly intense both from other department stores downtown and from the growing number of upscale suburban malls.

For the past few years, the store had been run by Thomas Bartley, the fourth generation of the family. However, he was looking to retire and hand on the business to the next generation. The good news was that his three children (Brad, Lex, and Mara) were all very bright and well educated. The bad news was that they did not get along and thus his optimal solution—having them run the operation as a team—wasn't a viable option.

Brad was the one who was best at looking at the overall big picture. He was also the most capable when it came to developing detailed plans and budget projections. However, he could be very abrasive in dealing with people. He didn't communicate too well and seemed to lack a great deal of political savvy.

Lex was the exact opposite. He got along well with everyone and was a born salesman. However, while he was good at taking a specific project and working out solutions, he was not too good at looking at broader issues.

Mara was the youngest and the quietest. She was fascinated by figures and would spend hours doing projections and plans. However, organizing and directing others was not something she felt comfortable doing.

Question: How would you rank the importance of the five managerial skills in terms of the future of Bartley & Sons?

Question: Which of the three children would be best suited to take over the company?

Question: Stepping "outside the box," what alternative solutions to Thomas Bartley's problems can you come up with?

THE EVOLUTION OF MANAGEMENT THOUGHT

1. Over the past one hundred and fifty years, there have been a number of different ways in which researchers have looked at organizations and how they function. The different approaches can be combined into six (6) stages in the development of management thought, namely, the:

   ■ Scientific . . . the application of the scientific method (observation and analysis) to business operations.

   ■ Administrative . . . placing the emphasis on the organization of people to maximize their effectiveness.

   ■ Human resources . . . the realization that organizations consisted of people (with their own interest, goals, and objectives) and that they could be influenced to achieve the organization's goals.

   ■ Quantitative . . . the application of modeling, statistics, linear programming, etc. to business problems (especially utilizing the power of computers).

   ■ Systems perspective . . . the realization that organizations (and their component parts) did not operate in a vacuum and that they had to be considered as part of a far broader system.

   ■ Contingency . . . the appreciation of the complexity of management and the need to develop strategies and actions consistent with the unique environment and features facing each and every organization.

   If you can remember the names . . . fantastic. More important is that you understand:

   ■ What led up to (or caused) each of these steps.

   ■ When approximately, they occurred,

   ■ What they involved.

2. *The Scientific Approach* . . . the first approach to understanding management and organizations came about following the industrial revolution (the period from 1750 to 1830 that transformed the United Kingdom—and other countries of the world—from an agricultural society to a town-centered society engaged in manufacturing) and it reflected the interests of scientists who applied the scientific methods (i.e., observation . . . formulation of a hypothesis . . . use of the hypothesis to predict other results . . . and experimental testing) to business operations.

   The primary emphasis of this approach was on increased productivity. This was a period in which the demand for products was beginning to increase rapidly and the question was: how can we produce more using the same equipment and the same workers? Some of the key researchers in this field were Frederick W. Taylor, Henry Gantt, and Frank and Lillian Gilbreth.

   > **Example:** "Whenever, one of the assemblers runs out of parts, he/she has to get up, walk all the way across the floor, grab a basket and fill the basket with parts, and then walk all the way back. They generally stop off at the candy machine and visit the restroom on the way. Some of the assemblers take up to twenty minutes . . . and, if they do that three times a day, they are losing an hour per day of productivity. That is not efficient."

> **Example:** A group of students was touring a local firm that manufactured metal tables and chairs. At the end of the tour, they were asked to write a report on what they had observed. One student focused on the flow of production through the plant. "It doesn't make sense to me. The parts inventory is in the wrong area. The completed products have to be pushed in a wide loop to get to the painting operation. And the shipping office is at the other end of the building from the shipping dock. I think this plant could be much more effective if they redesigned their layout."

3. ***The Administrative Approach*** ... at around the same time as the scientific method, business people and researchers started to look at the question of how the workers could best be organized and what rules they could develop to maximize this effectiveness. Again, the primary emphasis was on increasing productivity.

   In many cases, managers were dealing with immigrants who had limited English-language skills and thus they saw it advantageous to break jobs down in relatively small and simple elements. They weren't particularly concerned about the employees as about ways of organizing them more effectively. Some of the key researchers adopting this approach were Henri Fayol and Max Weber.

> **Example:** The assembly lines consisted of twenty-four positions each producing three units per hour or 24 units per day. Ira Levine did the calculation and immediately concluded that there was no way the company could fill the contract by the end of the month using the current methods. The solution lay in establishing three teams of eight and breaking the assembly task into eight steps with each person doing just one step. Henry Ford did the same thing back in 1908.
>
> **Example:** "Virtually every member of our workforce these days is either Korean or Vietnamese. Unfortunately, I don't speak either language. For a time I tried to communicate through the foremen. However, that resulted in all sorts of problems. So, last year, I analyzed the jobs and broke them down into a number of steps each of which I could demonstrate by signs and movements. I think it made the job rather boring for the workers but they are making far fewer mistakes.

4. ***The Human Resources Approach*** ... while it was not until the 1930s that the Human Resources Approach came into favor, there were earlier individuals who were concerned about the human aspect of their operations. They believed not only that they had a responsibility to the people working for them but that concern for the workers resulted in increased profitability. Robert Owen and Mary Parker Follett were among the leading researchers in this area.

Example: Beginning in 1924, a series of experiments were carried out at Western Electric's Hawthorne Plant in Cicero, Illinois. One of the earliest was to determine the impact of different levels of lighting on the productivity of the workers. As one might have predicted, productivity increased as the level of lighting increased. However, what was surprising was that the level of productivity increased as the level of lighting decreased. There clearly had to be another factor at work ... and the only variable was the workers themselves. They enjoyed being part of the experiment since they received a lot of attention. The conclusion was that productivity could be influenced by focusing on the interests and concerns of the workers.

Example: While Fensham Distribution was a good place to work, the boss, Harry Fensham was very rarely around. In fact, most of the employees wouldn't have recognized him. When he passed the business on to his son, Alex, who walked around the building at least once every day. He would stop and ask questions and joke with the employees. "I am new at this. I want to know what is going on and how I can make things better," he commented. The overall morale of the operation went up considerably as did productivity.

5. **The Quantitative Approach** ... while this approach had its origins back in the early days of scientific and administrative management (collectively known as the classical approach), it became increasingly important during World War II (1938-1945) when techniques such as modeling, statistics, linear programming, and decision tree analyses were used to solve a large number of complex problems faced by the military. Following the war, there was a growing interest in, and usage of, large main frame computers which allowed researchers to carry complex calculations. The introduction and growth of the personal computer in the late '70s and early '80s further stimulated the use of quantitative techniques.

Example: "What will happen to our sales in the southeast region if we increase the price from $1.20 per bottle to $1.27?" Historically, the answer would have been: your guess is as good as mine. However, the company had the advantage of a very sophisticated mathematical model which immediately gave the answer: a 2.3% decline in sales. The model also instantly calculated the impact on revenues and bottom line profitability.

Example: "When I first got into the oil drilling business, you dug a well and hoped it wasn't dry. If it was dry at 5,000 feet, you had a critical question: do we continue digging or move on to the next site? You could look at the geological map but it was largely guesswork. Then, they came along with decision tree analysis that looked at the probability that the well was dry and the wisdom of continuing. That really changed the way we evaluated our risks."

6. **The Systems Perspective** ... this approach emerged (in the mid-1960s) out of the growing realization it did not make sense to continue to look at departments and divisions as separate entities (as had been done in the past). It became increasingly apparent that changes in one area of a company invariably impacted on others.

Furthermore, as organizations continued to grow and expand, it was realized that they did not function in a vacuum. It was clear that an organization was not a closed system but one which interfaced with numerous external forces and that one needed to look at the organization as an open system taking into consideration the external environment.

Example: "We always regarded the company as a number of separate divisions that reported to the chief executive officer. It was his job to pull everything together. Then, we introduced a new line of products for which we had very high hopes ... and it didn't sell. So, we talked to the sales people and it rapidly became apparent that the problem was that the product was too complex and sophisticated for the customer. They wanted something cheaper and simpler. The sales people had been saying this all along ... and nobody was listening."

Example: "Our original plant was located in Springfield, Ohio. All we had to deal with was the production from this one plant and the local rules and regulations. Then, we opened plants in California and Texas. These were followed by new facilities in Australia, India, Italy, Japan and, most recently, in Mexico City and Taiwan. Now, we have to coordinate production worldwide and deal with a multitude of different governments and their unique rules and regulations. It is a complex open system."

---

7. *The Contingency Approach* ... up until the 1980s, much of the emphasis was placed on identifying one best approach to handle both people and the working environment. However, people began to realize that no single approach fitted all situations. What worked very well in one case was notably ineffectual in another. This led to the realization that the appropriate course of action depended upon the specific characteristics of the situation, specifically, the:

- Size of the organization.
- Degree to which the tasks and the technology are routine.
- Degree of uncertainty in the environment.
- Individual goals and objectives.

Example: "Working for a *Fortune 500* company gives you a sense of security. Tasks were divided among a number of skilled individuals. You monitored what went on in the external world and you pursued goals and objectives set by the corporation. Then, I started my own company. What a difference. Rather than designating somebody to do something, I had to decide whether I had time to do it. Nothing seemed to be routine. Everything was a challenge. Now we have a number of small clients rather than three very large ones. And, in the end, it came down to what I wanted to achieve. Same world ... but a totally different approach."

Example: "I used to have an IBM typewriter and, about once every couple of months, the local service guy came to the office to fix it. In fact, one of the reasons why people bought IBM was the quality of the service. Now, it really doesn't matter what brand of computer you buy. You expect it to work straight out of the box. The technology has become routine. If the unit needs extensive repair, most people now purchase a new one."

Example: Among the many products that Kostia manufactures are toasters and cellular phones. The company follows very different strategies in these two markets. As the head of development commented, "The toaster market is pretty certain. It is a slowly evolving market where design is the key. By contrast, the cellular phone market changes every other week and we are continually working to improve the technology of our products."

CASE 1.5

HENDAHL INDUSTRIES

Hendahl Industries was founded by the Hendahl family in 1865 who had always played an active role in the business:

- While demand for our materials is really starting to grow, our workforce is changing. Many immigrants do not speak English well. How do we take advantage of the changes and continue to compete? [Karl Hendahl, 1867].

- Without women, we couldn't have provided the materials for the war effort. Now, the soldiers are returning and they aren't very happy just being told to operate a machine in a particular way. We are starting to experience a lot of industrial unrest. Should we be taking another look at how we run the business? [Robert Hendahl III, 1947].

- The people at the local university think we can use some of the new quantitative approaches to come up with some better solutions to our manufacturing problems. They solved one of our design problems in just a couple of days. However, I'm concerned we're replacing the human element with numbers. Is this dangerous? [George Heyer Hendahl, 1957].

- Traditionally, we have always looked at the company from an inside perspective. However, the reality is that we are influenced by a number of external environments. Maybe, we should take them into consideration as well. [Marissa Hendahl-Burton, 1979].

- I've always felt that the solutions to the company's problems could be found in some books or magazines. Unfortunately, I can't find that book or article. [Roger Burton, 1986].

Question: What has happened to Hendahl Industries with the passage of time?

Question: How do these changes parallel the evolution of management thought?

Question: If Roger Burton can't find the answer in a book or a magazine, how can he handle a really complex organizational problem when it arises?

SUMMARY

1. A manager performs four (4) key managerial functions:

   - Planning ... determining the future directions and goals of the organization.

   - Organizing ... utilizing the human resources (i.e., personnel) in the most efficient manner.

   - Leading ... motivating the personnel to achieve the organizational goals.

   - Controlling ... monitoring the actual performance of the organization (in terms of production, sales, profits, etc.) relative to the organization's goals and objectives.

2. Management, within an organization, can be roughly divided into three levels:

   - First-level managers ... supervisors, office managers, crew chiefs, etc.

   - Middle-level managers ... branch managers, project leaders, department heads, etc.

   - Top-level managers ... the chairman of the board, the president, and the senior vice presidents of the various functional areas, etc.

3. The roles and responsibilities of the different levels are very different ... and moving from one level to another can cause serious problems for an individual.

4. A manager needs some or all of the following five (5) managerial skills:

   - Technical skills ... the ability to do a specific task (e.g., write a report or handle a welding torch) particularly well.

   - Interpersonal skills ... an individual's ability to communicate and work with other people and develop an effective team.

   - Conceptual skills ... the ability to see the organization as a whole and visualize its future.

   - Diagnostic skills ... an individual's ability to look at a problem and develop a solution.

   - Political skills ... the ability to pull together allies and supporters to achieve the organization's goals.

   The importance of each of these skills depends very much on the situation facing the organization or the specific department or group.

5. Management thinking has evolved dramatically since the industrial revolution and there have been at least six (6) major stages or approaches:

   - Scientific ... the application of the scientific method (observation and analysis) to business operations.

   - Administrative ... placing the emphasis on the organization of people to maximize their effectiveness.

   - Human resources ... the realization that organizations consisted of people (with their own interest, goals, and objectives) and that they could be influenced to achieve the organization's goals.

   - Quantitative ... the application of modeling, statistics, linear programming, etc. to business problems (especially utilizing the power of computers).

   - Systems perspective ... the realization that organizations (and their component parts) did not operate in a vacuum and that they had to be considered as part of a far broader system.

- Contingency ... the appreciation of the complexity of management and the need to develop strategies and actions consistent with the unique environment and features facing each and every organization.

6. No single approach has provided an answer to all the challenges of modern management. However, each has provided ideas and techniques which can assist a manager in terms of developing their own strategies to meet the needs of the specific situation. While these models or approaches may appear somewhat academic, they do include a lot of valuable "meat."

CRITICAL THINKING QUESTIONS

1. Do you agree with the definition of a manager? How would you improve it? What are some of the definitions used by other texts? And what are the pros and cons of alternative definitions?

_____

_____

_____

_____

2. Which of the four managerial functions (i.e., planning, organization, leading, and controlling) is the most important? *Note:* you may want to ask yourself whether or not this is a question that can be answered. What factors might influence the selection of one function over the others?

_____

_____

_____

_____

3. Why do you think very successful people often have problems moving up from one level in an organization to another (e.g., from first-level manager to middle-level manager and from middle-level manager to top-level manager)? What steps can a company do to help a person move from one level up to the next?

_____

_____

_____

_____

4. Moss Treadwell worked as a research chemist for a large corporation. When offered early retirement, he started his own firm manufacturing a line of insecticides. For a number of years, he managed the day-to-day operations. However, as the company continued to grow, he spent more and more time heading up the research program developing new products. The result was that the company began to flounder. A report prepared by an industry analyst contained the following phrase: "Treadwell Industries is at a turning point. It needs to make the transition from a small company run by one man to a major player led by professional managers." What do you think has happened here? If you were a stockholder in this company, what would you want to see occur?

_____

_____

_____

_____

5. Mary Hart has received job offers (as a general manager) from two companies. Company A is leader in its industry, very successful and very profitable. "Running like a well oiled machine" according to the outgoing general manager. Company B is struggling to break even. It has serious problems in a number of areas ranging from an ineffective sales force and extensive debts to an outdated product line. How would you rank the importance of the five managerial skills relative to these two positions? More importantly, why?

_____

_____

_____

_____

6. What do you think would have happened to the development of modern society if the concept of management had never been explored and developed? For example, what would have occurred if the scientific method had never been applied to business? Or if the computer had never been developed?

_____

_____

_____

_____

7. How do managers regard employees today? What differences can you identify that would differentiate a modern manager from his/her counterpart back in the early 1900s?

_____

_____

_____

_____

CASE PROBLEM

T&C DEPARTMENT STORE

Although only 35, Alexa Mishkin could look back on a very successful career. Joining T&C Department Stores out of high school, she started on the perfume counter in one of the smaller stores. She then moved up to a mall location, and shortly afterwards was made manager of the cosmetics section. Five years later, she was made regional manager for cosmetics. With her promotion to regional vice president, she was now responsible for cosmetics for the 22 northeastern stores.

Each year, T&C hired a consultant who spent time traveling around with each of the senior managers. Following are some of the consultant's notes:

- Alexa is a very active and motivated person. We were on the road very early and didn't get back until eleven o'clock at night. We visited all 22 stores in three days spending approximately an hour at each.
- At each stop, she walked around the cosmetic department accompanied by the department managers ... talking continuously. She gave instructions to a number of managers to completely revamp part or all of their display.
- From time to time, she consulted her data on the performance levels—by day, week, and month—for all the stores ... often commenting to the manager on the negative performance of his/her store.
- In half a dozen stores, she asked if they had resolved specific problems and, when told that they had not, said "You'd better get on with it."
- At the Eagleton store, the manager had a list of questions relating to the product mix. Alexa looked at the list and commented that the strategic plan would be coming down from headquarters within the next week or so.
- When the manager pushed her on another question, Alexa said she was running late and would tackle it next time she had a chance to visit.
- On our way back to headquarters, Alexa commented that she found it hard to get away from headquarters. "When I do, it is rush, rush, rush. However, it gives me an opportunity to get out into the real world ... see how things are done when we come face-to-face with customers.

Question: *Based on this limited information, how would you evaluate Alexa Mishkin overall as a manager? How would you rate her in terms of the four managerial roles?*

_____

_____

_____

_____

Question: *In which of the five technical skills does she appear to be strong? And where does she appear to be weak?*

_____

_____

_____

_____

Question: *If you were a manager of the cosmetic department for T&C, would you like to work for Alexa Mishkin? Why or why not?*

_____

_____

_____

_____

THE REAL WORLD OF MANAGEMENT

CHAPTER

2

OVERVIEW

Managers do not operate in a vacuum. They function in an open system and there are a number of factors that influence what they can and can't do. Management is carried out within a variety of constraints. One way of viewing these constraints is to look at the environments in which a manager functions (i.e., the environments that influence their decision-making and actions).

In this chapter, you will become familiar with the:

- General (or macro) environment ... consisting of the overall economy, socio-cultural influences, political and legal forces and technological advances.
- Operating (or micro) environment ... consisting of the organization's customers, competitors, suppliers and labor.
- Internal environment ... consisting of the various departments and divisions within the organization.
- International environment ... the unique features or characteristics encountered when a business moves from the United States into a foreign market.

THE GENERAL (OR MACRO) ENVIRONMENT

🔑 Key Points:

1. The general and external (or macro) environment consists of four (4) major forces, namely:

   1. Economic ... the forces in the general economy that influence the overall demand for products and services.
   2. Social-cultural ... the characteristics of the population (in terms of sex, age, race, religion, etc.) and the influence of these factors on the marketplace.
   3. Political and legal ... the laws and regulations passed by government (ranging from the international bodies to the federal government to the local township) designed to promote and protect the wellbeing of society.

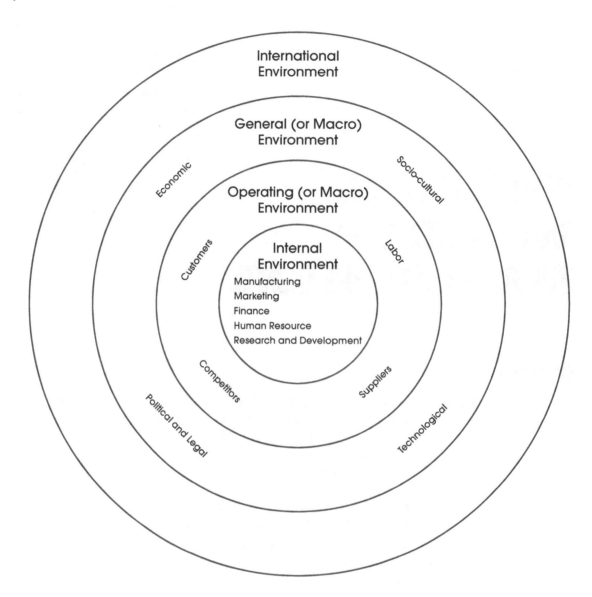

4. Technological ... the output of research and development activities that are introduced to the marketplace as new products and improvements.

2. ***The economic forces*** ... economies go through cycles. One year, the economy is booming. Jobs are plentiful, wages are going up, and people feel confident about the future. They have more money in their pockets after paying for essentials (such as taxes, the mortgage/rent, their automobile, etc.) and thus are in a position to spend money on discretionary items. When the economy turns down and people lose their jobs (or fewer new jobs are being created), people are less willing to spend. They become less confident in terms of the future.

Example: "Our timing was bad. I'd always wanted to open an upscale French restaurant in this area of town and when this location became available I grabbed it. We opened La Belle Époque and did well for a time ... great reviews. But then our regulars started coming in less frequently. So, we asked: why? The answer was the economy. Our client base was largely commission-based sales people and they were experiencing a dramatic downturn in their income due to the economy. Maybe, we should have opened another hamburger place. They have been much less affected."

3. *Socio-cultural forces* ... there are two main aspects to this social force. First, there is the demographics (i.e., the statistical characteristics) of the population. Demographics are vitally important because a male teenager will spend his money on a very different mix of products from his sister. And individuals in the 30-40 year old range will spend their money on very different products and services from those a mere ten years old. Likewise, a retiree will have a different pattern of expenditure from somebody in their mid-50s.

> **Example:** "These kids," Mrs. Johnson said in a tone of exasperation. "Emmy has just come back from the mall with two dresses and a new bag despite the fact that her room is covered with piles of dresses and she has more bags than I have ever had in my whole life. She doesn't need another dress. Why doesn't she save her money for her vacation? Or buy gas for the car?"

Secondly, there are the social values of the population (i.e., what they personally place value on). Over time, these can change quite dramatically.

> **Example:** "I always admitted to being a couch potato. However, when I read the latest report on the effects of obesity on one's health, I changed my behavior. I eat many more salads and fewer hamburgers. I bought myself an expensive exercise machine and I use it daily. Instead of buying a high definition television set, I bought a new tennis racket and a membership at the local club."

4. *Political and legal forces* ... every business is constrained by rules and regulations generated by one or more levels of government (federal, state or local). While they are designed to promote the well-being of the population as a whole, they can make life much more difficult for business operations and hence for the manager.

> **Example:** "The people from OSHA (Occupational Safety and Health Administration) paid us a visit last week and we were written up for a number of violations. They are requiring that we replace the safety guards on two pieces of equipment and improve the lighting in that area. In addition, they've instructed us to increase the width of the walkways, install guard rails in a couple of areas, and replace the doors. The total cost will probably be more than $50,000. All at a time when we are struggling to be competitive with overseas firms that don't have to meet these regulations."
>
> **Example:** "This used to be a thriving town with four large lumber mills. Look at it now ... dead!! Everybody has moved away. Why? Because some local bird was placed on the endangered species list. Apparently, this was the only place where it was found. Now, I'm all in favor of protecting nature but doing so destroyed this town."

5. *Technological advances* ... this is an ever present force in the modern world and has a dramatic impact on many industries. Firms recognize that, in order to be successful, they need a competitive advantage. Likewise, their competitors need to match or bypass this technology. Rarely does a competitive advantage last for very long and even companies with a dominant position in a marketplace can find themselves in difficulty due to innovation by one of their smaller competitors.

> **Example:** In the early days of the automobile industry, it looked as if the dominant power source would be the steam engine—the Stanley Steamer. The discovery of oil and the development of the combustion engine doomed that form of transportation. Today, the industry is starting to see a growing emphasis on electric and hybrid cars. There may well come a point in time when the gasoline engine is a thing of the past.
>
> **Example:** "We were number one in our industry for thirty plus years. Then, some small firm in Sweden came along with a totally different technology. We ignored them despite some of our customers saying they had a much better product. Now, they have 60% of the market and we are trying to work out how to stay in the business."

6. *Important note:* There isn't a great deal that a manager can do to influence these four general and external environmental forces.

> **Example:** No single firm (however large) can set out to dramatically impact the national economy (although strikes in major industries such as airlines and steel can have an irritating short term impact). As one manager commented, "we can respond to changes in the economy by cutting back on production or reducing our prices but that's the best we can do."
>
> **Example:** While the introduction of break-through products (such as the automobile, the computer, or the iPod) has undoubtedly changed the socio-cultural environment over time, an individual company has a limited ability to affect short-term changes in attitudes, buying behavior, etc.
>
> **Example:** Associations of firms can attempt to impact the political and legal forces through lobbying activities although there is no guarantee of success. "We support lobbyists in Washington who represent our point of view and concerns. However, there is always somebody lobbying for the other side."
>
> **Example:** "The best we can do vis-à-vis technological changes is to monitor them, continually evaluate the potential impact on our industry, and move as rapidly as possible to meet these challenges. The problem is that new technology often emerges from the most unlikely sources."

THE WORLD OF HI-TECH

Jim Stanton stared at his notes for the annual meeting at which each manager presented his/her projections for their division's sales for the coming year. These projections were then given to manufacturing for scheduling.

As manager of the Electronic Components Division (ECD), Jim was a key player in the planning process. Last year, he had projected that a total of 4 million A-47 chips would be sold and that estimate had been remarkably accurate. Up until recently, he had expected sales to increase to 4.2 million. However, recent events had made him question the accuracy of this number.

Over the past few months, the economy had started to turn down and consumers weren't buying at the same pace. This, in turn, meant that ECD's customers were slowing down their orders.

In addition, a recent article in a trade magazine had indicated that many marketers believed that, as the population aged, they would be less interested in buying the type of products currently utilizing the A-47.

Then, there was the announcement by Technico that they were introducing an improved chip that would be both faster and cheaper than the A-47. While they weren't saying when it would be available, ECD's customers were already asking when ECD would have a competitive product.

Also very worrying was the law suit brought against ECD by one of its smaller competitors for patent infringement. A decision was expected in two to three weeks. If ECD lost the suit, it would have to either license the technology or go back to using an earlier process.

Finally, the company was facing pressure from environmental groups with regard to pollution emitted from its U.S. plants. Complying with the proposed standards would dramatically increase the cost of production and thus might well force the company to outsource production to an Asian supplier.

Question: What are the general (or macro) environmental factors that impact on Jim Stanton's business and hence his projections?

Question: To what extent can Jim control each of these environment factors?

Question: Should Jim stick with his sales projection of 4.2 million units? If not, what figure should he use?

THE OPERATING (OR MICRO) ENVIRONMENT

🔑 **Key Points:**

1. In addition to the general or macro-environment, a manager has to deal with the more immediate or micro-environment consisting of:

   - Customers ... individuals or organizations that purchase the company's products or services.
   - Competitors ... other firms that offer similar product and services and compete in the same segments of the marketplace.
   - Suppliers ... the firms and organizations that provide raw materials, parts, equipment, supplies, etc. that the organization uses to produce its own products or services.
   - Labor ... the supply of skilled personnel able to perform the tasks of the organization in a cost-effective and productive manner.

2. *Customers* ... customers are the individuals or organizations who purchase the end product or service. A large number of factors effect the way they make decisions at a particular point in time. And they often make a different decision at a later time (i.e., they may well change their mind). Not only do styles and fashions change but so do relationships. To be successful, a manager has to track these changes and anticipate those that will impact on his/her business.

   > **Example:** "Last year, the big seller was our line of full-sized SUVs. We couldn't keep them on the lot. Now, we have rows and rows of them. Customers want the smaller models or, for the first time in years, they are going back to the sedans."
   >
   > **Example:** The health of the toy industry is extremely dependent on the level of sales in late November and December and it is critically important that the stores have adequate supplies of the items that children are going to want. "You bet that something like a cabbage patch doll is going to be in demand. If you are right, you're a genius. If that turns out to be last year's big seller and this year every kid wants something that you didn't stock up on ... you are in trouble!!"

3. *Competitors* ... only rarely does a firm enjoy a monopoly (i.e., operates in a market without competition). The vast majority have one or more firms (often hundreds) with which they compete directly. And it is important to recognize that these firms may well have a very different game plan. A manager cannot assume that the goals and objectives of the competitor are identical with their own.

   > **Example:** "About this time last year, our major competitor dropped their price per ton from $200 to $180. We decided we had no option but to follow suit. They then went to $160 per ton, which was very close to our cost of production. Again, we followed suit because it was an important product for us. The next thing we hear is that they are shutting down the plant and going out of business. All they were trying to do was to clear out their inventory."

> **Example:** "We started Altra Air about a year ago with flights out of a small regional airport. We flew into a couple of second tier airports in Florida. Ours is a very low cost operation so we offer very attractive prices. The big airlines have ignored us so far. As long as we stick to our particular niche in the market, they will leave us alone. However, I'm convinced that if we schedule cheap flights into, say, Orlando they will fight back. They regard that as their turf."

4. *Suppliers* ... all organizations have to rely on a network of suppliers to provide it with products ranging from equipment and raw materials to products to supplies (such as copy paper). Interruption of the flow of materials and goods for any reason can have a major impact on a firm. So, the emphasis is on establishing and maintaining strong relationships with suppliers.

> **Example:** "We used to manufacture domestically. However, we couldn't compete in terms of costs so now everything is manufactured in China. Initially, we dealt with anybody who could supply our needs. We just sent them the order. These days, however, we work very closely with far fewer firms and we're in continuous contact with them to ensure delivery times and quality."

> **Example:** One way of improving a firm's bottom line is to minimize its inventory levels (since investing in inventory ties up a firm's capital). One way of achieving this is to go to a "just-in-time" inventory system where new inventory arrives as the older inventory is being fully utilized. To achieve a seamless flow of goods and materials there has to be a very close relationship between the customer and the supplier.

5. *Labor* ... one of the key elements of management is the organizing and leading of people. In every area of business (e.g., sales, marketing, finance, production, accounting, etc.), a firm needs skilled people to perform the necessary tasks in a timely and cost-effective manner. The absence of such personnel can have a severe impact on the organization's performance.

> **Example:** "This is a union firm and we get our people from the local hiring hall. Since we have been in business for many years and are known as one of the best firms to work for, we generally get very good people. However, when we took on a project in Cleveland, we were viewed as outsiders and the people we got were ... not so good. It really hurt us on that project."

> **Example:** Simpson-Thayer projected sales of the new PM-432 at 150 units during 2004. Actual sales were closer to 60 units. "The product was well received by the marketplace and, in one sense, we've been very successful selling it. The problem is that we don't have enough trained sales people to really attack all segments of the market. And, even if we did, we don't have enough service personnel to support them."

6. *Important note:* Once again, one can ask: what can the manager do about these four operating environmental forces?

The good news is that a manager can influence these operating (or micro) environments to a rather greater degree than the four general external macro-environments. However, his/her ability to do so is still fairly limited.

Example: The local department store cannot tell or instruct customers in terms of what they should buy. However, to a degree, it can influence customers through its image advertising and promotional activities and by pricing its products to generate the maximum amount of traffic.

Example: "I would like to be able to influence what my competitors do but I really don't have a great deal of power. Right or wrong, they will implement their chosen strategy and there is little I can do other than pursue a competitive strategy."

Example: To a degree, a manager can control a supplier according to the terms of any agreement and by ongoing monitoring of production processes. However, even then the control is limited. The contract may call for 10,000 units per month but, if the supplier can only produce 8,000, there isn't a great deal the customer can do.

Example: Firms have the ability to hire new people ... and thus have some control over the labor function. However, hiring somebody does not mean that they have the skills to perform the necessary tasks effectively. Furthermore, it generally takes time to train and educate new employees. It is not easy, therefore, to rapidly affect changes in the labor environment.

CASE 2.2

ALANA JACKSON—MANAGER

In June 2004, Alana Jackson was hired by a nationwide chain of 120 department stores as the manager for women's coats. While she had a number of years experience in the retail business, this was her first position in charge of a fashion item.

Her first step was to schedule a meeting with her predecessor, Mary Scott. "Where do we stand in terms of the Fall and Winter lines?" she asked.

"Not as well as I had hoped," Mary replied. "The Fall line should be going out to the stores in about a month. However, many of the items haven't arrived yet. The biggest problem is with Wat San Industries in China. Much of their plant was destroyed in a fire earlier this year when it was too late to switch suppliers. They are only now starting to produce some of the items. Also, there is a rumor that our largest competitor, Hayley Bros., is planning to change its strategy and more directly compete with the discounters by reducing its prices by 6 to 8% starting this fall. That will make things very tight for us. Do we retain our current margins or do we cut into our profits to compete?"

"Then, the latest weather forecast is that it is going to be a very warm fall and a bitterly cold winter. When we placed our orders at the start of the year, everybody was predicting the opposite. So, it is quite possible that many of our items will not be what the customers are looking for. Finally, there is the shortage of good sales people in many of our stores. Unfortunately, we let many of our senior people go a couple of years back because we wanted to create a younger image by having younger people. That has backfired badly. Now, we are trying to hire people and struggling to train the new generation."

Question: What operating (or micro) environmental factors does Alana Jackson have to deal with (i.e., what factors does she have to handle)?

Question: To what extent can Alana control these factors?

Question: Does the fact that Alana is working in a fashion business (as opposed to a pharmacy) make responding to these environmental factors easier or more difficult?

THE INTERNAL ENVIRONMENT

⊙➤ **Key Points:**

1. An organization is similar to a football team and each manager and employee is a member of that team. The success of any one individual will depend, to a large extent, on the support and efforts of the other members of the team.

> **Example:** "The interdependence of all the people working here at Stayes and Bullock was beautifully demonstrated last week. Manufacturing did a fantastic job producing the new product. Distribution did its part by getting it delivered to the stores last week. Advertising did a great job on the winter catalog to promote the new product. But where is it? It is still sitting on the dock waiting to be mailed!! It will go out next Tuesday, they tell me!!"

Just as a manager has to be aware of the general or macro-environment and responsive to changes in the operating or micro-environment so they have to be attuned to the realities of the internal environment (i.e., the players and the forces within his/her own company). Failure to work closely with other members of the team can often result in a less than effective outcome.

> **Example:** "Bob Hansen had a great year last year. He sold three times as much as any other sales person. So, I asked him how he did it. He was very reluctant to say. However, I eventually found out. He was calling on the purchasing manager and then on the engineering staff the same way as everybody else. However, following the meeting with the engineer(s), he would walk back with them to the purchasing manager and have a three-way discussion. That sold the product. If he had told me this last year, we could have trained our other salespeople to have done exactly the same thing."

2. A successful manager needs to be able to work effectively with all the elements of the organization ranging from accounting, design, and engineering to human resources, manufacturing, and marketing to research, sales, etc.

Example: "Personally, I like Sandra (the president of the company). Overall, she has done a very good job. However, one area in which I would fault her is her dealings with my department. I know accounting isn't quite as sexy as some other areas but we keep the company on track. She has only visited the department once in the three years she has been in charge. And some of the comments she has made at meetings suggest she doesn't have a very high regard for us. Quite frankly, a number of my people don't like her."

Example: "I learned something shortly after I arrived here at Canter-Miles. Different departments have different ways of doing things. When you meet with the sales people, it has to be a short meeting. They aren't interested in long discussions. The people in human resources are only really interested in talking if they have a problem. The engineers, however, will sit and talk for hours. To get the most out of these people, you have to adapt your way of doing things to their style."

CASE 2.3

IN-HOUSE PROBLEMS AT VERTATEK

Following his appointment as the Manager for Manufacturing at Vertatek Corporation, Dan Wilson moved rapidly to get his department back on track. The previous manager had let things slide and the department had gained a reputation for turning out poor quality work and failing to meet critical deadlines.

His first step was to schedule two meetings ... one with the day shift (which employed 43 people) and other with the night shift (19 people). He then interviewed each of the employees on a one-on-one basis. At the end of two weeks, 28 of the employees were given their pink slip, the night shift was temporarily discontinued, and five employees were promoted to supervisor.

Within months, the department's reputation improved dramatically. Orders were now correct and going out on time. The improvement was so dramatic that he reinstated the night shift ... appointing one of the supervisors as the night manager.

Dan felt that he had done a good job. However, when he met with the president of the company, Mary Fisher, for his six month evaluation, he was stunned by her criticisms.

"Jim (V.P. of Marketing) was very unhappy about the way you handled the Archer account. He's been working on that account diligently for a couple of years and didn't appreciate you going over there and talking directly to their CEO. Also, Danielle (V.P. of Human Resources) complained that you made an offer to one of the candidates that was way above what we had been paying previously causing a number of problems. Furthermore, it has always been our practice to have HR make the actual offer. Finally, Vern (V.P. of Engineering Design) ... well, you put his nose out of joint. Apparently you told him exactly what you wanted and then left the meeting before he or any of his staff had had a chance to respond or comment."

"So, I am pleased with the way manufacturing is working but ... in other areas, we seem to have problems."

Question: What has Dan Wilson overlooked?

Question: Does Mary Fisher have reason to be annoyed?

Question: What plan of action would you suggest Dan adopt to overcome the criticisms?

THE INTERNATIONAL ENVIRONMENT

⚷ Key Points:

1. In one sense, being a manager overseas is just the same as being a manager here in the United States. You still have to handle people and problems on a daily basis. You still perform the same managerial functions. And, in general, you need the same managerial skills.

   On the other hand, what can make it so different is that the operating and internal environments have an added dimension, namely: the international environment, which can consist of many, many different factors. Among some of the more important are:

   - Language ... the knowledge and usage of a common language.
   - Face ... the reluctance of individuals to admit that they are at fault or subordinate.
   - Status ... the relationships (in the business environment) between two individuals within an organization (or representing different organizations).
   - Sense of time ... not everybody shares either the Western concept of time or the importance of meeting schedules.
   - Expectations ... different cultures have very different expectations of business meetings and relationships.

2. *Language* ... while English is widely utilized as the language of international trade, not everybody speaks it with the same degree of fluency or, for that matter, the same "brand" of English.

Example: "I spek very goot English." Any traveler outside the United States will find many people who do speak perfect English. However, there will be some who claim to speak English "very well" but only have a good knowledge of a particular area of the language or may be exaggerating their level of understanding.

Example: Winston Churchill, the British prime minister during World War II, once described the Americans and the British as a "single people divided by a common language." Quite a large number of words have very different meanings in American and English.

---

3. *Face* ... the concept of "losing face" is an oriental one. However, it is important to recognize that nobody (anywhere in the world) likes to be made to appear stupid or inferior. While people in foreign countries may admire and, sometimes, even envy the United States, they don't like feeling inferior or in any way subordinate. Nor, in many parts of the world, do they want to appear rude. So, speaking one's mind may not be acceptable.

> **Example:** "I was down in Mexico City for two weeks trying to get some data on our sales by customer. The people in the office struck me as very bright and extremely friendly. However, I could not get my data. Two days after I arrived back home, I received an e-mail with all the data I needed. Great!! My guess is that they held on to it until I left. That way, they maintained their dignity and independence."
>
> **Example:** The negotiations had gone extremely well and Alan Barnes flew back to London confident that the two companies would easily reach an agreement. Two weeks later he received a long letter from the Japanese firm raising a multitude of concerns and issues. "I don't understand," he commented to his boss. "They said 'yes' to everything I suggested. They said 'yes' to the schedule and now they are saying that we need to renegotiate it." "That's fine," his boss replied. "You are dealing with a culture where to say 'no' is extremely rude. Two or three more trips to Tokyo and we'll start to get close to an agreement."

4. *Status* ... while there are status differences in the United States, most Americans like to think of themselves as egalitarian. Americans have become used to a workplace in which the authority that goes with a specific position is fairly well hidden. By contrast, foreign environment may involve far greater distinctions in status between managers and their staff. As a result, relationships within the organization and the social expectations that go with those relationships can be very different.

> **Example:** "When I worked for a bank in the Philippines, the branch manager was always addressed as "Mr. Ochoa. I would never have considered calling him by his first name. In fact, I don't think I ever knew it. When I started work in the States, it was hard to call my boss Jim. But everybody did so. I found America to be much more informal and less status oriented."
>
> **Example:** Ransome Industries sent one of it best managers down to South America to take over its operations. As a way of getting to know his managers, he organized a cocktail party. At the party, playing the role of a good American host, he asked the managers what they would like to drink ... and then went and obtained it for them. His reputation was ruined. No managers in Latin America would consider getting a drink for somebody. That was what servants were for!!

5. *Sense of time* ... to an American, 9:15 a.m. means nine fifteen in the morning. It doesn't mean eight o'clock or ten o'clock. Why? Because he/she invariably has a tight schedule with further activities planned at 11:00 a.m. and noon. While many foreign businessmen have adapted to this same sense of time, there are still large segments of the world's populations to whom time has little relevance.

> **Example:** "When I was living in the Far East, I was invited to a party that, I was told, would start at 3:00 p.m. I was running late and was embarrassed when I arrived at four. I shouldn't have worried. I was the first person to arrive. Most of the guests started arriving closer to five o'clock."

6. *Expectations* ... there is the expectation among many Westerners that business is business and that the goal is to get the job done and move on to the next problem. They expect people to focus on the task at hand and take action. The problem in the international environment is that many of the people with whom one is dealing do not have this sense of urgency or commitment to rapid action.

> **Example:** "The meeting was scheduled to start at 9:00 a.m. and the regional vice president arrived ten minutes early. As soon as he sat down with his counterpart, he pulled out his presentation. However, it rapidly became clear that the other party was not ready to discuss the critical problem. He was clearly expecting a far more general social interaction before moving on to the business at hand. It wasn't until after lunch that the serious discussion began."
>
> **Example:** "At one stage in my career with Boston Industries (BI), I was sent out to Japan to meet with the people from a large company with whom we did business. I was introduced to the son of the owner and we spent quite a bit of time together—both in Japan and when he visited the U.S. Apparently, and I found this out when I left BI, the idea was that we would become close friends and, over time, our two companies would grow closer together and thus do more business together. They obviously had a very long-term perspective."

CASE 2.4

WHY DIDN'T I STAY IN ST. LOUIS?

It was only ten o'clock in the morning and it was already extremely hot and humid. Martin Sexton had been on the dock for three hours trying to get clearance of a shipment of equipment from the company's plant in Italy.

When he had accepted the job, he had viewed moving from the headquarters in St. Louis to Lagos, Nigeria as an opportunity to see the world and gain experience as a manager away from the constraints of headquarters. On the surface, everything was fine. He had a large, clean office with a great view of the harbor. The local people had found him a house about twenty minutes away where he had six servants and enough space to house a football team. He had a car and, somewhat to his frustration, a driver. And he was enjoying meeting with other American managers who gathered for lunch at the Majestic or drinks after work at the Henley Country Club.

He had a total of six office staff and four sales people ... two of whom worked out of small offices in Ibadan and Ngubu. They called in on a daily basis and flew down to Lagos each month for a visit. Every desk was equipped with a modern computer and internet connection.

Rather than enjoying himself as an independent manager, Martin was finding it extremely frustrating. He'd promised the president that he would increase sales by at least 50% this year. He had been in Lagos for six months and sales were actually somewhat down on the previous year.

Martin went to the main office to talk with the dock supervisor. "Milan states that the materials were shipped on the 3rd on the Maru Kibiti. Has it arrived? If it has arrived, where is it docked? If it docked, has it been unloaded? And, if it has been unloaded, which storage area is it located in?"

"I'm sorry I can't help you. I just don't know," the dock supervisor replied in very good English. "But I will look into it for you ... as soon as possible."

Question: What are some of the unique problems that Martin has experienced in Lagos? How is it different from being in St. Louis?

Question: How do you think Martin should deal with these differences?

Question: In view of the fact that the world is rapidly become a single "village," how rapidly do you think the way of doing business (in places like Lagos) will change?

SUMMARY

1. A manager has to deal with three (3) very different environments, namely:

   - General (or macro) environment.
   - Operating (or micro) environment.
   - Internal environment.

     And, if he/she is involved in international trade and operations, in the:

   - International environment.

2. The general or macro environment consists of four (4) critical factors or forces:

   - Economic ... the forces in the general economy that influence the overall demand for products and services.
   - Social-cultural ... the characteristics of the population (in terms of sex, age, race, religion, etc.) and the influence of these factors on the marketplace.
   - Political and legal ... the laws and regulations passed by government (ranging from the international bodies to the federal government to the local township) designed to promote and protect the wellbeing of society.
   - Technological ... the output of research and development activities that are introduced to the marketplace as new products and improvements.

3. ***Important note:*** A manager has very little, if any, control over any of these forces. However, he/she needs to monitor them and respond to changes in an appropriate manner.

   Furthermore, not all of these forces impact on any one specific situation. Technology may well be the critical factor in one industry while the changing social environment may be critical in another.

4. The operating or micro environment also consists of four (4) factors:
   - Customers ... individuals or organization that purchase the company's products or services.
   - Competitors ... other firms that offer similar product and services and compete in the same segments of the marketplace.
   - Suppliers ... the firms and organizations that provide raw materials, parts, equipment, supplies, etc. that the organization uses to produce its own products or services.
   - Labor ... the supply of skilled personnel able to perform the tasks of the organization in a cost-effective and productive manner.

5. ***Important note:*** A manager has very limited control over these forces. Sometimes, they are in a position to influence them. However, in most cases, their role is limited to the monitoring of trends and responding to the changes.

   Furthermore, once again, not all of these forces apply equally to all situations. The action of competitors may be the major concern in one industry (e.g., what Wal-Mart does may have a dramatic impact on the smaller supermarkets in the area) while working with suppliers may be the number one challenge in another field.

6. The internal environment consists of the various divisions, departments and groups within the organization company. Depending on the nature of the organization, these may include: accounting, design, engineering, human resources, manufacturing, marketing, research and development, sales, etc.

An effective manager has to be able to work well with each of these departments if he/she is going to be successful. A manager cannot isolate themselves from the other areas of the organization. An organization is a team and the "players" have to work together.

7. The international environment is an additional dimension; an overlay on top of the general, operating, and internal environments. To be successful, a manager must recognize, understand and appreciate the differences between the typical domestic culture and the one found in the foreign environment. Among some of the factors that need to be taken into consideration are:

- Language ... the knowledge and usage of a common language.
- Face ... the reluctance of individuals to admit that they are at fault or subordinate.
- Status ... the relationships (in the business environment) between two individuals within an organization (or representing different organizations).
- Sense of time ... not everybody shares either the Western concept of time or the importance of meeting schedules.
- Expectations ... different cultures have very different expectations of business meetings and relationships.

CRITICAL THINKING QUESTIONS

1. The text indicates that the general or macro-environment consists of four forces (economic, social-cultural, political-legal, and technological). What other external forces are there over which the manager has no control?

   _____

   _____

   _____

   _____

2. A manager cannot control the flow of technology. Breakthrough technologies can come from any company, of any size, located anywhere in the world. So, what do you do if you are a manager in a company where the technology is changing rapidly? What steps can you take to ensure that you are at least familiar with the status and direction of the relevant technology?

   _____

   _____

   _____

   _____

3. "We need to do a better job of controlling our operating environment." The speaker is the owner and manager of a small brewery. What steps, if any, could the company's management take to "control" its customers, competitors, suppliers, and labor?

   _____

   _____

   _____

   _____

4. Marley and Company imports items which it sells exclusively to gift shops nationwide. Due to increased competition from large discount stores, Alice Marley is looking to reduce her costs. "We currently purchase from approximately 200 suppliers located in China, Hong Kong, Taiwan and Thailand. Each year, we visit them. They show us what they have and at what price and we place an order. We have to cut our costs and this is one area in which we make substantial improvements." What course of action would you suggest to Alice Marley?

   _____

   _____

   _____

   _____

5. You have recently been appointed CEO of Raysat Industries which consists of four divisions (engineering, human resources, manufacturing, and sales). One of the first things you noticed was that the divisions seemed to operate as separate and independent "empires." Since you are a firm believer in the importance of teamwork, what would you propose to improve the coordination and interaction between the divisions?

_____

_____

_____

_____

6. After five years as a production manager with Ponting Steel in Pennsylvania, Carl Wickam is being promoted and sent to India to assume responsibility for the Ponting (India) Ltd. plant located twenty miles outside New Delhi. What training, if any, would you give Carl as part of his preparation for assuming this new position?

_____

_____

_____

_____

7. Carl had planned to go out to India on his own and see his family about once every two months when he visited the company's headquarters. However, at the last moment, his wife, Eve, and their three children (Sophie, May, and Lionel) decided to travel with him. What difference does this make? What problems will Eve and the children face?

_____

_____

_____

_____

CASE PROBLEM

JAZPRO TOY COMPANY

Roommates in college, Neil Jaza and Randy Proven met again at their tenth reunion. Both were frustrated with their current positions with large corporations and they decided to start a business together making toys. Specifically, they focused on the sort of toys that kids could sit in and peddle around the yard.

From the very start, their goal was to produce a quality yet safe product. Initially, they established a small factory in Maine because Neil, who handled production, commented that he felt more comfortable using American labor. "I can see what is going wrong immediately. I don't have to wait for the product to arrive from China to find that it isn't what I wanted."

Randy handled the office staff and sales to toy stores and, for a number of years, sales grew very satisfactorily. Their top two selling items were the fire engine and front end loader. However, in 1995, they experienced a severe drop in sales and, while it recovered somewhat the following year, sales were essentially stagnant.

The problem, according to Randy, was the growing sophistication of children. "It used to be that they liked toys you could use and rough house with. Now, they want electronics. It is not just the computer based games that have taken over. Look at this truck. If you say "engine" it makes the sound of an engine. If you hit the accelerator pedal, it roars. If you hit the turn indicators, the lights flash. If you put your foot on the brake, the brake lights come on. Now, if we add these sorts of features, it would increase the price to the point where the average parent wouldn't see the value. The cost would be prohibitive."

"Randy and I are in our mid 40s and aren't ready to retire. But we have to do something. Christmas is our big time of year and the figures don't look good. We may have to lay off some of the factory people ... something we have tried very hard not to do."

Question: *Looking at the four environments (general or macro, operating or micro, internal, and international), what can Neil and Randy realistically expect to control?*

_____

_____

_____

_____

Question: *What options do Neil and Randy have?*

_____

_____

_____

_____

Question: *As a consultant, what would you recommend they do? And why?*

_____

_____

_____

_____

THE IMPACT OF TECHNOLOGY

OVERVIEW

While the role of the manager continues to involve responsibility for those employees who report to him/her, the dramatic development of technology has had a major impact on both the nature of the manager's job and how he/she performs it.

This chapter focuses on some of the major innovations that have changed the way business is viewed and conducted. Specifically, we will begin with the impact of:

- Mechanization, interchangeable parts, and the assembly line.

And then focus on the development and impact of the computer. For those who have grown up in the computer age, it is difficult to fully appreciate its impact on:

- The way firms do business.
- Communications.
- Data collection and analysis, and
- The access to, and use of, information.

MECHANIZATION, INTERCHANGEABLE PARTS, AND THE ASSEMBLY LINE

 Key Points:

1. *Mechanization* ... the use of machines to replace human and animal muscle power. For centuries, humans had relied on their own strength and the pulling power of horses, bullocks, etc. This all changed with the development of machinery powered, initially, by the steam engine and, later, by electricity.

> **Example:** Thomas Savery patented the first crude steam engine in 1698 in an attempt to pump water out of coal mines. This was followed by improvements introduced by Thomas Newcomen (1712) and John Watt (1769).
>
> **Example:** In 1773, Eli Whitney patented the cotton gin that automated the separation of cottonseed from the short-staple cotton fiber. Whereas a laborer could produce only a pound a day, this machine could produce up to 50 lbs. of cleaned cotton per day.
>
> **Example:** Michael Faraday (1831) discovered electromagnetic induction which led to the modern electric motor, generator and transformer and, in 1837, resulted in the first industrial electric motor.

2. *Interchangeable parts* ... the idea that pieces could be made with such precision that one component could be substituted for another.

> **Example:** In 1819, John H. Hall, a New England gun maker, signed a contract with the U.S. army to produce 1,000 breech loading rifles. He spent several years tooling new workshops and perfecting precision machinery for producing rifles with interchangeable parts—a boldly ambitious goal for an industry which was traditionally based on the manual labor of skilled craftsmen.
>
> **Example:** In 1908, the Royal Automobile Club of England (RAC) challenged all automobile manufacturers in the world to prove the interchangeability of its parts. Cadillac accepted the challenge and won when the RAC took three cars off the showroom floor, dismantled them, mixed up all the parts, and added some new parts. Cadillac was then able to reassemble them.

3. *Assembly line* ... a process that led to increased production efficiency. Rather than the workers moving from one location to another, the product moves while the workers are stationery (i.e., the product comes to the worker) who focuses on a specific and discrete task.

> **Example:** In the 16th Century, the Venetian Arsenal, a dockyard, employed some 16,000 people who, it is said, worked on a production line basis and were able to build, outfit, and provision one new galley each day.
>
> **Example:** In 1901, Ransom E. Olds created the assembly line and quadrupled his factory's output. However, it was Henry Ford who, in 1913, improved on Olds' assembly line by installing conveyor belts and thus created the moving assembly line. The assembly line resulted in the ability to produce vehicles at a far faster rate and at a price that made them affordable.

CASE 3.1

ASSARA NATIVE CRAFTS, INC.

"I moved to the island of Assara about five years ago ... primarily because I was fed up with the rat race and wanted to get as far away from civilization as I could. It really is a beautiful island and I'm enjoying a very pleasant existence. I don't miss the outside world at all. However, I appreciate the fact that cruise boats drop anchor from time to time and bring newspapers, mail, etc."

"I swim and fish in the morning. In the afternoon, I sit at my typewriter. I must admit I miss my computer and the television but we don't have electricity on the island. Most evenings, I go for a walk along the beach and have a drink with some of the natives who are very friendly."

"The only thing that worries me about the island is the living standard of many of the islanders. I have everything I need. But there are so many things they don't have. They sell various items such as wood carvings and weavings to the passengers from the cruises. But they only generate enough money to pay for the bare essentials."

"Anyway, I sent some of the carvings and weavings to a former customer of mine in Chicago. He's very interested and I recently heard from him that he thought the weavings were fantastic and that he would be interested in purchasing 10,000 of them for distribution nationwide."

"Now, there is no way, the islanders could produce that number by hand in ten years. However, it struck me that, if we brought all the women together in one location, acquired a generator, introduced some simple weaving equipment, and set up an assembly line sort of operation, we could meet that target. The income would really do wonders for everybody on the island so I'm going to discuss the idea with the native leaders some time next week."

Question: What do you see as the pros and cons of this idea from the perspective of the native leaders (all male)?

Question: What do you see as the pros and cons of this idea from the perspective of the women of the island?

Question: What do you think is likely to be the long-term impact of going ahead with this project?

THE WAY FIRMS DO BUSINESS

⊙══ **Key Points:**

1. The introduction of computer-based technology has led to some major changes in the way firms do business in that it has:

    ■ Provided worldwide versus local coverage.

    ■ Enabled firms to replace human intermediaries by technology.

2. *Worldwide versus local coverage* ... without the computer, there would be nothing closely resembling the Internet, which has enabled firms to project a far larger presence outside their own local market areas. This is true of both small companies and large companies and of companies located in the developed and underdeveloped markets.

    > **Example:** A pharmacy located in Springfield, Missouri does more than 95% of its total annual business with customers located in Saudi Arabia. "The internet has enabled me to be competitive in a country I have never even visited," the owner commented.
    >
    > **Example:** While a web may represent a well-known firm such as Barnes & Noble, it is increasingly difficult to tell whether kgh.com is located in Boston or Beirut ... in Los Angeles or Mexico City.
    >
    > **Example:** "I thought I was dealing with a large company. They had a beautifully designed and extensive web site. However, when I visited the company, I found it was two guys working out of a garage."

3. *Replacement of human intermediaries by technology* ... tasks which used to be handled by an individual employee have been automated.

    > **Example:** "When I wanted a specific part or the cost of a product from a supplier, I used to either search through the company's catalog (if it had one) or call the company and talk to somebody in in-house sales. Using the computer is much simpler. I just go to their web site. More importantly, I know what products they have, whether they are in stock, and what the current price is."
    >
    > **Example:** "We used to have 105 branches. Then, we introduced ATMs. We closed down some of the branches and replaced them with machines. Now, we are very hopeful that the next generations of ATMs will provide 90% to 95% of the services that you can get from a full-service branch. My guess is that we'll be down to less than a dozen branches in ten years."

HORTON & SONS—ANTIQUARIANS

Located on a small side street in downtown Boston is the firm of Horton & Sons ... dealers in old and rare books. Founded in 1871, it is still run by a family member—Thomas B. Horton. Waiting in the wings (and chomping at the bit to takeover) is his son, Charles.

"Charles and I have very different views with regard to this business. I see it as a craft ... a highly personal business. I know virtually all our customers by sight and by name. I know specifically what they collect. I know how much they are willing to pay. And I know that, when I find something for them, they will purchase it. Only very occasionally does one of our clients turn down a book and, when they do, it is largely because of condition."

"We are computerized. We inventory all our stock on the computer and record all purchases and sales. And we do have a web site. It tells potential customers who we are, how long we have been in business, and where we are located. It also gives them a telephone number but we don't get many people calling. These are people who prefer to come in and browse and talk."

"My son has very different ideas. He wants us to use the web site to create a worldwide presence. He wants to put our entire catalog on the web along with prices, delivery conditions, etc. I think he sees us selling to Saudi Arabia and New Zealand and everywhere in between. His idea is to have all clients and potential clients complete an in-depth questionnaire listing their interests, requirements, etc. so that he can match this information with the various computer-based listings of available books. When there is a match, he will inform the customer as to the price (including our commission) and condition and then leave it up to the customer to say 'yes' or 'no.' I don't know. I understand what he wants to do but am not too sure it is the way to go."

Question: Is Horton & Sons—Antiquarians a business that could continue to function unchanged? If so, why?

Question: Has technology (specifically the computer and the Internet) had a positive or negative impact on this business?

Question: What do you think of Charles Horton's plans to revitalize the business?

COMMUNICATIONS

⊙━➤ **Key Points:**

1. From 1876, when Alexander Graham Bell invented his "electrical speech machine," until the late '70s and early '80s, the standard land-line telephone was the basic means of verbal communication if a face-to-face meeting were not possible. The impact of the computer and related technologies has been to dramatically change the business environment with the growth of:

   ■ Cellular phones.

   ■ E-mails.

   ■ Instant messaging/text messaging.

   ■ Interconnectivity.

   It has also raised an important philosophical question, namely:

   ■ Do we want to be connected 24/7?

2. *Cellular phones* ... this technology has enabled people to stay in contact with each other on a 24/7 basis irrespective of where they are in the world. Furthermore, it has also enabled people to become part of the business environment without requiring the traditional office or a fixed telephone line.

   > **Example:** A piece of machinery breaks in Lyon, France and the operator can immediately contact his/her supervisor, the local service representative, or the manufacturer of the equipment in Lisbon, Portugal at any time, day or night, without moving from the equipment.
   >
   > **Example:** People (especially the younger generation) have now become so attached to their cellular phones that they are rarely without them. As they advance in their business careers, they will expect others to be similarly connected ... and thus available to interact on business issues on a 24/7 basis.
   >
   > **Example:** In a number of countries in Africa, women (who have historically played a subordinate role) are now actively pursuing business opportunities since they now have a technology that makes them independent of their husband or other male members of the family.

3. *E-mails* ... here technology has replaced the letter and fax to a large degree ... and greatly reduced the length of time it takes for one person to communicate with another. However, the ease with which the message can be sent poses serious problems. E-mails lend themselves to shorthand and "off-the-cuff" remarks. They are unlikely to be proofed for tone or content and may not be read by the recipient.

   > **Example:** Calling somebody an idiot to their face may be laughed off as a joke or wisecrack. The same comment as part of an e-mail may be regarded very differently.

> **Example:** "The moment I hit the send button, I knew I had made a mistake. I had broken my own rule of waiting 24 hours before sending out something that I knew would put the cat among the pigeons."
>
> **Example:** A critical e-mail rescheduling the time of a meeting may be overlooked by the recipient who sees it as just one of a multitude of communications to be read at some future time during the day.

4. *Instant messaging/text messaging* ... two further technological advances that appeal to the younger generation. Many people now find it easier to send an instant message to a computer or a text message to a cellular phone than to actually speak to somebody. They have created their own language or shorthand in the process.

> **Example:** Two people text message each other on a regular basis and build up an effective working relationship. Yet, when they meet face-to-face, they find that they do not have adequate verbal communications skills.
>
> **Example:** During the aftermath of the December 26, 2004 Tsunami, text messaging proved to be an invaluable tool for communications when the cell phone signal was too weak to sustain a spoken conversation.

5. *Interconnectivity* ... the ability to connect to your computer from any point in the home or office or from designated points outside it.

> **Example:** "The laptop has been a marvelous invention. My first one weighed a ton and you had to be Hercules to cart it around. Then they introduced units that weighed ten or twelve pounds. My latest laptop weighs six pounds. But the most important thing is that, when I am in the office, I can connect to other computers and, when I am on the road, all I have to do is to find a Wi-Fi hot spot ... and I am connected."
>
> **Example:** "I carry a PDA (personal digital assistant) in my pocket and it goes everywhere with me. I store contact information (names, addresses, phone numbers, e-mail addresses), make to-do lists, take notes, track appointments (date book, calendar), perform calculations, etc. Most important, it enables me to connect via Wi-Fi and wireless access points.

6. *Important note:* the use of these technologies raises a number of serious questions, namely:

   - Do we really want to be connected 24/7?
   - What impact will this "closeness" have on the way we live?
   - Will these technologies lead to the impersonalization of communication?
   - Will there be a dramatic loss in effective writing skills?

Example: Fifty years ago, a senior executive went on vacation for four weeks. He didn't tell anybody where he was staying. And he never called the office once. He felt he had his priorities. He worked 46 weeks of the year and his vacation was his time to relax.

Example: The science fiction writer Isaac Asimov envisaged a world in which people could not physically bear to be in the same space as another human being and, as a result, communication between individuals could only be conducted on an impersonal basis.

Example: "My students can't write any more. They spend so much time writing in their own short hand that they don't know how to write a correct and effective English sentence. It is almost as if English were becoming a second language."

CASE
3.3

E-MAIL ... THE GREATEST INVENTION SINCE
SLICED BREAD

In June, approximately one hundred corporate managers of Richardson Corporation arrived at a resort in Sedona, Arizona for the annual manager's meeting. Each year, five managers were selected to give a fifteen minute talk on a topic of interest to them. It was regarded as something of an honor since it enabled the speaker to present themselves to top management. This year, Mary Feedler had been chosen and she had decided to speak on the use of e-mails.

Mary was a good speaker and had a well crafted audio-visual presentation. So, her talk went well as she briefly summarized the benefits of the use of e-mails. When she finished, she asked for comments and questions ... and quite a large number of people raised their hands. The first speaker was the manager from Pittsburgh, Carter Wilson, and from the nodding of heads, Mary concluded he was expressing a widely held view.

"Mary, I appreciate what you are saying. In theory, e-mail is a great idea. But, in reality, it is a nightmare. Let me summarize some of the problems for you." He then proceeded to list a series of objections to the use of e-mails.

"And I'd add another major problem," Alec Tiebault (one of the company's legal staff) chimed in. "I've had a number of legal issues cross my desk in the past few months ... all resulting from the use of e-mails."

Question: What advantages of e-mails could Mary have presented in her talk?

Question: What objections and problems might the sales manager from Pittsburgh have raised?

Question: What legal issues might be raised or exacerbated by the use of e-mails?

DATA COLLECTION AND ANALYSIS

1. Three of the areas in which the computer has had a dramatic impact are:

   - Record keeping ... the maintenance of, and access to, a wide range of data.
   - Modeling ... the use of mathematical models to illustrate the marketplace and project future impacts.
   - Data mining ... the analysis of sets of data to identify key factors and relationships.

2. *Record keeping* ... the growth of computer-based capabilities has dramatically improved the ability of organizations to maintain and rapidly update accurate records.

   > **Example:** Historically, it could take a firm eight to ten weeks to prepare consolidated monthly financial reports for multiple locations. Today, the information can be gathered and submitted electronically, and converted into a report that can be on the manager's desk the following day.
   >
   > **Example:** In the era before computers, determining the number of items in stock was a time-consuming process. Somebody had to physically count them ... moving from shelf to shelf with a pencil and paper. A full inventory count was done only infrequently. The introduction of stock keeping unit (SKU) codes enabled the computer to tie the sale of an item to the withdrawal from inventory and thus maintain a real-time count.

3. *Modeling* ... while numerous mathematical techniques have existed for many years, using them was extremely time-consuming. Teams could work on a single problem for months. The computer enabled these projections to be made dramatically faster. This, in turn, led to the development of new and improved software to take advantage of this high speed computing.

   > **Example:** During World War II, one of the great allied successes was the breaking of the German and Japanese military codes. This was achieved using strips of paper on which the code breakers wrote down sequences of letters that were then compared with other strips of paper. It required thousands and thousands of man hours to identify the code being used.
   >
   > **Example:** "When one of our competitors changed its pricing, we used to have to wait for weeks to see what the impact was. Now, we simply plug the new pricing data into our model of the industry and we have a projection of what will happen. Then, we can look at the variable and plot appropriate countermoves ... all without moving from this office."

4. *Data mining* ... this is the computer-assisted process of digging through and analyzing enormous sets of data and then extracting, through the use of models, the meaning of the data. These analyses predict behaviors and future trends and enable businesses to make proactive knowledge-driven decisions.

Example: Wal-Mart uploads approximately 30 million point-of-sale transactions on a daily basis. This is a massive amount of data and, through analysis and modeling, Wal-Mart attempts to turn this data into significant insights about its customers and markets.

Example: By sorting through its data, a manufacturer discovers that males earning between $70,000 and $90,000 who subscribe to a particular magazine are likely purchasers of a product. This enables them to advertise in this magazine using terminology that will appeal to this demographic segment.

Example: A company that sells drugs to the country's largest health care providers mined its data to determine hidden links between illnesses and known drug treatments. The result was more effective treatments that were less expensive.

CASE 3.4

MOUNT OLIVE HOSPITAL

Dr. Jacob Marmet nervously shuffled his papers.

"Roger Singletary was brought into surgery for the replacement of his left hip. The surgery went well. No complications. Let's see, according to his chart, he was returned to the ward at 4:30 p.m. on the 15th. I saw the patient at 7:30 a.m. the following morning and again at 6:25 p.m. that same evening."

"At that time, he seemed to be in some distress and I prescribed 3 mg. of Arazoline (a fictional drug) to be given intravenously. I left the hospital around 6:45 and was half way home when I received an emergency call. Mr. Singletary had gone into shock. I arrived back at the hospital at 7:20 when I pronounced the patient dead."

"According to an autopsy conducted, Mr. Singletary suffered a massive stroke as a result of being administered 30 mg. of Arazoline. The attending nurse misread my instructions. Furthermore, Mr. Singletary experienced a rare negative drug interaction which I had not anticipated."

The head of surgery sighed. "That's the third case this month where either an error has been made in the prescription or we've failed to pick up on a potential drug interaction."

Relative to other hospitals, Mount Olive had a relatively poor record ... especially compared with those that had invested in wireless laptops for both doctors and nurses, access to X-ray from the PCs, a digital drug-order entry systems, etc.

Question: A hospital would seem to be an ideal environment for computerization. So, why do you think Mount Olive has not computerized all its patient record keeping?

Question: How do you think the various members of a hospital—the doctors, the nurses, and the administrators would react to any proposed computerization?

Question: What disadvantages do you see to the computerization of the medical practice in a hospital?

THE ACCESS TO, AND USE OF, INFORMATION

1. The impact of the computer has been to dramatically improve:

    ■ Internal access to information.

    ■ Customer access to information.

    And has raised:

    ■ Serious questions about the security and use of information.

2. ***Internal access to information*** ... the ability of employees to obtain data and information to enable them to better perform their jobs.

    > **Example:** "When I first joined this company, having information meant having power. As a result, the people who had the information guarded it very carefully and, to get the data you needed, you had to work your way up the organization to identify the person who would release it. Today, I have immediate access to all the data I need to do my job. There is still information to which I don't have access but ..."
    >
    > **Example:** "Before I go into a meeting, I scan my computer for the names of all the people in the meeting ... to see what I know about them. For example, I know that George Fensham's wife's name is Mary, that they have two boys, and that the oldest, Hank, is starting college this fall. I can ask where he decided to go. My records also show that Carol Levy's mother died recently and I can express my sympathy. It is these pieces of information that give me an advantage in getting to know people."

3. ***Customer access to information*** ... through the use of the Internet, the consumer now has far greater power vis-à-vis the seller.

    > **Example:** "When I first opened my medical practice, patients would come in, tell me their symptoms, and wait for me to prescribe some sort of medication. Now, they come in, tell me their symptoms, and then pull out pages and pages of material that they have printed off the internet."
    >
    > **Example:** Rob Taunton had decided to purchase a digital camera. He visited the local camera store and then the local electronics stores. Then, he went on-line and found the best price from a firm a thousand miles away. Cliff Barstaires did the opposite. He started his search on-line, identified the features he wanted and then went to the local stores armed with this information.

4. *Security of information* … with the introduction of computer have come growing concerns over the usage, and misusage, of personal and sensitive information.

Example: A computer exists with data on your every telephone call. Another computer holds the details of every credit card purchase you have ever made. Other computers contains your medical history, the details of every loan you have applied for, every employment application you have filled out, every school record you have, your credit record, every web page you visit, etc. Combine this data in the hands of one agency and the dangers become obvious.

Example: Personal privacy has become a major issue. Software programs now enable a person to track every key stroke on another person's computer. Likewise, hackers can break through the firewalls designed to protect confidential data.

Example: "I had never thought of identity theft as something that would affect me. I am always very careful when I give out any information … especially on the internet. However, out of the blue, I received a bill from a credit card company. My name and my address but not my card. Then, I found that they had accessed my bank account and taken about a thousand dollars. Finally, they had applied for a $20,000 loan in my name. Fortunately, I knew the bank manager very well and the individual was arrested. However, I am still trying to clean up the mess."

CASE 3.5

ARBOR CONSULTING AND THE INTERNET

Arbor Consulting is an engineering consulting firm (headquartered in Houston) with more than 5,600 employees working out of twenty-three offices worldwide. For a number of years, the company has provided an informative web site in English, French, Spanish, Russian, Chinese and Japanese. While quite expensive to maintain, management has felt that it was a cost-effective use of the Internet.

In recent months, two issues have been raised with regard to the company's Internet usage. One of the company's major clients, LNG Industries, has asked why Arbor does not have an extranet (i.e., a system whereby their representatives in the field can place orders, check on the status of orders, etc.). At the present time, the field personnel phone or e-mail these inquiries to the local Arbor office which then e-mails the request to the headquarters. "It generally takes 24 hours to get a reply," the LNG contact observed. "And that is far too long if you are waiting for something. The people in the field need an immediate response."

The other issue resulted from a major problem with a project in Indonesia. The local manager had suggested and implemented a substantial chance in a local hydroelectric project with disastrous results. The client was extremely unhappy and their lawyers were preparing to file numerous suits.

When, the manager in Pakistan heard about the situation, he wrote to Arbor's president as follows, "When I heard about that problem, I was stunned. We ran into the same problem last year and came up with an elegant solution that left the client very satisfied. As a company, our reputation is hurt by doing one thing in one country and something totally different in another. Why don't we install an Intranet (i.e., a data base to which employees can input their ideas and solutions for solving various problems) so that the 'left hand knows what the right hand is doing'"?

Question: What are the pros and cons of establishing a system which customers can use to place orders, check on the status of orders, etc.?

Question: What are the pros and cons of establishing an internal data base of ideas, approaches, and solutions so that employees can see if a particular problem has previously been analyzed and handled?

Question: If Arbor Consulting goes ahead with these proposals, what are the risks associated with a hacker breaking into Arbor's computer system and gaining access to both the internal and external systems?

SUMMARY

1. The business world is continually changing and, to survive, businesses have to adapt. Complacency and stagnation are not viable options. The continuous stream of new technologies and the ever present need to cut costs and maintain profit margins mean that a manager has to continually evaluate his/her company's position relative to new approaches and technologies.

2. For many centuries, society used relatively little technology beyond paper, pen and ink, and candles. It relied heavily in human and animal muscle power. Yet, starting in the mid to late 18th century, three technologies (in a very broad sense) revolutionized the world of business:

   - Mechanization ... the growing ability to replace human and animal power by machines.

   - Interchangeable parts ... the development of standardized items that could be substituted one for another.

   - Assembly line ... the product moved not the workers.

3. The most dramatic impact has resulted from the growth of computer-based technology. It has impacted:

   - The way firms do business.
   - Communications.
   - Data analysis.
   - Access to information.

4. Two major changes have occurred with regard to the way firms do business, namely:

   - The provision of worldwide versus local coverage ... the ability of a firm to function in a global context rather than merely in the local environment.

   - The replacement of human intermediaries by technology ... the automation of many of the functions previously handled by individuals.

5. In the communications area, there have been numerous major changes in recent years:

   - Cellular phones ... which have enabled a person to maintain contact with another on a 24/7 basis.

   - E-mails ... that quick and easy form of communication that has largely replaced more formal approaches.

   - Instant messaging/text messaging ... two other technologies that enable quick and easy communications.

   - Interconnectivity ... the advent of the wireless technology which enable a business person to connect with their computer and receive message virtually anywhere in the world.

6. Data analysis ... the advances in computer technology have dramatically improved a business firm's ability to:

   - Record keeping ... the maintenance of, and access to, a wide range of data.

   - Modeling ... the use of mathematical models to illustrate the marketplace and project future impacts.

   - Data mining ... the analysis of sets of data to identify key factors and relationships.

7. Access to information … one of the computer's main contributions has been in the availability of information. Employees now have immediate access to data and information that previously would have required approval from one or more levels of management. Customers can now go to the Internet and gather information thus reinforcing their position vis-à-vis the suppliers.

8. This improved access to information has come at a price. There is a growing concern over the usage and misusage of personal information and the growing fear of a super computer that could put together all the information into one powerful data base.

CRITICAL THINKING QUESTIONS

1. Only forty years ago, a noted industrialist stated that there was a worldwide market for just three computers!! Now, there are a substantial number of households that have four or five computers. Why? Why did this leading industrialist so dramatically underestimate the market? And why have computers been so widely and rapidly adopted?

   _____

   _____

   _____

   _____

2. Many people are still very concerned over the security of personal information. There is a growing fear that the ability to pull together information (such as ones tax return, health history, driving record, telephone logs, etc., etc.) will destroy a person's privacy and leave them at the mercy of a variety of agencies. To what extent is this a realistic fear? And to what extent has it already occurred?

   _____

   _____

   _____

   _____

3. What do you see as the future of Internet-based sales? Each year, the volume of on-line sales has increased as people become more comfortable with this option. However, this growth has been slower than many predicted. Some felt that electronic purchasing would rapidly kill off the bricks and mortar operations. So far, it has not and many retailers have recognized the synergy between the two approaches. What do you see happening in the years ahead? Are some of retail stores likely to be put out of business? If so, what sorts of businesses? If not, where will the balance be between electronic retailing and the bricks and mortar stores?

   _____

   _____

   _____

   _____

4. Acme Tools and Parts used to have seven sales people who called on customers and four internal sales people who handled incoming calls. The internal sales people were kept busy by customers calling in to get quotes on specific items, checking delivery dates, etc. Then, in 2000, the company established an extranet – one of the first in its industry. Customers could sign up and obtain direct access to the company's catalogs and data bases. As a result, the numbers of calls to the internal sales force declined and, over the next four years, three of them were terminated. It also had an impact on the outside sales force. While they continued to make calls on customers, these calls tended to be shorter and less personal. As one salesman commented, "We used to really talk with our customers. Now,

they go direct to our web site. We only spend time with them when they have a serious problem." Has the extranet been a success? Has Acme lost anything as a result? Or has it gained an opportunity?

_____

_____

_____

_____

5. Jim Brown stuck his head around the door. "I plan to attend the meeting this afternoon, Bob," he said. "Great," Bob replied. "But you didn't have to walk all the way over here to tell me that. You could have sent me an e-mail." Bob paused for a moment. "It has just struck me. I used to get e-mails from you on a daily basis. But I haven't had one in weeks. What's going on?" Jim shrugged his shoulders. "I try to avoid e-mails as much as possible these days." What do you think is going on here? Why does Jim prefer face-to-face communications to the use of technology?

_____

_____

_____

_____

6. Cartwright Industries (a manufacturer of components) was in the process of upgrading its web site and two of its managers, Tom Ridgeway and Marlene Johnson, were discussing how much product information should be included. Tom's view was that customers should have access to all the product information they might need. "By providing all the information, we look professional and ready to do business." Marlene's opinion was very different. "I think we should provide just the basic data on each product. For example, the thickness of the component, its special features, the cost per unit, and whether or not it is in stock. Then, if the customer wants to make a purchase, they call up our in-house sales people. In this way, we maintain an ongoing and personal contact with the customer. If we go your route, we will never have occasion to talk with them." Where do you come out on this argument? What factors would influence your answer?

_____

_____

_____

_____

7. The last five years have seen a dramatic growth in the use of technologies which has changed the business environment. There is no evidence to suggest that the pace of technological development is going to slow down. Using your own personal crystal ball, what innovations would you expect to see occur in the next fifty years?

_____

_____

_____

_____

CASE PROBLEM

THOMAS JACKMAN & SONS

Thomas Jackman & Sons was established in 1925 and built up a reputation for its high quality electrical equipment which it exported to representatives worldwide who then sold the products to their customers.

When Peter Storey took over as president in 1998, a consultant warned him that the company was falling behind in terms of its use of technology. As a result, the company's management decided to cut back on its advertising and promotion and invest heavily in all areas of computerization. Peter now felt they were among the cutting edge firms in their industry.

In August 2004, Peter received a call from Mary Sturgess, president of Royce & Hill. Located just north of London, they accounted for 30% of Thomas Jackman's total sales. The key point of the call was that Mary was considering selling the business. "We have just received an offer from Horton (a firm that represented another manufacturer). That made me think, would you be interested in acquiring us?"

Peter indicated he would give the matter some thought. It was an interesting idea. The immediate problem that came to mind was that, unlike Jackman, Royce & Hill had not kept up with technology. They still had many more typewriters than computers. And the records were still largely kept on a manual basis. While they were a good firm with a good reputation, most of the people had been with the company for 25 or more years ... and the culture was one that focused on quality and personal service rather than competitiveness. Peter was often quite taken aback when he compared their operation with his own.

Question: What would be the pros and cons of the acquisition? Based on this analysis, what conclusion would you come to?

_____

_____

_____

_____

Question: If Peter decides to acquire Royce & Hill, what game plan should he adopt? Should he leave it the way it is? Or should he try to bring it into the 21st century?

_____

_____

_____

_____

Question: *If Peter decides to bring it up-to-date, what approach should be taken—given Royce & Hill's culture?*

_____

_____

_____

_____

THE IMPACT
OF DIVERSITY

●VERVIEW

The term diversity refers to a mixture of people with different group identities or characteristics within the same work environment. Diversity can result from two factors:

- Cultural factors (e.g., Hispanic, Jewish, Muslim, etc.).
- Demographic factors (e.g., sex, age, size, marital status, religion, sexual orientation, etc.).

This chapter focuses on the impact of this diversity on the role of the manager. Specifically, it covers:

- Immigration.
- The impact of changing demographics.
- The impact of a diverse workforce.
- Handling of diversity.
- Diversity training.

IMMIGRATION

 Key Points:

1. The impact of immigration can be seen in terms of the following:
    - Its importance to the growth and development of the United States.
    - Immigrants often assume roles that natives are not willing to handle.
    - Problems for managers.
    - Social pressures ... especially caused by illegal immigrants.

As a result:

- The issue of immigration remains controversial.

2. ***The importance of immigration to the United States*** ... the "melting pot."

> **Example:** A study conducted in March 2000 showed that 28.4 million immigrants now live in the United States. This represents approximately 1 in 10 of all residents. Furthermore, more than 1.2 million legal and illegal immigrants come to the United States each year.
>
> **Example:** Immigrants have added dramatically to the richness and progress of the United States. Among some of the more famous immigrants to this country have been Albert Einstein (science), Irving Berlin (music), Frank Capra (cinema), Felix Frankfurter (law), Henry Kissinger (politics), etc.

3. ***Immigrants often assume unpopular roles*** ... many of those coming to the United States have limited skills and limited knowledge of English. As a result, their first employment is often in a minimum wage position for which there are few, if any, native born applicants.

> **Example:** In many southern states, the picking of cotton, grapes, etc. is done almost exclusively by migrant workers. Without them, it is highly doubtful if growers would be able to find sufficient workers to meet the demands.
>
> **Example:** "This restaurant would go out of business if people stopped coming to the United States. We rely on them as cleaners, dishwashers, etc."

4. ***Immigrants pose unique challenges for managers*** ... resulting from their lack of skills, limited English, and different work habits.

> **Example:** "Taking over the manufacturing end of the business was a real challenge. I was used to working with people who wore suits and spoke fluent English ... and generally speaking, I understood their values and knew what they were thinking. This is a whole different world. I only have a couple of people who speak the same language."
>
> **Example:** "I have no problems with immigrants when it comes to working. They put in a good day's work. But explaining our personnel policies and medical benefits to them is a nightmare. Translating a complex policy with regard to job safety into simple English and then into a foreign language can be a real challenge."

5. *Social pressures* ... immigrants (both legal and illegal) place a burden on local communities.

> **Example:** "Back in the '70s, there was a major influx of Soviet Jews into this area. While many of them were quite well educated, they had no experience whatsoever of job hunting. They had done whatever job the government told them to do. Also, they weren't used to shopping in large stores where there were multiple choices. They were overwhelmed. So, we had to set up an extensive program to not only teach them English but also introduce them to American life."
>
> **Example:** States bordering Mexico find themselves faced with huge healthcare and education costs ... primarily from the need to provide services to illegal workers and their families. Likewise, the police forces in these areas are often overwhelmed by the continuing flow across the border.

6. *The issue of immigration remains controversial* ... the main areas of disagreement being with regard to:

   - The rate at which immigrants should be legally allowed into the country.
   - The continuing influx of illegal immigrants.

> **Example:** There are millions of people around the world waiting for permission to immigrate to the United States. Because of the quota system, applicants in some countries have to wait 15 or 20 years before finally being admitted legally.
>
> **Example:** Each year, thousands of individuals make their way to the United States illegally ... often risking death to reach these shores. Many hundreds die in the attempt. The United States remains the destination of choice for many from the third world and less developed areas.

CASE
4.1

VAN HEFLIN MANUFACTURING

Van Helfin Manufacturing is an unusual company. It manufactures more than 6,000 different tools for a wide variety of industries (such as upholstery repairing). These are tools for which the demand is very limited and thus they have no real competition. All the tools are hand made and each is made by one individual who is an expert. Each has their own small work area. Visiting Van Heflin is like visiting a factory in the early 19th century.

"Finding people to work here is the main challenge. We're located in an older area of town. Over the years, the more affluent residents have moved out to the suburbs and thus the place is badly run down. People don't want to come down here to work. And, in any case, they don't want to work in a hot and dirty environment making tools. They prefer a white collar job behind a computer."

Giselle Van Heflin was discussing the problems of running her unique sort of business. "While we do advertise positions in the local newspaper, we get very few responses and those are from people who either don't want to work or have serious mental or health problems. So, a number of years back, we started contacting various agencies that work with immigrants and refugees. People arrive in this country not speaking the language, with limited skills, no education, nowhere to live, etc. and the agency provides support for them. We have hired a lot of their clients. And they have generally worked out well. However, as they become fluent in English and comfortable with the American way of life, they tend to move on."

"Many of my peers complain that these immigrants and refugees are taking jobs away from the general population. I suppose that may be true but without them, I'd be out of business."

Question: Where do you think the United States would be today if immigration had been rigorously limited to, say, 10,000 per year for the last hundred or so years?

Question: What strengths and benefits have immigrants brought to the United States?

Question: What should the United States do about the continuing influx of illegal immigrants? What can it do? Should it throw open its borders to anybody who wants to come here?

THE IMPACT OF CHANGING DEMOGRAPHICS

 Key Points:

1. The impact of changing demographics can be seen in terms of:

   - The aging population.
   - Migration of the population.
   - The changing ethnic make-up of areas.

2. *The aging population* ... the population of the United States is getting older and this has serious implications since it not only affects the way people live and what they buy but also their needs and requirements in terms of medical and other supporting services.

   > **Example:** By the year 2010, it is estimated that 20% of the population of the United States will be over 65 (compared with 13% in 2001) due to the aging of the baby boomers.
   >
   > **Example:** The ratio of working age residents to those 65 and over will fall from 4.8 to 1 in 2000 to 2.7 to 1 in 2040. When the Social Security system was established there were 16 workers for every pensioner. There are now 1.7 workers per pensioner. And this is just one example of a major program faced with serious long-term problems.

3. *The population continues to migrate* ... from rural areas to the cities, from the cities to the suburbs, and from the north to the south.

   > **Example:** The census of 1800 estimated that approximately 94% of the total population lived in rural communities. This percentage has steadily declined over the past two hundred plus years ... to less than 23% today.
   >
   > **Example:** The movement of population—particularly the middle class—from city to suburbs has been occurring for more than a century, pushing the boundaries of metropolitan areas far from the city and prompting rapid development of outlying counties.
   >
   > **Example:** According to the 2000 census, the population of the United States is moving south and west with states such as Nevada experiencing a 66% increase, Arizona's population increased by 40%, Florida by 24%, and Texas by 23%. By contrast, New York's population increased by 1.1% and Massachusetts' by only 1.3%.

4. *The changing ethnic make-up of areas* ... reflecting both the influx of immigrants into specific geographic area and the migration of more established residents in common with the general population.

> **Example:** Between 1990 and 2000, Boston saw a 27.3% increase in the Latino or Hispanic population and the Asian/Pacific Islander population increased by 49.4%. The Black or African American population remained unchanged while the white population declined by 13.9%.
>
> **Example:** In the 1990 census, the white (non-Hispanic) population of California represented 57% of the total of more than 29.7 million. By 2000, the population had increased to 33.9 million of whom only 47% were white.

5. *Important note:* This population shift impacts on the availability of individuals willing and able to work in local businesses and also on where consumers go to purchase items.

> **Example:** A manufacturer of wooden trusses for homes and buildings found that he had to bus in teams of workers from the Korean and Vietnamese communities in the downtown area because no local residents were available and willing to work in the factory environment.
>
> **Example:** Mrs. Bradley used to shop downtown. She now goes to a brand new mall located on relatively inexpensive land in the suburbs. As she points out, "I don't have to drive from one shop to another. I drive to the mall, park, and everything I need is there."

CASE 4.2

BARTON & MAYHAN

Barton & Mayhan opened its first department store in Atlanta in 1947 and, by early 2004, had stores in more than twenty malls across the south-eastern United States. Overall, the company enjoyed many years of continued growth and profitability . . . largely because of the growth of the population in its market areas.

However, in 2000, the rate of growth slowed down dramatically and preliminary figures for 2004 suggested that per store sales were now starting to decline. Marcus Finney, the manager of the Allendale store was especially concerned about this trend since his sales were down by more than 3% over the previous year. So, he arranged to have lunch with a friend from the local university.

"The Allendale mall was completed in 1962 and, at that time, it was on the cutting edge of mall design and development. One magazine called it 'the mall of the future.' Now, we are just one more suburban mall. In fact, a recent analysis suggested we are close to being part of the decaying downtown area. Look at the University and the area around it. It was all farm land well into the late '80s. Now it is surrounded by residential areas and you're building another campus ten miles further north."

His friend nodded. "You're right about that. In fact, we are seriously thinking of selling our house and buying a new one out by the Northville campus. Much better house values and far less traffic!! But that doesn't help you. I'm teaching retail management this semester so why don't I arrange for the class to visit the Allendale mall and see what they come up with. Let's have them do an analysis. Let's see what sorts of observations and conclusions they come up with."

Question: If you visited Allendale Mall, what do you think you would notice in terms of the demographics of the customers (in terms of their age, ethnicity, social level, purchasing behavior, etc.)?

Question: During this same visit, what do you think you would notice in terms of (a) the number of stores in the mall and (b) the corporate names on the stores?

Question: Why do you think management has not responded to the changing nature of the environment? What could it do?

THE IMPACT OF A DIVERSE WORKFORCE

Key Points:

1. Issues relating to the impact of the diverse work force categorized in terms of:

   - Women.
   - Minorities.
   - Physical handicaps.
   - Sexual orientation.

2. *Women* ... a critical and growing force in the workplace. Many more women are opting to focus primarily on their careers and less on traditional female roles. However, despite passage of Title VII of the Civil Rights Act of 1964 (which prohibited discrimination on the basis of sex) and the efforts of Equal Employment Opportunities Commission (EEOC) women still face bias and discrimination in the workplace.

   > **Example:** According to an AFL-CIO report, only one third of the labor force was female in 1950. By 2010, women are expected to account for 48% of the workforce.
   >
   > **Example:** In 1990, the typical employed woman was more likely to be in an administrative support job than in a managerial or professional job. However, by 2000, the reverse was true. In 2000, 32.3 percent of women were employed in managerial or professional occupations, compared to 23.5 percent in administrative support occupations.
   >
   > **Example:** Experiments have shown that a male and female candidate with the same non sex specific name on their resume (e.g., J.G. Smith) are quite often treated differently with the male candidate more likely to be called back for a second interview.

3. *Minorities* ... while various racial and ethnic minorities are a critical component of the workforce and are protected by Title VII of the Civil Rights Act of 1964, they still face major barriers in obtaining both employment and promotion and remain badly under-represented at the managerial level.

   > **Example:** "First of all, there are very few Hispanics in this company. I know of only two others besides myself. As a result, there isn't the same support group that the white males have. When a promotion opportunity does come up, we always seem to be the second choice."
   >
   > **Example:** Although African-Americans account for 12.9% of the population, they make up less than 2.5% of senior-level managers.

4. *Physical handicaps* ... with the passage of the Americans with Disabilities Act (ADA) in 1990, the law extended protection to a person who has a physical or mental impairment that substantially limits one or more major life activities (like sitting, standing, or sleeping).

> **Example:** I always thought that ADA covered people who were deaf, blind, or required the use of a wheelchair. However, I found out that it covers a wide range of conditions. An individual who suffers from epilepsy, diabetes, HIV infection or severe forms of arthritis, hypertension, or carpal tunnel syndrome may be covered by this law.

5. *Sexual orientation* ... while some states and localities do bar discrimination on the basis of sexual orientation, there is no comparable federal law to protect the rights of gay men, lesbians, bisexuals, and people who are transgender.

> **Example:** "I worked for a company in Massachusetts which has laws prohibiting discrimination on the basis of sexual orientation. My boss was aware of my position and I didn't run into any problems. Here in Missouri, I have to be much more careful. There is no comparable protection."

> **Example:** In 1993, the Federal government passed a law making it illegal for openly gay people to serve in the U.S. military. This is known as "Don't Ask, Don't Tell" policy and is still the guiding principle despite the fact that this keeps many qualified personnel out of the military.

6. *Important note:* As a result of these changes, the role of a manager has become increasingly complex and fraught with potential pitfalls.

> **Example:** A manager is trying to decide between three candidates for a managerial position: a white male, an African-American male, and a white female. "They are all good people. The problem I have is keeping my own personal biases out of my decision. What do I do if I just feel more comfortable promoting one rather than the other two?"

> **Example:** A manager is trying to decide whether or not to send Alan, who is a paraplegic in a wheelchair, to a meeting in Atlanta. "I just don't want to make life difficult for him. After all, he'll be on his own."

CASE 4.3

BRAXTON INDUSTRIES

On either side of the corridor leading to the president's office were photographs of the company's staff ... starting in 1924. It was a company tradition. Each year, everybody gathered on the lawn outside the main building and lined up for the corporate picture.

"The first thing you notice is how the size of the staff has varied from year to year along with the fortunes of the company," Max Henderson, the director of sales, commented. "The other thing you notice if you compare the first and last pictures is that the workforce has changed dramatically. Look at 1924 ... all male except for three secretaries. And all white. Now, look at last year's picture. More than fifty percent of the employees are women. Twenty percent of the workforce is African-American, 18% Hispanic, and 17% Asian-American. English used to be the first language of all employees. Now, it is the second language of as many as 40% of our people."

"The good news is that our workforce is representative of the local population and we pride ourselves on our hiring practices. Also, it means that we have a number of people who can relate to different segments of the population. However, in my opinion, it has made management more difficult. According to legend, the main problem in 1924 was the fights between the English and the Welsh workers in the plant. Today, there are no fights but there are a lot of problems that need to be handled in a diplomatic way."

"Look at last year's picture again. There are four employees in wheelchairs who are covered by ADA and three others who have conditions that complicate their employment. In addition, there are eleven employees who either work from home or work half days and share their job with another employee."

"It has certainly made being manager much more interesting and considerably more difficult."

Question: *What would you think has been the impact of the growing percentage of female employees on a manager's role?*

Question: *What impact would you think the growing number of employees of different ethnic and linguistic backgrounds has had on the manager's role?*

Question: *What special problems arise for a manager as a result of having handicapped and home workers?*

HANDLING OF DIVERSITY

 Key Points:

1. From the perspective of the manager, the key elements in handling diversity are:

   ■ The law.
   ■ The responsibility to take action.
   ■ The weakness of the "I didn't know" defense.

2. *The law* ... as previously indicated, Title VII of the Federal Civil Rights Act of 1964, states that "it shall be an unlawful employment practice for an employer to discriminate against any individual with respect to his compensation, terms, conditions, or privileges of employment, because of such individual's race, color, religion, sex, or national origin."

> **Example:** Prior to 1964, application forms regularly included questions about a candidate's sex, race, religion, etc. and similar questions were asked during the interview. These questions were deemed discriminatory and thus were eliminated.
>
> **Example:** "We had a situation recently. I was walking down the corridor about six o'clock in the evening and I came across two members of my department (of the same sex) in a very passionate embrace. They were embarrassed and so was I. Since I didn't want to overreact, I called the company's lawyer the following morning and he is looking into the law in this state. Do I need to take action or should I ignore it? I don't know."

3. *The responsibility to take action* ... every manager has a responsibility to take all possible steps to ensure that the workplace is free of any behavior that may be deemed illegal under the law.

> **Example:** "I knew that Sara was making life very difficult for Barbara. She was always making snide remarks with definite sexual overtones. To be honest, I didn't want to get in the middle of the problem. However, I decided I had to say something so I took Sara aside and talked with her. I'm glad I did. I gather that Barbara was just about to hire a lawyer and bring a suit against me and the company."
>
> **Example:** "One of the managers had a picture on his wall of a very attractive young lady. Personally, I wasn't offended by it but one of my staff was. What was surprising was that it was one of my male employees who complained about it. I talked with the manager and he replaced the picture with one of his children."

4. ***The weakness of the "I didn't know" defense*** ... lack of knowledge of a problem is not *per se* a valid defense. Courts have increasingly concluded that employers (and thus managers) are responsible for the behavior of their subordinates and thus need to know what is occurring in their department.

Example: Alice Rosett brought a lawsuit against her employer, Tabor Industries, charging that she had been sexually harassed for many months by another member of the department. Her boss, Virginia Manton claimed that she was totally unaware of any harassment. However, other people in the department admitted they were aware of the situation and the court decided that Tabor Industries and Ms. Manton should have taken action.

Example: When Mike Corwin was passed over for promotion, he complained of discrimination. "I think the only reason I wasn't promoted was because of my age. I know I only have a few more years with this company but I believe I should have been given the opportunity." His immediate boss and the divisional manager dismissed the complaint as unfounded. However, the president of the company requested that a study be made of Corwin's complaint. "I just don't want to find myself in a court room looking stupid," he commented.

CASE 4.4

LINWOOD ENGINEERING

Angela Vaccaro could still hear her boss' instructions ringing in her ears. "Go down to Linwood and clean up that mess. I sometimes think we have more complaints and problems down there than we have employees. Do whatever you have to do but get the place cleaned up."

The general manager, Jens Logan, had given her a run down on the overall situation. "We have a group of older white males who can only be called 'rednecks.' They have no time for any of the ethnic minorities and regard the women as second class citizens. Then, there are two groups of younger white males—one is well-trained and very professional and the other I would describe as a group of unpleasant thugs. Finally, we have four or five ethnic groups that dislike each other for some reason and will not work together. As a result, the atmosphere here is pretty bad. Each week, we get two or three complaints of sexual harassment or discrimination."

As a skilled lawyer, Angela was familiar with both the laws regarding sexual harassment and discrimination and the recent court decisions in these areas. There were more than fifty files and the first thing Angela noted was that the date on some of them was more than a year old. After a careful review of all the materials, Angela began to think about a plan of action. In the long run, she would need to establish a training program. Of greater concern was what she should do immediately.

Having toured the plant and office facilities and visited the ladies' room and the cafeteria, Angela placed a call to her boss. "Jim, do I have the authority and funding to bring in the painters and heating people to clean this place up? It is filthy, cold and depressing."

Question: Why, if you were Angela Vaccaro, would you see cleaning the plant up as a high priority?

Question: What would you (as Angela) do with the more than fifty files currently pending?

Question: What steps would you (again playing the role of Angela) take to change the culture of Linwood Engineering with regard to the treatment of personnel?

DIVERSITY TRAINING

🔑 **Key Points:**

1. The keys to an effective diversity training program are:
   - Top management's commitment.
   - Regular reinforcement.
   - Follow-up.
   - Enforcement.

2. *Top management's commitment* ... if the leadership of an organization is not fully committed to the program then it is very unlikely that it will be effective.

> **Example:** A medium-sized firm in Illinois had serious problems with both sexual harassment and discrimination so, at the recommendation of the board of directors, the company introduced an ongoing program to improve the situation. Top management did not support the program and, as a result, most employees felt that it was a waste of time and thus very few benefits were realized.
>
> **Example:** "The company for which I work organized a "Diversity Day" when they held a series of programs (which we were required to attend) informing employees both about the law and its policies and procedures. It was a good program and the president was there all day enthusiastically supporting the program. However, none of the division heads attended. So, we all came away with very mixed feelings. Was this just window dressing ... or did the company really plan to enforce its policies?"

3. *Regular reinforcement* ... it is also important that the training be conducted on a regular basis. A program held every four or five years isn't likely to have a great deal of impact.

> **Example:** When he joined the company, Bob Squires was told that, as part of his orientation program, he would be required to attend a diversity training program. That was the last he heard about it."
>
> **Example:** Sophie Fischer was accused of sexual harassment by her assistant, Andrew. Management claimed that Sophie had attended at least two training seminars and thus knew what was acceptable and what was not. However, discussions with Sophie indicated that it had been four years since she had last attended a session and that her views were way out of date.

4. *Follow-up* ... even the best of programs are worthless unless there are clearly defined procedures for monitoring and responding to all complaints and concerns.

> **Example:** When Tanya Portman took over as human resource manager for JayBar Enterprises, she was impressed by the programs in place at the company. In addition to the annual update meetings held at different sites, there was a large policies and procedures manual explaining which forms should be used and what steps should be taken at each stage of any complaint. However, when she had lunch one day with a group of employees, she was amazed to learn that none of them had ever seen any of the forms and didn't have a good idea of the procedures to be followed. The policies and procedures manual had never been distributed to the employees. Her first task, therefore, was to create a brochure, summarizing the key points of the manual, which went to every employee.
>
> **Example:** One of the older members of the company, Ian Bradley, was known to have an eye for young and attractive ladies. So, when the director of human resources heard of a potential problem with Debra (one of the company's new hires), she immediately scheduled a meeting with both parties. She warned Ian of the penalties for any further transgressions. And she made it clear to Debra that the company was watching out for her best interests and explained the steps she should take if the problem arose again.

5. *Enforcement* ... no policy or program can be effective if the employees know that the organization is unlikely to take any action. On the other hand, if they know it will take swift and severe action if they fail to adhere to the company's rules and regulations, then they are far less likely to do so.

> **Example:** Jim had asked Teresa out on a number of occasions. Each time, she said "no." The next time he asked her for a date, she reported him to the appropriate corporate manager who warned Jim that one more time and he would be severely punished. Jim persisted and, after a verbal warning and a one week suspension, he was terminated.
>
> **Example:** "Different people find different words offensive. Something that you may find perfectly acceptable may make somebody else very uncomfortable. I sent out a memo stating the company's policy in this area and explaining what would happen if this occurred again. The first person who fell into this "trap" was the chief executive officer who made a comment at a meeting to which a couple of our minority employees objected. We followed our rules and made it clear that they applied to everybody in the company ... from the very top to the bottom."

CASE
4.5

DIVERSITY TRAINING AT THE UNIVERSITY

"A total waste of time and effort." This was the observation of a number of those who attended the University's diversity training program.

A key phrase in the University's mission statement was that "everybody in the University community has an obligation to create and maintain a climate in which respect and tolerance are recognized as part of the institution's commitment to educational quality."

Despite the words in the mission statement, each year the University experienced a substantial and growing number of complaints with regard to sexual harassment and discrimination. So, as part of its annual diversity program, the University organized a day-long program. Staff and administrators were required to attend and all faculty were invited to attend. The average session had approximately 45 attendees ... young and old, male and female, white and African-American, etc.

The first part of the program was devoted to a review of the law and its current interpretation and application. The speakers emphasized the cost of law suits and the need to be extremely careful in handling and working with personnel. Then, the participants were given a series of ten short case situations. In each case, they were asked to determine whether or not the characters described were guilty of sexual harassment and discrimination. These cases were then discussed at length with wide variations in opinions.

"I thought it was quite a good program," another participant commented. "Unfortunately, I had a meeting this morning and didn't get to the session until 10:30 a.m. And then I had to leave at 2:00 p.m. for a meeting with the president. But what I saw was good."

Question: Do you think the University's holding of these sorts of programs is a good idea? Should all organizations do the same?

Question: Would you expect the participants in the session to agree on whether or not the ten cases reflected situations involving sexual harassment or discrimination?

Question: Why have the twin issues of sexual harassment and discrimination become so important for a manager these days?

SUMMARY

1. Diversity in the workplace has added another level of complexity to the manager's role. And, to be successful, a manager has to be able to effectively handle this diversity, minimize any problems it may cause, and take advantage of the benefits that it provides.

2. The United States likes to call itself a "melting point" with regard to its ability to absorb and integrate immigrants from all areas of the world. The key points with regard to immigration are:

   ■ Its importance to the growth and development of the United States.

   ■ Immigrants often assume roles that natives are not willing to handle.

   ■ Problems for managers.

   ■ Social pressures ... especially caused by illegal immigrants.

   As a result:

   ■ The issue of immigration remains controversial.

3. Another key factor related to diversity is that of the changing demographics, specifically:

   ■ The aging population ... aging, like taxes, is one of life's certainties.

   ■ Migration of the population ... from rural areas to the cities and from north to south.

   ■ The changing ethnic make-up of areas ... resulting from the inflow of ethnic groups into the specific area and the outflow of previous migrations to the suburbs and their integration into the general population.

4. The results of all these changes has been the diversification of the workforce ... and here the key impacts stem from:

   ■ Women ... an important and growing force in the workplace.

   ■ Minorities ... the ongoing attempts to ensure that they are represented in the senior levels of the workforce.

   ■ The physically handicapped ... the extension of civil rights to individuals with any condition that will limit their ability to do a job.

   ■ Sexual orientation ... while not protected by federal law, this is an issue that is going to remain a serious issue for many years to come.

5. As indicated above, these changes have made the role of a manager far more complex and he/she needs to be familiar with:

   ■ The law ... in particular Title VII of the Federal Civil Rights Act of 1964.

   ■ The responsibility to take action ... a manager is responsible for taking every step possible to try to ensure that the work environment is consistent with the law.

   ■ The weakness of the "I didn't know" defense ... lack of knowledge of a problem is not per se a valid defense. A manager is expected to be aware.

6. Finally, a manager needs to be familiar with the key elements of diversity training:

   ■ Top management's commitment ... senior personnel have to fully support the program.

   ■ Regular reinforcement ... training has to be given on a regular and frequent basis.

   ■ Follow-up ... there has to be an effective methodology for following up on complaints, etc.

   ■ Enforcement ... all policies must be strictly enforced.

CRITICAL THINKING QUESTIONS

1. When immigrants arrived in the United States, in say, 1850 from Germany, Italy or Russia, what do you think would have struck these new arrivals as being very different from the environment they had left?

   _____

   _____

   _____

   _____

2. Where do you stand on the question of illegal immigrants? Should anybody who reaches these shores be allowed to stay? Or should the government follow a rigorous policy of deporting all such illegal immigrants back to their country of origin? What are the implications of the policy you select?

   _____

   _____

   _____

   _____

3. What are the differences between two women—one 20 years old and the other 70 years old—in terms of the amount of money to spend? Do they purchase the same types of items? Do they need the same sort of services? Do they live in the same area? Do they work in the same area? Are their attitudes and perspectives the same?

   _____

   _____

   _____

   _____

4. You run a dental practice in an old part of town. The customer base is largely white coming from the Italian, Polish and Russian communities. Our employees, however, are almost exclusively Hispanic, many of them recent immigrants to the United States, and they speak Spanish among themselves. One of your long time patients complains that "it is like visiting a foreign country." He claims he doesn't understand what the staff is saying. How would you address this problem?

   _____

   _____

   _____

   _____

5. As a manager of twenty employees, you do your very best to obey the law. You carefully avoid any form of racial or sexual discrimination. You attend seminars on the subject and ensure that the company's policies and procedures are up-to-date and that everybody is aware of them. "I don't care what their sexual preferences are as long as they do their job" is your motto. Now you are faced with a problem. There is a lesbian couple that kisses whenever they get the opportunity and there is a gay couple who goes everywhere together (including the rest room) usually holding hands. It makes you feel a little uncomfortable. For some time, the other members of the staff have been making adverse comments. And now, two of your customers have commented on the situation. "Are you running a home for sexual deviants?" was one of the comments. What would you do in this situation?

_____

_____

_____

_____

6. One of the first things you noted, when you took over as general manager of the Manufacturing Division of Carter Industries, was that there were a number of serious problems with regard to the extremely diverse workforce. The shop floor seemed to be divided into a number of antagonistic groups. There was an awful lot of shouting and obscenities, and hand painted signs had to be removed from walls on a regular basis. What steps would you take at this point in time? Do you have to do anything?

_____

_____

_____

_____

7. You walk into your office one morning to find two very irate female members of your staff. They are your most productive and cooperative subordinates and thus you are stunned to learn that they are suing you and your company for both sexual harassment and discrimination. What would you do immediately? And what would you put at the top of your "to-do" list over the next month or so?

_____

_____

_____

_____

CASE PROBLEM

RICHMOND COMMUNITY BANK

Hiring, especially at the entry level teller position, was always a major challenge for the human resource manager at Richmond Community Bank.

"There are a number of large firms located in the area that are attractive places to work. That makes it hard for us. We try to be competitive in terms of salaries and benefits. However, the available labor pool is very limited. So, hiring is a serious problem."

"I interviewed five people this morning. Carl A was a white male in a wheelchair. He had a bachelor's degree and has taken some graduate classes. Quite sharp. Two problems with him. First, I think he is overqualified. Second, our main need is in the Downtown office and that is an old building that really isn't wheelchair friendly. Then, there was Bob B. He's African-American and bored with retirement. I'd guess he's in his late 60s. He's never worked in banking. And he seemed to have health problems."

"Candace C. is a middle-aged white female. She has worked in banking. However, I thought she was a somewhat disagreeable person. Very aggressive ... and we are a generally laid back company. Without prompting, she told me she is a single mother with three small children. Danga D. is a Nigerian who has just arrived in this country to join her husband. She's an attractive younger woman but I had a serious problem with her English. She claims to be able to speak English but I found her very hard to understand."

"Finally, there was Rajah E. He's a Sikh with a colorful turban and a long moustache that he twirls with some regularity. He speaks good English and could certainly do the job. However, he made a couple of comments which seemed to me to be somewhat disparaging to women and other religious groups. We employ a large number of women ... many of them in very senior positions. And there are a number of substantial ethnic communities among our customer base and I ended up wondering how he would handle them."

Question: How would you determine which of the five candidates (if any) to hire?

_____

_____

_____

_____

Question: What possible legal issues do these five candidates raise? What areas of possible discrimination do you see here?

_____

_____

_____

_____

Question: *What steps would you take to ensure that the Bank follow a sound and non-discriminatory approach to hiring?*

_____

_____

_____

_____

ETHICS AND SOCIAL RESPONSIBILITY

CHAPTER 5

OVERVIEW

In recent years, the questions of ethics and social responsibility have taken on increased importance. Why? It is hard to say that they have become more common. What has changed is there is a far great lens placed on them these days. The explosion in terms of television channels and the dramatic growth of the Internet have led to far greater scrutiny. And since misdoings make for far better products than reports of success and performance, behavior in the business world (such as that at Enron and Worldcom) has led to a far greater awareness on the part of managers.

In this chapter, we will focus on:

- Ethics.
- Values.
- Social Responsibility.

And we will look at the

- The interests of stakeholders.
- Ensuring ethical behavior.

ETHICS

 Key Points:

1. Ethics ... what are ethics? Ethics is:

> *A set of rules or principles that define whether conduct is deemed right or wrong.*

95

You may be more familiar with the phrase:

> ***Do unto others as you would have them do unto you.***

2. While the definition is relatively straightforward, defining what is ethical is not. Whether or not a person sees their actions as ethical depends on a number of factors, namely their:

   ■ Values . . . those factors that are important to an individual; the aspects of their life on which they put a high value.

   ■ Personality . . . the personal identity or individuality of each distinct person.

   ■ Experiences . . . those events in their life that caused the individual to reevaluate their expectations of society and the business world.

Example: Jim Smith grew up in a very rough neighborhood in a highly dysfunctional household. His father was a heavy drinker and regularly abused his wife and children. He grew up fighting many of the local thugs. Although he obtained a college degree and eventually became a manager, his values were still heavily influenced by his upbringing and he carried many of these values into the business environment.

Example: Angela and Mary Hayes were twins. However, their personalities were totally different. Angela felt that she was in control of her life whereas Mary did not (loss of control), Angela was very manipulative of other people whereas Mary tried to be very straightforward (Machiavellianism), Angela had a very strong self image and saw herself as able to do anything. By contrast, Mary always doubted her own abilities (self-esteem). Angela adapted very rapidly to changing circumstances while Mary was most comfortable in a static environment (self-monitoring). Finally, Angela made decisions very rapidly and took risks while her sister always took a long time to make decisions and tried to avoid risks (risk taking).

Example: When Martin initially worked for Peter Candless, he was very uncomfortable with many of Peter's actions. He often questioned the ethics of his boss' actions. However, over the years, he watched Peter rise up through the organization and receive ever greater rewards. And, over the years, Martin became more comfortable with Peter's behavior and adopted them as his own.

---

3. Different groups and different cultures have very different perceptions of ethical behavior.

Example: "In the United States, we have laws against meeting with ones competitors to fix prices and bids. However, in some parts of the world, this is seen as expected behavior. You are not going to be successful if you don't play the game by the local rules."

> **Example:** Vinton Industries, headquartered in New Orleans, had very strict policies with regard to payments to either firms or officials. As Steve Walker observed, "in its policies and procedures manual, the company makes it clear that it doesn't condone such behavior. If a person is found guilty of breaking this policy they are immediately terminated. However, in this country (located in Central Africa) nothing happens without making a payment to somebody. Normally, as little as ten dollars will get things moving. I know I'm breaking the company's policies but I don't see any other way of conducting business."

4. Ethical and legal ... whereas a person's ethical values are determined by their own personal values, personality, and experiences, the legal system is a set of laws put in place by society as a whole. This means that an action can be legal and ethical, illegal and unethical, legal and unethical, and, in rare cases, ethical but illegal.

> **Example:** It is perfectly legal and ethical to advertise a used car for sale at $9,995 yet not include the fact that the purchaser will have to pay a delivery fee of $559.
>
> **Example:** Some years ago, the American Bar Association regarded advertising by lawyers as unethical although there was nothing illegal about doing so. The American Bar Association later changed it position and thus advertising became an accepted practice.
>
> **Example:** Dumping toxic waste is both unethical (since it hurts the environment and the people living in the area) and illegal (since there are laws against doing so).
>
> **Example:** It may be perfectly ethical for a doctor to prescribe a specific medication for a patient (since their objective is to aid their patients) but illegal to do so.

CASE 5.1

WORLDWIDE TOBACCO

The popularity of tobacco in the United States had decreased significantly in recent years as a result of a number of factors. The Surgeon General's report in 1964 showing that cigarettes were a major cause of lung cancer and various respiratory diseases led to the banning of cigarette advertising in 1971.

Placing warning labels on packs of cigarettes and focusing on keeping the product out of the hands of teenagers also added to the decline as did introducing bans on smoking in public places. Counter advertising and public education programs have also been effective to some degree.

Major law suits brought against the cigarette companies by both individuals and states (to compensate them for the increased health care costs) have led to substantial financial penalties. Today, even the companies themselves run advertising to either prevent smoking or help people to quit.

These changes have posed major strategic challenges to the large tobacco companies since they have a very large investment in the tobacco business. As a result, they have been forced to look for new markets. Initially, they focused on segments of the U.S. market where smoking was less common (e.g., African-American women) but that resulted in extensive protests from consumer groups. So, in recent years, the tobacco companies have focused on building up their brands in foreign countries.

Question: Is it ethical for cigarette companies to focus on those segments of the adult U.S. market that do not currently smoke?

Question: Is it ethical to emphasize the sale of cigarettes in those countries (such as China and Korea) where there are far fewer restrictions on the sale of tobacco products?

Question: What other examples can you think of that represent actions that are legal and ethical? Legal but not ethical? Ethical but not legal? And illegal and unethical?

VALUES

 ## Key Points:

1. A person's values are defined as:

> *The levels of worth that an individual places on various factors in their life.*

2. An individual's values are based on a large number of factors:

   - Interaction with parents and siblings.
   - Contacts with their peer group.
   - Their life time experiences.

3. Interactions with parents and siblings. Children recognize what is acceptable behavior within the family and what actions produce the desired effect.

> **Example:** Cara and Laura were sisters three years apart. Cara, the elder always complained that Laura could always get money out of her parents while she found it very difficult to do so. This was true. Laura had watched her older sister, seen which strategies worked and which did not, and had adopted values and behavior patterns that worked.
>
> **Example:** Harriet Hayes grew up in a very conservative household. Her parents had always voted Republican and she did so automatically. She never considered voting for any other party.

4. Values continue to develop in high school and college (through interactions with one's peers, one's team mates and, occasionally, the instructors).

> **Example:** In his first year in college, Jim shared a room with two guys who were into binge drinking. Most of the time, the room looked as if it had been hit by a tornado. At the start of his second year, Jim moved into an apartment with a couple of other friends who were moderate drinkers and liked to entertain in the apartment. The room, while not perfect, was relatively clean and tidy. By the time he graduated, Jim enjoyed an occasional drink and was regarded by his mother as a "neat freak".
>
> **Example:** Arthur played on a soccer team that usually lost its game by a wide margin. The captain didn't expect them to win ... and they didn't. Then, a couple of outstanding players transferred to the school and they started winning. Arthur began to put much greater emphasis on being fit and playing well. His values changed.

5. And individual's values continue to change throughout their life. They are influenced by their experiences, the environment, and by their own growth and maturity.

> **Example:** In high school, Scott had a great group of friends. They were known as the Red Barber Gang and they would do anything. Vandalizing cars was fun for a time. Then, they moved on to robbing liquor stores. Scott was probably heading for a life of crime when the principal of his high school organized a visit to the local prison. Most of Scott's friends thought it was fun day out. Scott saw it as truly frightening. The prospect of spending even one day behind bars appalled him. His values changed in a second.
>
> **Example:** After leaving college, Cynthia had a series of unsuccessful jobs. She worked for bosses who tended to be somewhat unpleasant and unhelpful. As a result, she saw this as the way to get things done. She then went to work for a local university where she was pleasantly surprised to find how friendly people in the office were. Her boss was extremely helpful. After a few months, Cynthia recognized that she much preferred the current environment and, when she was promoted, she adopted these new values in the handling of her people.
>
> **Example:** Brian was a risk taker in his youth. Sky diving, bungee jumping, rock climbing were his favorite activities. He drove a Corvette at high speed and he rarely had a penny to his name. Along came Gillian, they married, bought a house in the suburbs, and had three children. Brian's values changed. His family became more important than the thrill of jumping out of planes. Providing for their security and well being led to a far more conservative approach to money and life in general.

6. The values of a business organization are set, to a very large degree, by those values shared by the members of top management. If they enforce a particular set of values then the entire company will usually adopt those values. On the other hand, if they have loose values or do not enforce their values, then it is likely that the lower levels of the organization (or groups within the organization) will develop their own set of values ... often directly contrary to those espoused by the company as a whole.

> **Example:** Drayton Industries had a strict policy against drinking and the use of drugs on company property. This policy reflected the views of the founder, Andrew Drayton, who was a teetotaler and a leading advocate of drug prevention programs in the area. His senior managers all followed the company policy but they were relatively lax in enforcing it ... especially with new managers. It wasn't until one of the facilities had a serious accident caused by alcohol, and the police arrested four employees for selling drugs outside a plant, that the company realized that words were not enough. Their values had to be rigorously enforced.

CASE 5.2

TO THYSELF BE TRUE

Brian Cox and Tom Edwards joined the Color-Glow Company on the same date in 2001 as part of a management trainee program. They became good friends despite the fact that they came from very different backgrounds.

Brian lived with his mother in a tough neighborhood and, over the years, joined a couple of gangs as a way of gaining acceptance. His main achievement in high school was on the football team. After a couple of jobs with fast food franchises, he worked in a retail store but was let go. He was somewhat surprised when an uncle was able to get him into the trainee program at Color-Glow.

Tom on the other hand, grew up in a relatively affluent suburb, excelled in school, and sang in the local church choir. His father worked for a brokerage house and believed in self reliance and honesty. His mother was a school teacher in the local high school. They were a very close knit family.

In January 2005, the two of them attended a trade show in Atlanta and, on their return, prepared their travel expense forms. Tom estimated his at $650 while Brian's figure was well over a thousand. "You will have to pad yours to make it look consistent with mine," Brian said. "Look add a "1" here and put in $50 for dinner on Thursday and . . ." "But that isn't right," Tom replied. "Maybe not," his friend admitted. "But that's what Walt [their boss] always does."

At the trade show, Color-Glow introduced a new line of paint accompanied by extensive trade and consumer advertising. The ads implied that this new paint would not chip or peel for 20 years. However, the company's own research showed that, in the middle of summer, it could blister and chip. In this case, Tom didn't see a problem with this. As Tom said, "If the president is comfortable with this material, I am not going to argue with him." Brian, however, felt very uncomfortable.

Question: Why do you think Brian and Tom seem to have different values?

Question: How would you respond to Brian's suggestion with regard to the travel expenses and Tom's comment about the inaccurate statement?

Question: To what extent does the senior management of a company establish the organization's values?

SOCIAL RESPONSIBILITY

☞ Key Points:

1. Social responsibility is defined as:

> *The responsibility of an organization to take action to protect, and even promote, the welfare of the society in which it functions.*

The argument behind this definition is that businesses make money by "taking advantage" of the society in which it operates and thus has a responsibility to give back to the society.

> **Example:** Pat Scales, president of Thaltec Corporation, is a great believer in giving back to society. "We support a local hospice for battered women. We release our manager to work with local non-profit organizations. We support local sports teams at all levels. And we are very active in a group that is helping clean up the local river. We believe the public expects this sort of activity, that it creates a better image for the company and that, in the long run, it improves our profitability."

2. Not everybody agrees that a business has a social responsibility to the society. At the opposite end of the spectrum is the view that a company has one responsibility, namely: to make money for the stockholders. And thus anything which reduces profitability is inappropriate. If the stockholders want to use their dividends to support societal aims and goals then they certainly have the right to do so . . . but it should be their choice.

> **Example:** As Roger Corber, Senior Vice President of Allied Products said, "our stockholders have made it clear that we should be working towards profit maximization. Getting involved in socially responsible activities dilutes our primary purpose. Furthermore, we are good at manufacturing rubber products and don't have any real skills in social engineering. And, to be honest, there is very little support in the local community for our getting involved."

3. An organization's philosophy with regard to social responsibility is often determined by the personal interests and desires of top management or the majority ownership.

> **Example:** "When I acquired this company, we did absolutely nothing in the local community. We didn't have a bad reputation. I don't think we had a reputation at all. So, I set up a plan to encourage employees to become active. We now have people working in the local schools. We've been involved in a voter drive. We donated some land to one of the boy's clubs. And we provide free medical screening at the local mall. People think more kindly of us as a result of these activities. It has improved our image. And our people feel better knowing they are making a contribution.

CASE 5.3

ARISTO PHARMACEUTICALS

In early 1999, Gina Parcek (the president of Aristo Pharmaceuticals) identified five major targets for the company's research efforts. These targets included the development of a new drug for the treatment of Alzheimer's ... a rapidly growing problem as the population ages.

The first trials of Peritan on rats were extremely encouraging. Signs of Alzheimer's were largely reversed. So, the company obtained permission to conduct a test on 30 patients with advanced symptoms. The results were mixed. Six patients showed dramatic improvements. Ten showed some improvement and 9 showed none at all. Unfortunately, 5 patients died during the test ... far more than Aristo had predicted.

"The FDA [Federal Drug Administration] would never give us approval for Peritan as it stands," Ms. Parcek commented. "The problem is that Aristo has already spent $800 million on development and we are looking at another $500 million if we decide to continue to work on this class of drugs. All with no guarantee that we will come up with a product that will be approved."

"Ironically, Peritan has proven to be very effective against river blindness, a disease that afflicts millions in Africa and South America. The normal treatment is repeated doses of Invermectin ... and Peritan is much more effective without the side effects. The problem is, even if we set up a facility to manufacture Peritan, the price will be way beyond the resources of the markets that need it."

Question: Does Aristo have a social responsibility to continue with the development of Peritan and others in the same class of drugs? After all, it has proven effective in 1 out of 5 patients.

Question: Given that there are people who react negatively (sometimes fatally) to all drugs, at what point in time should the FDA ban or limit their use?

Question: Does Aristo have a social responsibility to offer Peritan at a cost which would enable the compound to be used to treat river blindness?

THE INTERESTS OF STAKEHOLDERS

Key Points:

1. A stakeholder is defined as:

> *An individual or groups of individuals who are impacted by the activities and policies of an organization.*

2. Most people are more familiar with the term "stockholders." These are individuals and organizations that own shares in an organization and benefit from increases in the price of the stock. By contrast, "stakeholders" are a far more diverse group and stockholders are only one of a broad range of individuals who have a stake in a company.

> **Example:** Wal-Mart is trying to obtain approval to build a new supermarket on the edge of town. Some stakeholders favor the development believing that the:
>
> - Town will benefit from an increase in taxes.
> - Store will be a potential employer in an area where unemployment is quite high.
> - Require new roads, more police, additional firefighters, etc.
> - Residents will be able to save money by being able to buy cheaper goods.
>
> Other stakeholders oppose the development because construction of the new store will:
>
> - Change the pace of life in the area.
> - Put many existing store owners out of business since they will face dramatically increased competition.
> - Result in increased air pollution, destroy the habitat of the local beavers, and infringe on plans to construct a green zone around the town.

3. Resolving conflicts between groups of stockholders is rarely easy since they often have dramatically different interests and goals.

> **Example:** A pharmaceutical company develops a new drug that is very effective against a disease common in South East Asia. The company (and its stockholders) goal is to make a substantial profit on the sale of the drug to cover not only the development costs but also costs associated with the development of drugs which were unsuccessful. Thus they want to price the drug at $200 per 50 tablets. Individuals suffering from the disease (and their governments) in South East Asia cannot afford this price. They want it to be priced at $2 per 50 tablets.
>
> **Example:** A university decided that, rather than construct a new building on its existing site, it would acquire and renovate an office building about a mile from the main campus. Most stakeholders were reasonably happy with this move. The main exception was the township which saw the building being removed from the tax roll. They had hoped the building would be acquired by a corporation which would continue to pay taxes.

4. Resolution of conflicts between stakeholders often depends on which stockholders have the greatest power and bring the most to the table.

> **Example:** A logging company wants to build a road into the mountains to bring out lumber. Environmentalists oppose this road on the grounds that it increases the probability of land slides into the lake below. The company argues that it will bring much needed revenue to the town and will provide additional jobs in an area of high employment. In this case, the road was approved.
>
> **Example:** Albert Industries purchased a large parcel of land close to the Interstate with the intent of building a distribution center on it. However, when it announced its plans, there was an outcry from a number of environmental groups who claimed that the site was home to a species of field mouse that was on the endangered species list. The company offered to move them to another site. However, the nature lovers began a nationwide campaign with placards showing the cute little mouse. Representatives appeared on television to plead their cause. The company lost its battle to use the land because, as the president commented, "we would have won if only it had been a large black spider rather than a cute little mouse."

5. In some cases, the two parties can reach a mutually acceptable compromise.

> **Example:** Representatives of Ranier Chemical Company met with the mayor, the town council, and representatives from various local groups from the town of Elkhorn to try to resolve a major conflict between the town and the largest local employer. Ranier was planning to ship drums of waste through the center of town; a move that the council and other civic groups strenuously opposed. After much heated discussion, somebody remembered the old railroad track that ran from the plant to the highway beyond the town. With only a small investment, the track could be put to good use. The company had a way to transport its waste and the downtown area remained waste free.
>
> **Example:** Jim Brandywine believed he should receive a very substantial increase in salary for the coming year. As he said to his boss, "I'm the lowest paid person in the group. With a 10% increase, I would only just catch up with the other salaries." Unfortunately, his boss was under instructions to keep all wage increases to 3% or less except in rare situations. In the end, Jim and his boss agreed that Jim would receive a 5% increase for the coming year (less than Jim was seeking but an exception to the guidelines given to his boss) and that the company would pick up the cost of Jim completing his MBA at the local university. Both parties were thus reasonably comfortable with the compromise.

CASE
5.4

THE WEST SIDE STADIUM

In March 2005, the Olympic Site Selection Committee visited New York as part of its evaluation of its bid for the 2012 Olympics. One of the key elements of the New York bid was the construction of a new stadium on a rail yard site owned by the Metropolitan Transit Authority (MTA). Under the plan, more than $1 billion of taxpayer money would be spent on the new stadium.

The proposal to build a stadium on the West side of Manhattan has provoked a major battle between those who support the idea and those who vehemently oppose it. Former mayor, Rudy Giuliani, is one of the supporters claiming that, "a city that continues to grow, that continues to build, is a city that can put teachers and firefighters and police officers and tens of thousands of New Yorkers to work." Even the supporters admit that construction of the stadium does not guarantee that New York will be awarded the 2012 games.

Opponents of the stadium fear that building on the MTA site will create a sea of skyscrapers and gridlock. They feel the development will displace and destroy many moderate-income communities and that the money could be better spent on the firefighters and police.

Further confusing the situation is the fact that the MTA put the site out for bids and the leading bids are those from the New York Jets who want to build a new stadium and Cablevision (which owns Madison Square Garden) which wants to build 6,000 new apartments, a mall, etc. Finally, the National Football League added its voice by awarding New York the 2010 Super Bowl ... contingent on the building of the new stadium.

Question: Who are the stakeholders in this battle over the West Side Stadium?

Question: What basis for power do each of the major stakeholders have?

Question: Is it possible to satisfy the wishes of all stakeholders? Is there a solution that will satisfy everybody?

ENSURING ETHICAL BEHAVIOR

 ## Key Points:

1. The ethical behavior of an organization flows from the top down. The standards of behavior of a business reflect top management's perceptions of what is right and wrong.

> **Example:** "Whenever a project started to run over budget, the previous president would tell his purchasing people to substitute cheaper products for those specified … without telling the client. There was no great danger but it was unethical. Also on cost plus contracts, he charged clients for all sorts of expenses that had nothing to do with them. As a result, this became the standard for the organization. There was a phrase when I arrived, 'If the big white chief does it, we do it.' As a result, everybody was cutting corners and padding their costs."

2. There has to be a clear and written understanding of what is acceptable behavior and what is not. This is known as a code of conduct. In the absence of such a code, employees will not know exactly what is permitted and what is not allowed.

> **Example:** "Somebody said to me, 'I didn't know I wasn't supposed to let the manufacturer's representative pay for my lunch. They always paid at my last company.'" My reply, "Well now you do and, by next week, everybody in this company will know that it is unacceptable."

3. Having established a code of conduct, the code has to be strictly enforced for all personnel. If it isn't, then it is no more than words on a piece of paper.

> **Example:** "We have a rule at this company that we will continue to work with a client at no additional cost until they are satisfied with the project. At times, this rule has cost us quite a bit of money. Last year, I received a call from a client complaining that one of our division heads had told him that there was nothing further that the company can do for him. I called in the division head and informed him that that was not our policy. He went away grumbling. Two months later I heard the same thing from another client. I gave the division head a final warning. And he is now no longer with us. He was one of our best employees and yet he wouldn't follow the rules. We enforce our policies."

4. There has to be a training program. Different organizations have very different sets of ethical values and it is unrealistic to expect that all employees will know and understand the specific values of the company. Training for new employees has to be provided as do regular programs for all employees to ensure that they are following the company's guidelines.

> **Example:** "We were extremely busy last year and hired four sales people who did not receive the standard training program. We found that they were acting in a manner that we felt was unethical. More importantly, their perspectives were starting to influence some of the other sales people. So, we scheduled another training program. We were very glad we did. In the middle of that program, it became clear that some of the sales pitches were both unethical and illegal. We immediately took steps to change the policies."

CASE 5.5

I'M IN CHARGE NOW!!

Mary Figueroa had been promoted to general manager of the Engine Division. As such, she was the first woman to head up one of the company's heavy machinery divisions.

She spent the first two weeks visiting with all levels of the divisional personnel ... and became increasingly concerned about the ethics of the division.

For example, it was clear that:

- The recent large and important contract with AGT Industries had involved a bribe to at least one or more members of their top management.
- Critical items were being shipped despite the fact that production had concerns over the quality and safety of the products.
- There was considerable animosity between the various departments ... they often acted as adversaries rather than as members of the same team with the same goals.
- Attitudes towards female workers were extremely sexist.
- Expense reports were being "padded" to an outrageous degree.
- Illegal aliens were being used for a number of positions ... paid "off the books."

And so the list went on. When Mary mentioned this to her predecessor, his comment was, "We have always had these problems. That's typical of this industry. Don't worry about it."

Question: Should Mary worry about these problems? Or should she "turn a blind eye" and adopt the same philosophy as her predecessor?

Question: Is there anything Mary can do to change the ethics and values of the division? If so, what?

Question: Which of these problems should she address first? What would be your priorities?

SUMMARY

1. Ethics is defined as:

> *A set of rules or principles that define whether conduct is deemed right or wrong.*

2. Each individual has their own set of ethics. They are a result of a number of factors including their:

   - Values ... those factors that are important to an individual; the aspects of their life on which they put a high value.
   - Personality ... the personal identity or individuality of each distinct person.
   - Experiences ... those events in their life that caused the individual to reevaluate their expectations of society and the business world.

3. *Important Note:* Different groups and different cultures often have very different perceptions of what is right and wrong.

4. An individual's values are influenced by their interactions with their parents and siblings, their friends, their experiences, and by their growth and maturity ... and thus continue to grow and change over their life time.

5. The values of an organization are generally established by top management and, if they are to be widely adopted within the organization, employees have to know what the values are and they have to be strictly enforced.

6. Stakeholders are individuals and groups who have an interest in an activity or event. It is a far broader term than "stockholders" who are the owners of a company. While there may be only one group of stockholders, there may be hundreds of stakeholders ... all with their own perspectives, goals and objectives.

7. Social responsibility is defined as the responsibility of an organization to take action to protect, and even promote, the welfare of the society in which it functions.

8. Not everybody agrees that a business has a responsibility to society. There is a broad spectrum of opinion. Some believe a business has a responsibility to maximize the profit enjoyed by the stockholders. Others see business as benefiting from its place in society and thus has a responsibility to assist wherever it can.

CRITICAL LEARNING QUESTIONS

1. Why doesn't the government (of the U.S. or elsewhere) just get out of the regulation business? Why doesn't it say to business leaders, "Do whatever you want to make the United States competitive in the world marketplace?"

_____

_____

_____

_____

2. Should a company (and its management) apply one set of ethics (i.e., what is right and what is wrong) in one country and a completely different set of ethics in another country? How does it handle business in a country where certain practices are accepted as an acceptable way of doing business and yet, in the United States, such behavior would not only be unethical but also illegal?

_____

_____

_____

_____

3. After college, you decided to take a job with the packaged goods division of a large company. The job is a great one which pays well and has great benefits. However, over time, you become concerned about some of the things that are being done in the organization. They don't sit particularly well with your values. This is made worse by the fact that the president of the company is very active in local politics and appears on television regularly with views that you find unacceptable. Furthermore, you have just been offered a new position (more money and prestige) with the tobacco products division. While you respect the rights of individuals to smoke, you do not smoke yourself and will not eat in a restaurant that doesn't have a well-ventilated non-smoking section.

_____

_____

_____

4. Traffic jams in the downtown area have become increasingly bad in recent years and planners have proposed that a new highway be constructed running from the west side of the city, through the downtown area, and linking up with the Interstate to the east. Much of the area consists of run down industrial plants and houses built in the early 1900s. However, it would also go over the top of the city park. Who are the stakeholders in this situation? Who would probably be in favor of building the new highway? And who would be against it?

_____

_____

_____

_____

5. As a member of the city council, you have to decide whether or not to vote in favor of the development of a new shopping mall on the edge of your ward. Your constituents have been calling and e-mailing you in an attempt to influence your vote. Some argue that the city needs new development and the mall will not only bring in new taxes but will also spur development on that side of town. They also feel it will increase the level of competition in the area and thus reduce costs. The opponents argue that it will greatly increase the level of traffic in that part of town and will change the "small village" atmosphere which many of them enjoy. Also, the city will have to use the principle of eminent domain (forced purchase) to obtain more than a dozen houses to build the new mall, and they feel that this is an inappropriate use of eminent domain. How are you, as a conscientious council member, going to make a decision on how to vote?

_____

_____

_____

_____

6. "If we build on the proposed site, we are going to run into extensive opposition from the residents of the area. Just the rumor that we are going to build a new plant has started people talking and organizing. Do we have any responsibility to the residents? We are going to be providing more than 100 well-paying jobs. And, apart from the need to widen Jackson Street, it is not going to have a great deal of impact." The speaker was Diane Little, head of development for Austin Chemical. Does it have a social responsibility in this situation? What would you do? Would you be influenced by the fact that people in the area generally have an unfavorable view of Austin Chemical?

_____

_____

_____

_____

7. Mark Scholto is the number one sales person for the company. He is a very pleasant individual who establishes a very good rapport with his customers. However, Mark does three things that are contrary to the company's policies. The maximum discount that a sales person can offer a client is 3% without approval from the sales manager. However, Mark often offers 5% and occasionally 7% on large orders without first getting approval. He also gives all his main customers expensive holiday gifts despite the company's policy of limiting such gifts to $25. Finally, he promises his clients that all orders can be returned at any time. The company policy is that orders must be returned within 30 days of delivery for a refund. Other sales people feel that Mark is cheating. Do you agree? What would you do in this situation?

_____

_____

_____

_____

CASE
PROBLEM

A DIFFERENT WAY OF DOING THINGS

As a young rising star within PGI Industries, Karl Westerman was excited when he was offered the opportunity to take over as manager of the company's construction operations in Wichita Falls, Texas. Karl saw this as an opportunity to really make his mark. However, after three months in the position, he wasn't so sure. He was reminded of his boss' advice, "You will find that things are very different there so take some time to get to know the place and the people."

The first thing Karl noticed was that the employees in Wichita Falls were considerably older and far more laid back than those at the headquarters in Pittsburgh. The old boy's network seemed very strong with considerable emphasis on who you knew and who your friends were.

The first issue that really concerned Karl was the Vickers Tower project. Karl was talking with one of the senior managers, Peter Leeds, about the major (and largely unexpected) project that had been awarded to PGI. "How did we get that project?" he asked. "Well, I guess we offered more than anybody else," Mr. Leeds commented. It turned out that Mr. Leeds and other senior personnel had made substantial under the table contribution to both the client and his family. When Karl pointed out that this was not only illegal but against the company's rules, Mr. Leeds shrugged his shoulders. "That's the way things get done in this neck of the woods. If you don't like it, you don't get the business."

Then, there was the Rasnell project. While there was no evidence of anything illegal having occurred, Karl was surprised by the bid. The lead manager on this project, Andrew Barstow, admitted the bid was low. "The Rasnells are an old family in this area and, in recent times, have been having financial troubles. So, we reduced our bid drastically to help them out. This is how we support local industries". "But what about people like me and my boss who receive a bonus based on the profitablity of this operation? Is a low bid in our best interest? And what about PGI stockholders? Don't you have a responsibility to them to maximize your profitability? They invested in this company to enjoy a growing return not to support local businesses."

Finally, at a meeting of the management committee, the question arose as to the company's donations to local charities and other nonprofit organizations for the coming year. The company generally gave three donations totaling approximately $90,000. Karl had proposed that $40,000 be donated to a local women's shelter which need to add additional space. The rest of the committee were in favor of giving the money to the local high school football team for a new club house. "Football is big in this part of Texas and we don't want our boys to be embarrassed when other teams see our facilities," the head of manufacturing commented. "And, in any case, the women in those shelters need to go home to their families and get on with their lives."

Question: Should Karl try to change the ethics and values of the people in the Wichita Falls office? Or should he just go along with the prevailing attitudes and behaviors?

_____

_____

_____

_____

Question: *If Karl decides to try to change things, how would you suggest he proceed? What series of steps should he take?*

_____

_____

_____

_____

Question: *Why should the Wichita Falls office give any money at all to local charities and nonprofit organizations? Isn't it primary responsibility to maximizing its profitability and thus the funds available to PGI Industries for distribution to its stockholders?*

_____

_____

_____

_____

PLANNING—
THE OVERALL
STRATEGY

OVERVIEW

Planning is the first of the four functions of management. It can be best described in terms of the phrase:

If you don't know where you are going, the chances of getting there aren't very good.

In this chapter, we will look at:

- The organizational mission and/or vision.
- Establishing the baseline.
- Developing overall strategies.
- Completing the planning processes.
- The pros and cons of planning.

THE ORGANIZATIONAL MISSION OR VISION

 Key Points:

1. The exact meaning of the terms "vision" and "mission" have become somewhat confused in recent years.

   Not too long ago, the mission of an organization was a statement of its long-term dream. It was essentially unachievable. But it was something that the company ultimately wanted to be. Today, this is more often called the "vision" of the organization.

   By contrast, the "mission" of an organization has become a statement of what the company intends to become or achieve within a relatively short time frame. It usually defines a challenging but achievable goal. It focuses on the purpose of the company, what it does as a business, and the values of the organization.

Both statements are designed to give the organization a sense of overall direction (i.e., what it wants to be at some future date).

2. The development of these statements is important because they force management to focus on its future directions. Since an organization has limited financial and personnel resources, it cannot do everything it might wish to do. So, it has to determine its priorities. By doing so, it comes up with a definition of what its mission should be.

3. There is a school of thought that believes that a mission statement should be the company's rallying cry and thus as short as possible. It is reported that Honda's motor cycle division's mission was to:

> *Crush Yamaha*

4. The important point about both mission and vision statements is that they should be "living" documents. They must be part of the organization's culture and picture of itself. If they are just words on paper then their value is greatly diminished.

CASE 6.1

QUE SERA ... SERA!!

In March 2005, the Board of Directors of The Williams Auto Group sat down for their annual meeting. These meetings were not overly serious affairs. All the directors were friends of Tom Williams and had known him for years. Their main function was to give him advice when he asked for it.

The previous year had seen steady growth and bottom line profitability had exceeded expectations so the meeting was going well until Bob Ainslie, the manager of the local bank, commented that The Williams Auto Group seemed to be diversifying into a number of largely unrelated businesses. "In 2003, you purchased AA Auto Parts and we agreed that the acquisition made sense. However, last year, you acquired the Porter Travel Agency in January and then Barnard Medical Supplies in July. Personally, I don't see the synergy. They are good businesses but I don't see that you and your staff have the knowledge to bring a great deal to these areas."

"Does everything have to fit into a nice box?" Tom asked. "They were available ... we had the funds ... and we bought them. And I'm very pleased with their bottom lines. So, what if they don't tie in nicely with the auto dealership or the parts distributor?"

"I think the question you have to ask yourself, Tom, is: what you want to do with this business? What's your ultimate goal?" The questioner was Mary Perkins the owner of a chain of dry cleaning stores. "A number of years back, I made the decision that I wanted to be one of the largest firms in the dry cleaning business in the area. And I have achieved that objective. In my opinion, you have to make the same decision."

"I've never really thought about it," Tom replied.

Question: Why is it important for Tom Williams to know what he wants to achieve with The Williams Auto Group?

Question: What are the pros and cons of diversifying into a number of different businesses?

Question: Why do you think Tom has never given any thought to his long term goals for the company?

ESTABLISHING THE BASELINE

⚷ **Key Points:**

1. A strengths, weaknesses, opportunities, and threats (SWOT) analysis consists of both an internal and external evaluation:

   - Internal—the strengths and weaknesses of the organization.
   - External—the opportunities and threats facing the organization.

2. The *strengths* of an organization are critically important. However, they tend to be relatively generic in nature (e.g., the organization's personnel, its image and reputation, its financial resources, its manufacturing or R&D capabilities, etc.) ... and quite difficult to change in the short term.

   The *weaknesses* of an organization tend to be more specific (e.g., the lack of planning, lack of depth in the sales force, an aging product line, etc.) ... and are usually (but not always) rather easier to change.

   The *opportunities* enjoyed by an organization are the openings or avenues that it could pursue (e.g., expanding into new markets, developing new products, changing the organizational structure, etc.).

   The *threats* to an organization are external factors that could seriously impact on the company's future (e.g., the entry of an IBM or a Microsoft into a small company's market, a new government regulation, a serious shortage of raw materials, etc.).

3. A SWOT analysis is an ideal tool for generating vigorous discussions as to the current status of the organization.

   However, different people within the organization may have very different views of its strengths and weaknesses. For example, the vice president of marketing may see his/her group as outstanding and the accounting department weak while the head of accounting may view marketing as the weak link.

   Furthermore, a person (such as the president) may be seen as both one of the organization's greatest strengths and its greatest weaknesses.

CASE 6.2

THE LUDLOW ADERTISING AGENCY

The Ludlow Advertising Agency was founded in 1983 by Peter Ludlow to provide advertising and promotional materials to local businesses. Originally a two man shop, it had grown to the point where it now employed eighty-four full time people in three offices spread over the entire state. It generated approximately $10 million in billings and had an outstanding reputation for highly creative advertising campaigns and effective public relations.

When her father suffered a heart attack in late 2004, Barbara Ludlow took over and continued to implement his plans and philosophies. However, at the first meeting of the management team in 2005, she asked them to think about the future of Ludlow. "My father ran this company for more than twenty years and I have great admiration for what he achieved. Now, I hope to sit in this chair for at least another ten years. So, my question to you is: what should we be trying to achieve over that period? As my kids always say to me, 'what do you want to be when you grow up?' What do we want to be in ten or fifteen year's time?"

"I think that's a very good question ... and we should certainly address it," Mike Hardin, head of the company's Public Relations Group commented. "However, I think there is a more fundamental question that needs to be asked first, namely: where are we now? Most of the time, we are rushing to complete assignments and never really step back, look at ourselves, and where we are."

"Good suggestion, Mike," Barbara responded. "Why don't we do a SWOT analysis? Why don't we start by looking at our strengths? And our weaknesses? Let's do an internal audit. And then let's go outside the company and look at the possible opportunities and the possible threats? That will give us a clear understanding of where we currently stand."

Question: Does doing a SWOT analysis sound like a good game plan?

Question: What sorts of strengths and weaknesses might Ludlow come up with? What sorts of opportunities and threats?

Question: Assuming each of the members of the management team develops their own SWOT analysis for the company, what problems do you see arising as a result of this analysis?

DEVELOPING OVERALL STRATEGIES

🗝 **Key Points:**

1. Any organization has four fundamental business strategies:

   - Market penetration.
   - Market development.
   - Product development.
   - Diversification.

2. *Current product–current market* (market penetration). This strategy focuses on obtaining a larger market share of the organization's current markets.

> **Example:** A manufacturing company with a 10% share of the U.S. market might implement an advertising campaign to increase its market share to 15%.
>
> **Example:** A hamburger chain, with four locations, might place additional restaurants in the local military bases, colleges, etc. in order to gain a larger share of the hamburger market.

Current product–new market (market development). This strategy focuses on finding new markets for existing products.

> **Example:** A restaurant chain with thousands of outlets might decide that there were few opportunities to expand domestically and turn to Europe and the Fair East as offering better potential for growth.
>
> **Example:** Hodkins Industries supplies small electrical motors to a variety of industries. However, increasing competition from a couple of very large companies led it to evaluate other potential markets for essentially the same product.

New product–current market (product development). This strategy focuses on finding new products to sell into the current markets.

> **Example:** A convenience store may conclude that its sales of groceries have reached a plateau and may decide to add video rentals and the sale of gasoline to improve its position.
>
> **Example:** For a period of time, BigBurger had little or no competition. Then, Wendy's opened a place half a mile away ... followed by McDonald's and a Burger King. In an effort to compete with these nationwide chains, BigBurger decided to expand its menu by offering both Chinese and Mexican dishes.

New product–new market (diversification). This strategy is pursued by a company that decides that it has basically saturated its current markets and opportunities and needs to identify a new product line that would sell into totally different markets.

Example: A chain of discount stores might well decide that, rather than continuing to expand by building new discount store locations, it will diversify into another unrelated business area such as office supplies or baby goods.

Example: "Why did we acquire Doncaster Materials? Well, I had known the owners for many years and was impressed by their business model. While there was no obvious synergy between their product line and ours, I liked the fact that their sales peaked in the summer while ours maxed out in the winter. We were both engaged in cyclical businesses and I felt that this acquisition would smooth out sales during the year."

CASE
6.3

PARSON'S DILEMMA

Alan Parson had been elected president of Little Tommy's Groceries ... a chain of 200 locations headquartered in Casper, Wyoming and covering Idaho, Montana, North Dakota, South Dakota as well as Wyoming. Established in 1949, it had always been very profitable (in contrast to chains such as 7-11 which had experienced severe financial problems) because of its founder's basic strategy of only locating its stores in very small towns. This meant that it usually had no competition and thus experienced few, if any, price wars. The fact that it was usually the only gas station in town helped.

Looking at the projections for the coming year, Alan was painfully aware that growth was slowing down and profitability was beginning to slide. "We're only planning to open another 22 stores this year in the five state area because it is becoming harder to find good new locations. Also, we are starting to see some of the industry leaders expanding into our traditional small town markets."

"I think it is time to rethink our fundamental strategy. We have a very successful business in our five state area. The question is: where do we go from here? What are our options now?

Question: Given that continuing with the current strategy (i.e., the current business in the current market area) may not be particularly attractive, what alternative strategies might the company consider?

Question: What are the pros and cons of each of the alternative strategies?

Question: Which of the potential strategies has (a) the greatest risk and (b) the greatest potential?

COMPLETING THE PLANNING PROCESS

 Key Points:

1. Just because top management has decided on a specific course of action doesn't necessarily mean that anything is going to happen.

> **Example:** Prager & Prager (a well-respected law firm) decided to open a new office in Atlanta as the first step in an expansion program. This decision was incorporated into its annual strategic plan and the same commitment appeared in the annual plan for the next four years. It remained nothing more than words on a piece of paper because the details of the action were never clearly delineated.
>
> **Example:** "I think we should open a facility in the European Union and really focus on that market. Let's achieve this goal this year." The chairman of the company liked Europe and saw numerous possibilities. Unfortunately, none of the company's managers shared his enthusiasm . . . and thus nothing happened.

2. Somebody has to be specifically responsible for ensuring that the action is taken. In some instances, responsibility can be assigned to a group or department. However, this leaves open the possibility of finger pointing and falling between two stools. "I thought you were going to do that."

> **Example:** "When the board meeting broke up on March 31, I was under the impression that the key questions regarding personnel would be handled by the three senior vice presidents. However, at the meeting today, it became clear that the senior vice presidents had each assumed that the problems would be resolved by the vice president of human resources. As a result, nothing had happened."
>
> **Example:** "About five years ago, we decided to get into the Phoenix market . . . preferably by acquiring one of the local firms. Since one of our senior people knew the principals at one of the companies, he started negotiations on our behalf. When those negotiations fell through, he moved on to other activities . . . and nobody stepped in to make contacts with some of the other firms. So, even today, we don't have an operation there."

3. A time frame has to be established by which date the action will have been taken.

> **Example:** "Our annual strategic plan stated that we needed to expand the size of our warehouse ... and that Jim Furby (the warehouse manager) would be in charge of the expansion. However, the volume of business increased dramatically last year and Jim became extremely busy. When I asked Jim how the expansion was coming along, he looked quite shocked. Because there was no time frame assigned to the expansion, he had essentially ignored it."
>
> **Example:** "I am going to have to spend the next couple of weeks interviewing potential sales people. According to the annual plan, I am supposed to hire two new people by the end of this quarter ... and I know the president is going to ask me where I stand. When we sit down and agree on a specific plan and a specific time table, you know that is what the president will focus on."

4. A detailed budget has to be established and the resources provided to enable the action to be implemented.

> **Example:** A company opening a new office has to prepare a budget covering the cost of the lease, the purchase of furniture and equipment, the hiring of personnel, etc.
>
> **Example:** The management of Jensen and Foster agreed that the time had arrived to purchase a new high speed laser cutter and funds were allocated for the cost of the equipment. However, there was nothing in the budget for either the installation or training of personnel and, as a result, the department head was reluctant to move ahead with the purchase.

5. A senior monitor has to be appointed. This is an individual who, representing the overall interests of the organization, makes sure that the planned action is implemented on time and on budget.

> **Example:** Bob Martini was asked to complete the development of a new module for a software package. The deadline was October 1 and the budget was $18,000. Since nobody was overseeing his activity, the end of the year arrived with virtually no progress having been made.
>
> **Example:** "I meet with my sales people every Monday morning for about an hour. In front of me, I have a listing of the major potential clients and who is going to call on them. And I ask the same question over and over again, namely: have you called on XYZ yet? If I don't continually prod them, there is a high probability that they will focus solely on their existing clients and ignore cold calls on the firms on the list."

CASE 6.4

THE LAW FIRM OF WALLACE & WALLACE

Wallace & Wallace is based in Columbus, Ohio and specializes in corporate litigation for clients throughout the region. With more than thirty partners, it has a strong reputation in the field.

In May, the managing partner of a law firm (known as HHW) located in Cincinnati (approximately a hundred miles from Columbus) contacted Ryan Wallace with the suggestion that the two firms merge. "A number of our senior partners are planning to retire in the very near future and we haven't been too successful growing replacements in-house. They are good people but they aren't quite ready to take over. Since you know many of them and we tend to handle the same types of clients, I thought it made sense to see if a merger would benefit both our firms."

At the next partners' meeting, Ryan Wallace raised the issue of a merger with HHW. Sixteen voted in favor of seriously considering the proposal. Three were against it and another three felt that, if the company were going to consider an acquisition or a merger, they should look at other firms in the area. The remaining eight chose to abstain. A team of five partners was then selected to investigate the benefits of the acquisition.

The recommendations were positive and, by October, Wallace & Wallace had acquired HHW with its twenty partners, fourteen non-partners and eighteen paralegals and secretaries.

Question: Having made the decision to acquire HHW, what steps does the management of Wallace & Wallace need to take to ensure that the takeover goes smoothly?

Question: How much detail should the takeover plan contain?

Question: What problems do you see with Wallace & Wallace taking over HHW?

THE PROS AND CONS OF PLANNING

Key Points:

1. There are both pros and cons to planning ... and different people have different views as to its value.

2. Supporters of planning believe that the advantages of conducting a planning process are that it:

   - Requires the company to take the time to sit down and discuss the future directions of the organization.

   - Emphasizes priorities within the activities of the organization and thus the allocation of resources.

   - Provides an opportunity for all employees to be involved in the development of the organization's future directions ... and hence develops a sense of team involvement.

   - Leads to the development of operational plans which identifies who is going to be responsible for a specific action, how it is going to be done, and when it is going to be done.

3. Those who take the opposite view see the following disadvantages:

   - It can be very time-consuming.

   - Employees can become disenchanted with having to read the reports and attend meetings.

   - The emphasis can be on creating the report rather than on the implementation of the plan.

   - The final draft of the plan can sit on the shelves for much of the year ... essentially unused.

   - The organization can fail to review actual progress against the plan.

   - The plan can give a false sense of security ... and cause the company to be reluctant to change to meet new challenges in the marketplace.

CASE 6.5

WICKLOW DISTRIBUTION COMPANY

For a number of years, Wicklow Distribution Company had prepared an extremely detailed annual plan primarily because the company's president, Porter Hayes, was a great believer in the value of planning.

"I think it gives us an opportunity to think about what we are doing as a company. The plan lays out our long-term objective and our specific short-term goals. We get everybody involved."

"The process begins at the departmental or group level. They get together and discuss their thinking and plans. These plans then go to the division heads who combine them into a divisional plan which they then review with the department and group heads. The divisional plans are then combined for each of the four companies to give us company plans. At the same time, the board of directors and I are working to come up with a top-down plan. It is more of an overall set of objectives for Wicklow as a whole."

"Usually, we find that there is a gap between what the four companies are proposing and what we would like to achieve. This leads to a series of interactions with the corporate and divisional personnel which are often quite heated. However, out of this process comes the annual plan which is then distributed to the companies and divisions. This is their bible."

Not everybody agreed with the use of this process. Carla Reyes, president of one of the subsidiaries, commented that "It is a case of overkill. We tend to analyze things to death. Paralysis through analysis is what I call it. The entire process focuses on the creation of a document that is out of date when it is finally distributed. I think Porter would be better off to tell us what he wants us to do . . . and just let us get on with it."

Question: Does this sound like a reasonable planning process?

Question: What are the advantages of having a planning process such as that used by Wicklow?

Question: What do you see as the disadvantages of this type of planning process?

SUMMARY

1. The first step in any organizational planning process is to identify the ultimate goals of the organization (i.e., what it wants to be or become). There are two terms that are often used in defining the ultimate goals:

   ■ Vision ... a statement of its long-term dream. It may be unachievable but it defines what it ultimately wants to be.

   ■ Mission ... a statement of what it wants to become or achieve within a relatively short time frame (usually 3 to 5 years). It is a challenging goal but an achievable one.

2. It is important that the vision and mission of an organization should be part of the organization's culture and philosophies not just words on a piece of paper.

3. The second step in the planning process is to determine where the organization currently stands. One of the techniques for doing this is a SWOT analysis which focuses on the internal **S**trengths and **W**eaknesses of the organization and the external **O**pportunities and **T**hreats.

4. Step 3 in the planning process is to determine the organization's fundamental strategy. One way of considering this is in terms of a matrix showing the product and the market. This gives four alternative strategies:

   ■ Current product–current market. Expanding the sale of the existing products in the existing market (exemplified by opening new locations). **Market penetration.**

   ■ Current product–new market. Introducing existing products into new markets (such as other parts of the country or overseas). **Market development.**

   ■ New product–current market. Creating growth by selling new products in existing markets (such as a hamburger chain selling tacos). **Product development.**

   ■ New product–new market. This strategy focuses growth by introducing new products into new markets (an example might be a chemical company's decision to market consumer goods in developing countries). **Product diversification.**

5. Having established the long term objectives and the strategy to achieve them, an organization needs to convert these into a short term operational plan (i.e., what it is going to do in the next twelve months or so to move it towards its longer-term objectives).

6. A short-term operational plan should make it clear as to:

   ■ Who is going to be responsible for the action?

   ■ What will be done?

   ■ When the action will be completed?

   ■ What budget and resources are allocated to implementing the action?

   ■ Who will be responsible for overseeing that the action is completed?

7. There are a number of advantages to implementing a planning process. The main ones are that:

   ■ It enables the organization to take a long-term view of its goals and directions. It gets it away from the daily emphasis on "putting out fires."

   ■ It provides an opportunity for members of the organization to develop a sense of involvement and commitment.

   Among the major disadvantages are that:

   ■ It can be a time consuming exercise with extensive meetings and discussions.

   ■ Emphasis can be shifted from action to planning for action.

   ■ The resulting plan can become merely a document rather than an active game plan.

CRITICAL THINKING QUESTIONS

1. What are the differences between a mission statement and a vision statement? Does a firm really need both or would either one be sufficient? Suggestion: identify an organization that has both ... and analyze the differences.

   _____

   _____

   _____

   _____

2. What should be the mission statement for a college or university? How would you develop this statement? And what problems would you expect in terms of establishing a statement to which everybody could agree?

   _____

   _____

   _____

   _____

3. Stella Linman was talking about the company retreat that she attended the previous month. "The company booked a suite of rooms at a resort about twenty miles from here ... and we all drove up there on Friday evening. The purpose of these annual retreats is partly social and partly business. Anyway, one of our first assignments on Saturday morning was to fill in the four parts of a SWOT analysis. It was an enjoyable exercise. However, I was amazed how different the responses were. I would have thought we would be in agreement on the strengths, weaknesses, opportunities, and threats. However, we spent the rest of the morning arguing over them." Why do you think the members of the management team disagreed on the company's SWOT? Given that they disagreed so dramatically, was the SWOT analysis a worthwhile exercise?

   _____

   _____

   _____

   _____

4. How applicable do you think a SWOT analysis is to an individual? What are your personal strengths and weaknesses? What are the opportunities and threats you face? Would an in-depth analysis of this sort help you plan for your future?

   _____

   _____

   _____

5. Which of the four basic or overall strategies (i.e., market penetration, market development, product development, and diversification) do you think a company would find most challenging? Which strategy has the greatest and least risk? And which has the greatest and least potential for substantial corporate growth?

_____

_____

_____

_____

6. You and a group of friends have decided to organize a holiday party. You expect at least 200 people to attend. Identify ten (10) actions that need to be carried out to ensure this party (a) actually goes off without a hitch and (b) is a success. What would an operational plan look like for planning this party?

_____

_____

_____

_____

7. Put yourself in the shoes of a consultant. You are talking to the owner of a very successful, yet totally disorganized, surfboard manufacturer and are trying to sell him on the benefits of developing a long range (i.e., strategic) plan for his business. The owner argues that both sales and profits are growing satisfactorily. "Developing a plan would be a waste of both time and money," he states. What arguments would you use to convince him of the benefits of hiring you to help him develop a five year plan?

_____

_____

_____

_____

CASE PROBLEM

ROBERT HANSON–ENTREPRENEUR

Bob Hanson dropped out of community college after one semester with a cumulative GPA of 1.34. He then went to work for a steel distributor. After three years there, he borrowed money from everybody he knew and established his own company which prospered.

Five years later, he sold that company and invested the money in four rather beat-up barges which carried goods up and down the Mississippi. Seven years later, he had a fleet of twenty-three barges which he sold at a substantial profit. He then invested in real estate and bought a series of properties which one of the national mall builders purchased giving him a 15% equity in the mall. Bob later did five more malls with the same company.

And so it went on. One move led to another ... and each was successful. When he died, his estate was worth $724 million. His brother who graduated from an ivy league university died two weeks earlier with an estate worth $305,000.

Before his death, Bob Hanson was interviewed for a major magazine and it was during this interview that he made the following statement.

"I don't believe in planning. I never have. It has always struck me as a total waste of time and effort. My brother was a planner all his life and look where it got him. I look at something and, if it smells right, I go for it."

"I appreciate the need for bean counters. They keep you honest and on track. But planners!! They just analyze things to death. They screw up the natural flow of things. When I bought Tennyson Industries (a publicly listed company), they had a whole department of planners and couldn't make a profit. I fired the whole damn lot of them ... and that was the start of the revival."

Question: *How was Bob Hanson so successful given his obvious lack of enthusiasm for planning?*

_____

_____

_____

_____

Question: *Why then do management texts put so much emphasis on the importance of planning?*

_____

_____

_____

_____

Question: *Do you think Bob Hanson was the exception? Or the rule? Can others be as successful as he was without planning?*

_____

_____

_____

_____

CHAPTER

7

DECISION MAKING

OVERVIEW

Decision making is a critically important skill for any manager. He or she has to take the available information and make a decision.

In this chapter, we will look at:

- Individual decision making.
- Group decision making.

And at four techniques that can help in decision making:

- Forecasting.
- Gantt charts.
- PERT/CPM charts.
- Break-even analysis.

INDIVIDUAL DECISION MAKING

Key Points:

1. Decisions (whether made by an individual or a group) are generally made under time and information constraints (i.e., there is enough time or funds to gather perfect information). The decision maker has to make his/her decision with the available information within a specified time period.

133

> **Example:** You are buying a birthday present for somebody. Their birthday is to-morrow. You need to purchase the present on the way home and you can only afford to spend $100. Time and resources limit how much effort you can put into shopping and what you can purchase.

2. The first step in decision making is to carefully define what you want to achieve ... the focus of the decision.

> **Example:** Wanting to take a vacation is a very general statement and isn't likely to be particularly helpful. Wanting to take a week long vacation in Florida and sit on the beach is far more specific. The more specific the goal, the easier it is to work through the decision making process.

3. The second step is to determine the alternatives that will achieve the specific objective.

> **Example:** You could fly to Florida, drive to Florida or even take the train. You could stay at a five star hotel, a one star hotel, or a bed and breakfast, etc. There are an infinite number of alternatives. However, most people limit the number they seriously consider. If you evaluate a large number of options, you may never go on vacation.

4. The third step is to evaluate the pros and cons of your selected alternatives.

> **Example:** The construction of a new office building on a main street might well have certain advantages to constructing the same building on a side street ... advantages such as visibility and prestige. On the other hand, it may have limited parking and a noisy location. The pros and cons of the side street may be equally distinct.

5. Based on the evaluation of the pros and cons, you then need to make a decision. It may not be the perfect decision but it will be a logical (and, hopefully, best) decision based on the available information.

> **Example:** A company may decide to purchase a new piece of equipment. The decision is made and the order is placed. One month later, another company introduces a new model with upgraded features at a lower price.

6. There is a final step in the planning process that will be discussed in a later chapter, namely: evaluating the effectiveness of the decision. Was it a good decision? If so, why? If not, why not? What could be learned from the decision and the decision process?

CASE 7.1

TO BUILD OR NOT TO BUILD?

Not long after being appointed as the company's manager for South East Asia, Lisa Twining was faced with a major decision, namely: whether or not to recommend that the company build a new production facility (possibly in Thailand) for Xanthan—one of the company's major chemicals.

Her boss, the president of the company, asked her to have a firm recommendation for the board which was scheduled to meet on October 2 . . . less than five weeks ahead.

"The problem, quite simply," Lisa explained. "Is that we don't have enough capacity in South-East Asia. We have a medium-sized plant in India and another small plant in Malaysia. But both of them are running at or close to capacity. In the short-run, we could probably export from our plant in Australia. They are running at less than 80% of capacity.

The Board was known for becoming very irritated with managers who failed to come up with a specific recommendation. So, Lisa couldn't just discuss the issue which, given the time frame, she would have preferred to do.

Question: What alternative strategies could Lisa present to the Board on October 2?

Question: What should she do when she has identified the viable alternatives?

Question: What problems does she face in reaching a decision on a course of action?

GROUP DECISION MAKING

🗝 **Key Points:**

1. There are a number of advantages to having a group or team make a decision. Specifically:

   ■ A group or team can (in theory) come up with a better decision than a single decision maker.

   ■ It spreads the effort over a number of individuals ... and allows the project to be completed which a single individual could not handle.

   ■ Different people bring very different views, attitudes, and perspectives to the decision making process.

   ■ One individual will have specific skills and capabilities that other group members do not have.

   ■ Being part of the decision making usually means that the members are more committed to the outcome and thus are likely to work harder at implementing their decision.

2. On the other hand, there are a number of disadvantages:

   ■ It usually takes longer to make a decision and, given a situation in which there are very different points of view, the group may be unable to reach a conclusion.

   ■ Group decisions are more costly than individual decisions because of the involvement of a number of people.

   ■ Groups are often dominated by one individual either as a result of his/her personality or his/her status.

   ■ Members of a group may come to a specific conclusion merely to maintain friendly relationships among the members of the group. This is often called *groupthink*.

3. There are a number of techniques which can help groups make decisions:

   ■ *Brainstorming.* This is a technique where anyone can suggest anything they like. No negative comments are allowed until everybody had made their contribution and thus no suggestions (however odd or unrealistic) are counted out. The suggestions are recorded by the group leader and then placed before the group for discussion.

   ■ *Nominal Group Technique.* This is a variation on Brainstorming. Instead of presenting the ideas to the group, each participant writes down his/her ideas and suggestions and then presents them to the group to be written on a board or flipchart. There is then a spontaneous discussion of the ideas by the entire group followed by a secret vote. The idea receiving the most votes is the one chosen.

   ■ *Delphi Technique.* This approach involves circulating a questionnaire to those participating in the study. The questionnaires are collected and summarized and the results fed back to the participants. This sequence can be repeated a number of times. Each time, the participant can stick with their previous submission or change their opinion based on the feedback. These steps are then repeated until the members of the group reach an agreement.

MOVING DEPARTMENTS TO A NEW LOCATION

"We have been in this building since 1973 when my brother and I founded the company. We occupied only part of the second floor. Now, we occupy all four floors and are bursting at the seams. Some of the sales people have to work out of their own homes and others work out of temporary offices about a mile away."

The speaker was Rutherford Barnes, president of Arloa Industries. "We are going to have to divide the company between this building and a new one being constructed on the other side of this office park. Somebody is going to have to move and the key question is: who goes and who stays? R&D is by far the largest group followed by marketing, accounting, design, human resources, finance, and advertising."

"I made a suggestion at the last general staff meeting that I thought made sense and was inundated with calls and e-mails from employees complaining that it was unfair, that it would make their job more difficult, etc. It is an issue which seems to arouse considerable passion."

"So, when one of division heads suggested we set up a task force to look into the matter . . . drawing members from all areas of the company and all levels of the organization, I said fine."

Question: How should the members of this task force be selected? Does it make any difference?

Question: What are the advantages of using a task force made up of employees to address this problem?

Question: What are the disadvantages of having a group make this decision?

FORECASTING

🔑 Key Points:

1. Forecasting is an attempt to project the future. In business, a projection is extremely important since it gives management a sense of what it needs in terms of resources (people, equipment, etc.).

> **Example:** Patton Industries manufacturers 200,000 tons of Celdar per year and has four sales people. If a forecast shows that they will sell 400,000 tons next year then they will have to increase production and that may mean additional equipment or a second shift. On the other hand, if sales are projected to decline to 150,000 tons then they may need to lay off some of the manufacturing personnel and one of the sales people.

2. One approach to forecasting the future is to assume that whatever happened in the past will continue in the coming year. So, if a value has gone up from 100 to 120 to 140 then one would naturally assume that it would reach 160 in the coming year. However, rarely do data follow a straightforward pattern and different mathematical processes applied to the data will give widely differing projections.

   Quite obviously, the more data one has to work with the better. Ten years of monthly history is far more likely to give an accurate projection than three years of quarterly data.

3. Another approach frequently used is to ask the company's sales force to estimate what they, individually, think they will sell during the coming year ... and then add the estimates together to generate the corporate projection. While the sales people have the best knowledge of what is likely to occur in the marketplace, they tend to be optimistic ... assuming that they will pick up new clients without losing any of the existing customers.

> **Example:** Peter Ross sold $1.4 million in 2003 and projected that sales to his existing customers would grow by 5% in 2004. He also projected that he would pick up two new customers with total purchases of $200,000 for a grand total of $1.67 million. Both his assumptions were correct. However, he also lost two customers who accounted for $350,000 in sales ... and thus ended up with total sales of only $1.32 million.

4. Another approach to forecasting is to ask a group of "experts" in a field. These are individuals who actively track a particular market and thus are in a position to make an estimate of the total market. Based on this projection, a company can then make an estimate of its own sales by making an assumption about its market share in the year ahead.

> **Example:** A panel of experts gathered in Phoenix, Arizona to discuss the market for golf cart batteries. They agreed that it would be close to 1.9 million units in 2004. However, due to economic conditions and the lack of new golf course construction, they estimated that sales in 2005 would drop to 1.7 million. Based on this estimate, Clifton Industries (one of the manufacturers) reduced its sales projection from 190,000 to 170,000 ... assuming that it would continue to hold a 10% market share.

CASE 7.3

YOUR GUESS IS AS GOOD AS MINE

In November of 2004, the management team for the Appliances Division sat down as a group to develop sales forecasts for the coming year for each of its five main product lines. This year the major uncertainty was with respect to its line of kitchen blenders.

Among the comments were the following:

"Looking at sales for the last four years, we sold 391,000 units in 2000, 395,000 in 2001, 425,000 in 2002, 304,000 in 2003, and the best estimate is that will sell 327,000 this year." [Bob Fano]

"The sales people are optimistic that they can sell 479,000 units in 2005. The North-East region thinks they will pick up two new accounts and increase sales from 85,000 to 158,000. South-East also thinks they will pick up at least one new account and grow from 73,000 to 105,000. Mid-West is expecting to sell 81,000 (up from 66,000) and the West region expects to add 32,000 to its projected sales for this year (selling 135,000) units." [Carol Tomaso]

"Did anybody read the article in *Appliance Daily* which projected that total sales would drop next year to 3.7 million units. Assuming we maintain our current 7.6% share of the market that means we will sell approximately 281,000 units." [Bailey Coutts]

Question: Why wouldn't you automatically adopt the projections made by the sales personnel? After all, they are the closest to the actual market and should have the best "feel" for what they can sell.

Question: How do you think the estimate of the total market was derived for the Appliance Daily article? How much weight should be given to this projection?

Question: What is your projected level of sales of kitchen blenders for 2005?

GANTT CHARTS

Key Points:

1. A Gantt chart is a scheduling device which visually represents the resources or activities needed for a project against time.

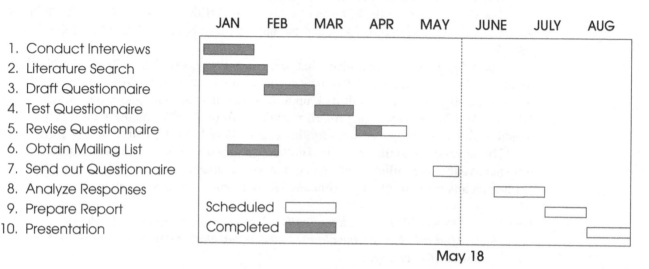

2. It is important to note that a Gantt chart does not necessarily show a relationship between activities (i.e., it does not show when one activity has to be completed before another can be started). However, it clearly implies some of those relationships.

> **Example:** In the above diagram, sending out questionnaire clearly follows obtain mailing list ... although it doesn't show a direct relationship.

3. By highlighting the current date, a Gantt chart will indicate the progress of a project.

> **Example:** In the diagram above, both revising the questionnaire and sending it out are clearly behind schedule.

CASE 7.4

A TIGHT SCHEDULE

As regional vice-president for the Mexicali chain of restaurants, one of Maria Valasquez's main tasks was to identify sites for new locations ... with the goal of opening one store every three months.

Maria was explaining to a reporter for the local newspaper that her job consisted of seven basic yet important tasks which she repeated for each location. From day one, I start looking for and securing a site. That takes about six weeks. At the same time, I begin the process of obtaining the necessary building permits. That is time consuming and can take 20 weeks. However, I can start that activity immediately as well. I can also identify and hire a contractor (8 weeks) since that isn't dependent on the site or obtaining the permits."

"Construction takes 12 weeks and obviously we can't begin until we have the site and the contractor. Landscaping takes 6 weeks and generally begins about eight weeks into the construction. The other two main activities are hiring and training a manager and hiring and training the staff. Both of these activities take about 12 weeks and are not critical ... as long as they are completed by the time the restaurant is ready to open. We use what is called a Gantt chart. "This is a visual approach to showing the various activities and where we stand relative to the goal."

"So, it takes 19 months from the start of the site search to the actual opening of the restaurant," the reporter commented adding up the numbers. "Oh no ... it is much shorter than that," Maria replied. "It normally takes about 8 months."

Question: What assumptions was the reporter making in calculating that it would take 19 months to open each new site?

Question: How can these seven activities be condensed into an 8 month time frame?

Question: How would a Gantt chart appear for this project with an 8 month deadline?

PERT/CPM CHARTS

 Key Points:

1. PERT (Program Evaluation and Review Technique) and CPM (Critical Path Method) use the same basic diagram. In fact, in recent year, the terms have begun to be used interchangeably.

2. Both diagrams show the sequence of events that have to be followed to complete a project:

PERT NETWORK

EVENT	ACTIVITY	ESTIMATED TIME (DAYS)	PRECEDING EVENT
A	Select Date	3	None
B	Rent Facilities	4	A
C	Identify Keynote Speaker	7	B
D	Arrange for Catering	3	B
E	Identify Program Speakers	15	C
F	Prepare Advertising Materials	12	D, E
G	Mail Invitations	6	F
H	Advertise Program	12	F
I	Prepare Handouts	5	G,H
J	Finalize Program	3	I

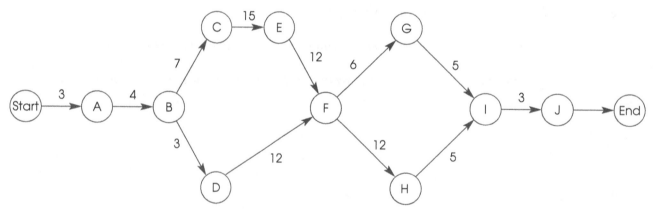

Example: Quite obviously, in the example given above, the company must first rent facilities before preparing advertising materials.

3. The key step in both techniques is to clearly identify all the activities and the predecessors (i.e., those activities that have to be completed before the next activity can begin).

> **Example:** In the above diagram, omitting activity G (i.e., mail invitations) would have a disastrous impact on attendance at the program ... as would sending out the mailing before activity E—identifying program speakers.

4. Using the Critical Path Method (CPM) involves identifying that path that will take the longest time to complete. Each of the activities has a single time estimate (in hours, days, weeks, months, etc.) and, by adding these estimates together for each of the paths from the start to finish of the project, one can determine the longest path ... and hence the critical path.

5. The Program Evaluation and Review Technique (PERT) differs in that there are three time estimates for each activity:

   - The optimistic time (O) ... this is the shortest period of time the activity will take if everything goes perfectly.

   - The pessimistic time (P) ... this is the longest period of time the activity will take if everything goes wrong.

   - The most probable time (M) ... this is the most realistic estimate of how long it will take to complete the activity.
     The expected time for this activity is then calculated using the following formula:

$$\text{Expected time} = \frac{O + 4M + P}{6}$$

6. If you are completing an activity for the first time then all you can estimate is the most probable time. On the other hand, if this is an activity which has been carried out many times then one can easily estimate all three values.

> **Example:** A sculptor generally takes four weeks to build a work from scrap metal. This would give him/her the value of M. However, he/she has completed one in a week (the value of O) and once took as long as 13 weeks to complete a sculpture (P). The expected time to complete a sculpture, therefore, would be 5 weeks.

CASE
7.5

DECLINING USE OF THE LIBRARY

"In recent months, the usage of the town's library has declined dramatically," Alison Forbes, the librarian explained. "I know the weather has been bad this winter but we have experienced a 37% decline in usage and none of the other townships around here have suffered anywhere near so badly. So, we have decided to mail out a questionnaire to the town's residents to see if we can find out what is going on."

Ms. Forbes laid out the following twelve steps in the process ... indicating the length of time each would take and what steps would have to be completed before the next step could begin. Next, she developed a PERT/CPM chart for the project. "PERT stands for Program Evaluation and Review Technique and is a way of showing the sequence in which activities have to be completed. CPM stands for Critical Path Method and is the longest path through the activities. If the project is to be completed on time then this critical path has to be maintained."

		Predecessor
1	Develop draft questionnaire (2 weeks)	—
2	Test draft questionnaire (3 weeks)	1
3	Revise/finalize questionnaire (1 week)	2
4	Selection of sample (1 week)	1
5	Prepare mailing labels (2 weeks)	3
6	Print up final questionnaire (2 weeks)	3
7	Develop data analysis program (5 weeks)	3
8	Mail questionnaires and get responses (6 weeks)	4, 5
9	Test data analysis program (3 weeks)	6
10	Input responses to questionnaire (4 weeks)	7, 8
11	Analyze results (4 weeks)	9
12	Prepare/present report (3 weeks)	10

Question: What would the PERT/CPM chart look like for this project?

Question: What is the critical path for this project?

Question: How could the time frame for this project be shortened?

BREAK-EVEN ANALYSIS

Key Points:

1. A break-even analysis is a relatively simple technique in which you compare the revenue generated by the sales of a unit (i.e., the number of units sold multiplied by the selling price) with the cost of producing this same unit.

     The cost of the unit consists of two components: the fixed cost and the variable cost:

   - Fixed costs. These are the costs (such as the cost of the building or equipment) which the company has to cover irrespective of whether or not they produce a single product.

   - Variable costs. These are the costs (such as raw materials, labor, etc.) which are directly related to the production of each specific unit.

BREAK-EVEN ANALYSIS

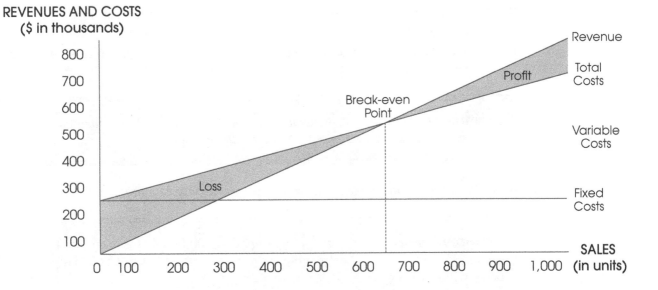

> **Example:** You purchase a new car and agree to pay $250 per month for 36 months. You have to pay $250 each month even if it sits in a garage unused. This is a fixed cost of ownership. On the other hand, if you drive it, you will have to purchase gasoline and the amount you have to buy will depend on how far you drive.

2. The break-even point is the level at which the fixed cost per unit plus the variable cost per unit exactly equal the revenue per unit.

     The formula for this is:

$$\text{Break-even point} = \frac{\text{Annual fixed cost}}{(\text{Selling price} - \text{Variable cost})}$$

> **Example:** A new plant cost $5 million. Management estimates that the plant will handle production for 10 years so assigns a fixed cost of $500,000 per year. Management also estimates that the cost of materials and labor will be $6 per unit and that it can be sold for $11 per unit. So, on each unit sold, the company will generate $5 which will go towards covering the fixed cost. Therefore, in order to cover the total fixed cost, the company will have to sell 100,000 units per year—the break-even point. As soon as it has sold 100,000 units, the company will have covered all the costs associated with the product.
>
> **Example:** If the sales price is increased to $16 then the company will generate $10 per unit ... and the break-even drops to 50,000 units. On the other hand, if the price is reduced to $8 then the company generates only $2 per unit and the break-even increases to 250,000 units.

3. While this is a useful "order of magnitude" calculation, it has a number of weaknesses:

   - All the lines are drawn as straight lines ... and the reality is that none of them are straight over a wide range.
   - The more the company produces the better the price per unit they receive on the raw materials.

   > **Example:** Go to the local auto dealership and order 20 cars. You will get a much better price per car than you would if you purchase just one.

   - As the volume sold increases, the selling price typically declines.

   > **Example:** One person may be willing to pay $4,000 for a home entertainment center. However, somebody else will wait until the price drops to $2,000 before being willing to purchase.

   - The fixed costs tend to increase as the volume produced increases.

   > **Example:** As the volume produced increases so does the wear and tear on the equipment.

   - The length of time that the plant will be used to produce a specific product cannot be determined in advance. A change in technology or design may make a product obsolete. So, the best a manager can do is to "estimate" how long the plant will last ... and the break-even point is very sensitive to this estimate.

CASE 7.6

HOW MANY WILL WE HAVE TO SELL?

"The current estimate of the cost of the new building is $2 million and we anticipate that the production lines will cost another $1.4 million. Assuming that the raw material costs remain essentially unchanged at $2.50 per kilo, the question is: does it make sense to go ahead and build the plant?"

This was the dilemma facing the planning group at Hayes Chemicals, a small manufacturer of organic chemicals. It would be a major investment for the company and they wanted to be sure that they were making the right decision.

"Well, that depends on the selling price," Andrea observed. "It has been fairly steady at $11.25 per kilo over the last year or so but it has been as high as $15.50 and as low as $9.75."

"And it also depends on how rapidly we want to write off the cost of the building and production lines. Top management wants us to use 10 years these days, which is pretty aggressive in my opinion," added Walter.

Question: At a selling price of $11.25 per kilo, how many kilos will the company have to sell per year to break-even?

Question: If the total annual market for this product is 290,000 kilos, what share of the market will they need to achieve?

Question: If the selling price drops to $9.75, what will the break-even point become?

Question: If the company decides that they want to write-off the cost of the building and production lines in 5 years, what does this do to the break-even point?

SUMMARY

1. Decision making is one of the critical functions of a manager.

2. The manager invariably has to make a decision based on incomplete or inaccurate information within a specific time frame. It may well be what is known as a *satisficing* decision (i.e., one that satisfies the needs of the organization) as opposed to an optimal decision (i.e., the best possible decision).

3. The key steps in making a decision are:

   - Define the goal or objective ... the focus of the decision.
   - Identify the alternatives that will achieve the specific objective.
   - Evaluate the pros and cons of the decision.
   - Make and implement the decision.

4. Following implementation of the decision, it is important to review the outcome to determine whether or not it was a good one ... and what can be learned from the decision process.

5. Decisions can be made either by individuals or by groups. There are a number of advantages and disadvantages to group decision making. A group takes advantage of the skills, abilities and perspectives of a number of people and often generates more commitment to the outcome. On the other hand, groups consist of people and this may make the process more complicated and time consuming.

6. There are a number of techniques that can be used to facilitate group decision making, namely:

   - Brainstorming ... participants are free to suggest ideas however wild. No negative feedback is allowed until everybody's ideas have been presented.
   - Nominal Group Technique ... each participant writes down their suggestion on paper and presents them orally. The group then discusses all the suggestions and, by means of a secret ballot, votes for the best idea.
   - Delphi Technique ... a questionnaire is circulated to the participants and the results are tabulated and then shared with the participants. They can then either stick with their prior opinion or change it based on the responses of others. This process continues until there is a consensus regarding the issue.

7. There are a number of techniques that a manager can use to assist in the planning process:

   - Forecasting ... methods of determining the future demand for a product.
   - Gantt charts ... a visual representation of the resources or activities for a project.
   - PERT/CPM chart ... visual representations of the sequence in which events have to be completed for a project to end on schedule.
   - Break-even analysis ... a means of estimating the number of units that will have to be sold for the organization to break-even.

CRITICAL THINKING QUESTIONS

1. What sorts of decision are easy to make? What characteristics do they have which tend to make them relatively easy to resolve? How do these differ from decisions which are often very difficult to make?

   _____

   _____

   _____

   _____

2. Your boss has asked you to evaluate the pros and cons of opening a new store on the edge of town. After driving around the area and interviewing the people in that part of town, you have come up with a listing of seven arguments in favor and five arguments against. When your boss asks for your recommendation, you point out that the pros outweigh the cons and thus the company should go ahead with the new store. Why is this an inappropriate or ineffective analysis? And what could you do to make it more realistic and useful?

   _____

   _____

   _____

   _____

3. Your organization has established a project team to develop a comprehensive training program ... and you were asked by the president to chair this committee. The first meeting was useful and friendly. However, half way through the second meeting, one of the eight members walked out in disgust complaining that another member was dominating the discussion. Two other members were at loggerheads because they disagreed over the objective of the committee. And two others left to attend another meeting. What has happened here? And what should you do to get the committee back on track?

   _____

   _____

   _____

   _____

4. While preparing the budget for the coming year, the planning committee looked at the following figures for the past six years:

1999	124,500 units
2000	175,000
2001	154,000
2002	145,000
2003	106,000
2004	184,000

Based on these figures, each member of the committee had developed his/her own projection for 2005. The five projections were 195,000; 137,000; 128,000; 164,000; and 151,000. Why do you think the five projections are so different? How could the committee convert these projections into a single forecast?

_____

_____

_____

_____

5. What can you tell about the status of the project from the Gantt chart given below:

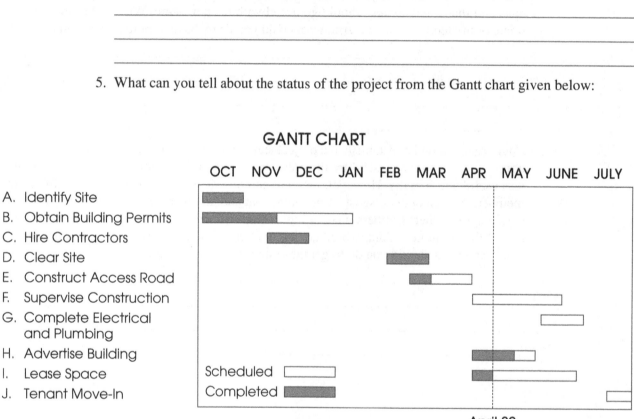

GANTT CHART

April 20

_____

_____

_____

_____

6. What is the critical path in the diagram given below? Initially, the client requested that the project be completed in 142 days. Is this possible? This morning, you have received an e-mail stating that the project has to be completed in 102 days. How would you meet this new schedule?

PERT NETWORK

EVENT	ACTIVITY	ESTIMATED TIME (DAYS)	PRECEDING EVENT
A	Review Product Specifications	5	None
B	Develop Prototype	30	A
C	Test Prototype	15	B
D	Review with Client	5	C
E	Reengineer Prototype	15	C
F	Manufacture Units	20	E
G	Identify Potential Customers	10	D, F
H	Beta Test Units	30	F, G
I	Conduct Interviews	15	H
J	Prepare Report	5	I
K	Presentation/Recommendations	5	J

_____

_____

_____

7. Should we automate the Jacksonville plant? That's the question facing the management of Arturo Construction. At the present time, the present plant produces 10,000 tons of Resicol per year which sells for $340 per ton. The fixed cost is estimated at $2 million per year and the raw materials are currently costing $30 per ton. Does Arturo currently make a profit? If it were to spend another $20 million on automating the plant, it would extend the life of the facility for another ten years and could increase its annual production to 20,000 tons per year. Management believes it can sell the additional production at the current rate. Should management go ahead with the automation?

_____

_____

_____

CASE PROBLEM

DAVIDSON INDUSTRIES

Alan Davidson looked around the room at the grim faces of the members of the management team.

"Well. The rumors you have heard are correct. I've received a written offer from Jim Candless of Endicott & Fayer to purchase Davidson Industries. From a personal perspective, the dollars are rather more than I'd expected."

"That's the good news. The bad news is that I would expect them to close down this operation and merge it with their plant in California. They would essentially be buying our client base. The question is: how should we respond?"

"It's your company, Alan. So you should make the decision," Mark, SVP of manufacturing commented. "I don't think it has anything to do with us."

"I disagree entirely," his counterpart in marketing exclaimed. "We have all worked hard for this company for many years. It's a great company and I don't want to see it disappear. I don't know about you but I have no intention of moving my family out to California ... even if they did offer me a job."

The head of sales shook her head. "It would be a mistake to sell the company at this time. We've just introduced two new product lines and are starting to pick up new clients. We have a fantastic opportunity to grow this company and, whatever you are being offered Alan, I don't think it's enough."

"Well," Alan observed. "Jim said he would give me time to think about the offer. So, let's assume we have three months. What shall we do?"

Question: *Who should make the decision in this case? Should Alan make the decision or should the management team be involved?*

_____

_____

_____

_____

Question: *What are the pros and cons of Alan making the decision alone? Or of having the management team be involved in the decision?*

_____

_____

_____

_____

Question: *Which, if any, of the various techniques described in this chapter should Alan Davidson and his management team use in analyzing the situation and coming up with a conclusion?*

_____

_____

_____

_____

CREATING THE ORGANIZATION

OVERVIEW

This chapter begins a study of the second of the major functions of a manager, namely: organizing. Organizing is the creation and development of an organizational structure. It can also be described as:

Making the most of the available human resources.

In this chapter, we will focus on:

■ The Organizational Planning Process.
■ Span of Control and Chain of Command.
■ Basic Organizational Structures.
■ The Matrix Organization.
■ The Virtual Organization.

THE ORGANIZATIONAL PLANNING PROCESS

Key Points:

1. The organizational planning process consists of a number of important steps.
   First of all, management needs to determine the specific goals of the organization and develop a clear understanding of the ultimate objectives (i.e., what is the organization designed to achieve?).

> **Example:** Bob Mazziotti had recently taken over as head of the purification division and was amazed to read in the company's strategic plan that the goal of the company was to become a leader in the field of industrial water purification. "But we do very little R&D and our sales force is almost exclusively focused on sales to retail outlets. So ... what exactly is the goal of this division?"

2. Having clearly defined the goals and objectives of the organization then you need to identify the major tasks that need to be taken to develop the desired organization.

> **Example:** In recent times, firms such as Procter & Gamble have dramatically reduced the number of products sold. They have sold off or discontinued a large number of also-ran products in order to focus their efforts and their energies on a relatively small number of leading brands. Having identified the goals and objectives of the company, they identified the major tasks which would have to be implemented, namely: reducing the number of brands sold and acquiring other major brands (such as the acquisition of Gillette with its well-know brands).

3. Each of the major tasks is usually broken down into a series of sub tasks.

> **Example:** A Los Angeles-based commercial real estate firm decided to open an office in San Francisco and responsibility was assigned to Harry Redknap. It was agreed that the new office should be up and running by August; thus giving Harry four months to complete the assignment. He determined that the task needed to be broken down into four sub-tasks, namely: (1) identifying a location for the office, (2) acquiring desks, computers, etc., (3) hiring sales and office personnel, and (4) implementing an advertising and promotion campaign. If all four activities were completed by the end of July, the office would be ready to open in early August.

4. The fourth step is to allocate resources to each of the sub tasks.

> **Example:** Harry Redknap next decided that he himself would handle the search for a location. The acquisition of desks, computers, etc. would be contracted to two local firms. He, along with one of his associates, would handle the hiring of sales personnel while a local firm would be assigned to hire the office personnel. Finally, the advertising and promotion campaign would be given to the company's existing agency in Los Angeles.

5. Finally, having established the organization, a manager needs to evaluate how well it is doing against the goals and objectives.

> **Example:** Jim Moore was great when it came to setting up organizations. He worked for the Aztec Company and had set up their entire network of office throughout South America. Once the organization was established, Jim lost interest. He was ready to move on to the next country. As a result, many of the countries had weak and ineffective organizations. And it was not until Jim retired and a new manager took over that somebody took the time to evaluate the organizational structures and make the appropriate changes. Two years after Jim had left, sales were five times the original level ... essentially because of the closer "fit" between the organization and the needs of the marketplace.

CASE 8.1

AMANDA VECCHIO

"Come on in Amanda. Let's talk." The speaker was the head of the International Division, Petra Semovich. "Well done on the Bolivian assignment. That was great, the client was very satisfied. Now, I have something a little more challenging for you. As you know, the board recently decided that we really need to move in to the European market starting with offices in London, Paris and Milan. In fact, they would like to see Europe accounting for 20% of our sales within five years. Since you speak fluent Italian, we'd like you to head up the Milan operation."

"There is virtually nothing on the ground there at the moment. We've rented office space not far from La Scala so you can enjoy the opera. And we've arranged with a temporary service to provide a secretary and driver whenever you need them. We have also booked you in to the Metropole Hotel. And, most importantly, we have put funding for the next year into a local account. In the folder are a copy of the Board's authorization and a summary of the last meeting. If you need any assistance ... I am always here."

As the plane made its way from JFK to Milan, Amanda pulled out her lap top and began making notes on the various things she needed to do. In the United States, the parent company sold equipment to four very different industries. However, 50% of exports to European clients had been to the baking industry and another 25% to agricultural customers.

Question: What should Amanda focus on as a first step?

Question: What would be the top three questions that Amanda needs to ask prior to taking any action?

Question: What steps should Amanda follow to plan the organizational structure?

SPAN OF CONTROL AND CHAIN OF COMMAND

 Key Points:

1. A manager can only supervise and manage a limited number of people effectively. As the number of employees reporting to a manager increase, the effectiveness of the supervision tends to decline. It is generally felt that a manager can effectively supervise between 6 and 10 employees.

> **Example:** A manager works 8 hours or 480 minutes per day. If 5 employees (or customers or suppliers) each spend 30 minutes with the manager then the manager has 330 minutes left to work on other matters. If he/she has 10 people, then the available time drops to 180 minutes. And, with 15 people, his/her day is essentially filled.

2. The number of people a manager can handle depends on the nature of the tasks they are doing.

> **Example:** Jim Brown manages two groups—commercial and industrial. The commercial group's activities are reasonably standardized and Jim rarely spends more than a few minutes with any of them. The industrial group, however, deals with very complex situations and he often spends much of the day working with them to resolve problems. The five people in the industrial group take ten times as much of his time as the much larger commercial group.

3. All organizations need a chain of command consisting of two elements. First, there is the unity of command which means that each person reports to one and only one boss. Second, there must be a clear and unbroken line of authority running from the president down to the lowest employee. *Note:* some of the newer forms of organization violate this rule.

> **Example:** Peter Hart works for a family owned business. "I love the people. They are great to work for but they drive me crazy. The president tells me to do one thing. His father comes in and tells me to do something else. Then, his mother comes in with another set of instructions. And then the president comes back and asks what I am doing."
>
> **Example:** Martina Biale sent out a memo summarizing the outcome of a lengthy staff meeting. "It went to all the participants and I assumed that they would send it on to their people. Some did and some didn't. When I asked the three people who didn't forward it why they hadn't done so, they either said, 'I didn't realize you wanted me to circulate it.' Or 'I thought you were the only person who had the authority to circulate those memos.'"

CASE 8.2

AN EXHAUSTED AND FRUSTRATED PRESIDENT

"Let's get away from this place and go and have lunch. Sometimes I think this job will drive me crazy."

Over lunch, Carla Riisse explained the situation.

"It wasn't so bad when there were just the six of us in the office. Everything was relatively calm and orderly. If you needed something or wanted to talk with somebody, you just stuck your head around the door. Now, there are twenty-five of us spread out over two floors of the building. It doesn't seem to be working."

"I arrived at 7:45 this morning in an attempt to get some work done on a proposal. Standing outside my office were two of the salesmen, the production manager, the vice president of finance, the office manager, and my secretary (with a large pile of messages). No sooner had I managed to handle them but two other sales people arrived along with a couple of representatives from suppliers and two of the project managers. It is now lunch time and I still haven't returned any of the calls and I haven't looked at the proposal yet."

"There is another problem that is arising with increasing frequency. Somebody comes to me and I tell them what to do. I assume they have passed this information on to the others in the team. But they don't. So, things are increasingly falling through the cracks. Then the manager comes in and complains that I never gave him the message. So, he's thinking his people are working on one activity and they are actually doing something totally different."

"I'll have a mineral water but what I really need is a double scotch ... and no rocks."

Question: What are the fundamental problems in this small company?

Question: What does Carla need to do?

Question: What are three to five things Carla should do ... in order of priority ... to get better control of her life and her company?

BASIC ORGANIZATIONAL STRUCTURES

🗝️ Key Points:

1. Initially a company has a very simple organizational structure ... with the vast majority of the employees reporting directly to the president. It tends to be a flat organization (i.e., all the positions are on the same level).

> **Example:** Arthur ran a small family-owned supermarket. By 2004, he had a total of ten employees ranging from the meat and deli managers to the cashiers. If any of them had any questions or concerns, they came to him.

2. As the organization grows so does the structure. Because of the span of control issues, the president doesn't have time to work with everybody so he/she introduces a new line on the organization chart (i.e., one or more managers).

> **Example:** Ted started out with just one sales person. However, as the company grew, the number of sales people increased from three to eight by the end of 2004. "I recently appointed a sales manager who is in charge of the other seven sales people," Tom explained. "I should have done it earlier, I just couldn't find the time to work with them. The disadvantage of having a sales manager is that I am now only dealing with one person and don't have the same 'feel' for what is going on in the marketplace."

3. Further growth often causes additional organizational changes as the company attempts to organize in the most efficient manner.

> **Example:** "When we acquired Porter-Randall, we added an entirely new line of products. And, for a time, we had their sales force report to Alec Muldroom, our sales manager. However, he complained that he couldn't manage both groups so we appointed two assistant sales managers—one for each group. This arrangement was better. However, as the sales of both lines increased, it was clear that we needed to make a further change. So, we split the sales people into two separate divisions each with their own sales manager."

CASE 8.3

RETHINKING THE ORGANIZATION—PART A

"When I founded this company in Boston, there were just myself, the guy who handled production, a couple of salesmen, and a secretary/bookkeeper. That was back in 1987 and we could just about hold a company meeting in a telephone booth. We had just the one product—what we now call the VZ."

"By 1991, we had 25 people and they all seemed to be reporting to me. So, I appointed a sales manager, a production manager, and an office manager. That worked well for a time until we added the HT product line. That meant that the sales and production managers had two assistant managers—one for VZ and the other for HT. That worked reasonably well for a time."

"However, three years later, we moved the production of HT to Austin, Texas along with the sales and supporting staff. In effect, we split the company into two separate divisions . . . and then into three when we added the RS line in St. Louis in 1997. All that we retained at headquarters was the financial operation. There were some advantages to this structure. However, communications became a problem. On one occasion, we had three sales people (one from each division) waiting on the same customer. That didn't make us look too good. Also, each division had its own R&D operation and we found there was tremendous duplication.

Question: What did the organization look like between 1987 and 1993?

Question: What were the advantages and disadvantages of this organizational structure?

Question: What did the organization look like between 1993 and 1998?

Question: What were the advantages and disadvantages of this organizational structure?

⌐○══ **Key Points:**

1. A company can establish a geographically-based organization either domestically or internationally. It does so when it believes that the problems and issues faced in a specific geographic area justify the additional organization.

> **Example:** "We started our own operations in Europe in 2003. Initially, they reported to me. But that didn't work so I appointed a general manager and they reported to him and he reported to me. That also didn't prove too efficient. So, last year, we appointed a president for Europe. She reports to me but is essentially running her own operation over there. They have their own accounting, finance, manufacturing, and R&D groups.

2. A company can also organize itself around its customers. It adopts this organizational structure when it finds that it has different types of customers who want very different things.

> **Example:** A manufacturer of paper for office copiers sells to a number of different market segments. It has its own sales force that sells direct to government agencies and very large companies. It has a second sales force that sells paper to the leading office supply chains such as Office Depot, Office Max, etc. And it has a third sales force that calls on distributors who sell copy paper to smaller stores and offices.

3. There is no single organization structure that works perfectly in any situation. Each structure has its advantages and disadvantages. With the growing emphasis on satisfying customer needs, organizational structures have tended to change from being internally driven (i.e., the way management prefers the company to be organized) to customer driven (i.e., the way the customers want to interact with the firm).

> **Example:** Ratzer Industries had offices throughout Asia which provided sales and technical support. Major customers, however, complained that the R&D was still being conducted at the company's headquarters in the United States. They wanted to be able to work more closely with people who knew their part of the world. While it was an expensive move, Ratzer established R&D groups in each of its major Asian markets.
>
> **Example:** Fisher & Co. had an extremely effective technical support group. The sales people sold the products and then, if the customer had problems, they contacted the technical support team. From Fisher's point of view, this system worked well. However, the larger clients wanted the sales person to be able to solve technical problems and Fisher decided to begin to merge the two groups and provide the sales people with additional advanced technical training.

CASE 8.3

RETHINKING THE ORGANIZATION—PART B

"So, in 1998, we went through a major reorganization. We split the company into four geographic regions (North-East, South-East, Mid-West, and West). In each region, communications among the sales force improved. However, in some areas, we were still sending two or three sales people to the same customer. And, quite frequently, we didn't have the right sales person in the correct geographic area."

Also, we were discovering that we had different types or classes of customers who wanted different things. The large customers required extensive technical assistance and support. The medium-sized companies required more training and marketing support. And the small customers wanted a personal relationship with the salesman. That meant we really needed three different types of sales people with different skills."

"In 2002, we changed the organization again. Now, we have three divisions each calling exclusively on one class of customer. Class A accounts are serviced out of Boston, Class B out of St. Louis and Class C out of Austin. The sales people don't like it because they feel uncomfortable selling all three lines. And not all the customers are happy. A Class A company wants top quality technical service on all three products . . . and sometimes the representative can't provide it. And, if they are located in California, they don't like the fact that the headquarters is in Boston.

"Believe it or not, we are considering changing the organization again. We are looking at the possibility of separating the sales and technical support functions. That would make it easier for the sales people and our customers would have better access with regard to technical issues."

Question: What did the organization look like following the 1998 reorganization? What are the advantages and disadvantages of this structure?

Question: Assume that finance, marketing, production, and R&D remained centralized, what did the organization look like following the 2002 reorganization? What are the advantages and disadvantages of this structure?

Question: What would be the pros and cons of separating the technical support function from the sales function?

THE MATRIX ORGANIZATION

⊙━▱ **Key Points:**

1. Organizations adopt a matrix organization when there is a fundamental need to better coordinate the activities of the organization. Companies typically begin with a two-dimensional organizational matrix in which one group focuses on the product and the other on the sales.

> **Example:** "We have a total of ten different product lines which are sold to retail outlets around the world. Most of the sales people sell all ten products and have a good understanding of the needs of their customers. However, they don't have a full appreciation for the manufacturing and selling of the products worldwide. As a result, we often find that they aren't selling all the products we are producing. And they are selling them in different ways in different markets. So, we introduced a product manager for all ten lines. Now, the sales people report to both their local manager and to the product manager here at headquarters."

2. As a further step, some firms utilize a three-dimensional matrix ... focusing on the product, sales, and the regional aspects of the business.

> **Example:** "The product manager system worked well. They established a very good relationship with the local personnel. Unfortunately, the sales people were motivated to sell wherever they could. So, our people in Korea started selling to China. Those in Thailand started selling in Malaysia and Indonesia. The Japanese sold in all three countries and so on. The problem was not only that they were tripping over each other but they were selling at widely different prices. So, we appointed a regional vice president and all sales outside the home country have to be approved by him."

3. One of the fundamental rules of organization is that a person should report to only one superior—the concept of unity of command. The matrix structure contravenes this rule. In a three dimensional matrix a person can end up reporting to three bosses. Clearly, making the "three boss system" work requires considerable ability and negotiating skills.

> **Example:** Bill Carterolo was a salesman in Brazil. Under the current matrix structure, he reported to his immediate boss in Sao Paulo, a product manager in London, and a regional vice president in Mexico City. "I have never had any problems here in Sao Paulo and the woman in Mexico City is great. It was the product manager in London who drove me crazy. He was always sending memos and e-mails telling me to do this and don't do that. And he didn't have any idea about our problems. Fortunately, the company promoted him and I am now working with a new guy who had a different view of the world. He doesn't tell me what to do. He merely gives me suggestions, advice, and guidance."

CASE 8.4

THORNTON INDUSTRIES

Thornton Industries is a **Fortune 500** company headquartered in Baltimore, Maryland. It consists of more than 100 companies and subsidiaries that sell a wide variety of products in all the major markets around the world. An example of the company's product line is Teldrin, a pesticide.

Up until 1999, each of the Teldrin representatives reported only to a local manager. However, there were growing concerns that they were not sufficiently knowledgeable and up-to-date about the material and its features. So, at the end of that year, the company established a product development division. As a result, the Teldrin representatives reported to both the local manager and to the Teldrin product manager back in Baltimore.

The Teldrin product manager was in continuous contact with the production facilities and would send out daily memos with instructions to the local personnel with regard to pricing and the materials to be promoted.

In 2003, each of the regional managers was charged with increasing exports. As a result, they began to look more aggressively at opportunities outside their own local market. The general manager for Australia, for example, placed far greater emphasis on selling to China and other developing Asian companies. Unfortunately, this had an undesirable side effect. A Chinese company received five bids on an order of Teldrin ... one from Thornton USA, one from Thornton U.K., Thornton Japan, Thornton India, and Thornton Australia. All five bids quoted different prices.

The company's reaction to this embarrassment was to set up a network of six regional vice presidents. The Teldrin representative in Australia now reports not only to his own local manager and the product manager in Baltimore but also the regional vice president located in Hong Kong.

Question: What do you see as the advantages of the current organizational structure? What are the disadvantages?

Question: What steps would you take to ensure that this organizational structure works effectively?

Question: What basic rule of management does this type of organization break?

VIRTUAL ORGANIZATIONS

🔑 **Key Points:**

1. Historically, companies handled all aspects of the business internally (i.e., they had departments devoted to all the major functions). However, the growth of technology and the need to focus on basic skills in order to be competitive led to the growing outsourcing of activities and the emergence of virtual organizations.

> **Example:** A *Fortune 500* company traditionally handled its payroll internally. However, an independent company proposed taking over this function. Due to its technology and volume of business, it could offer a very attractive rate. The *Fortune 500* company decided that maintaining internal control over payroll was not critical and decided it made sense to outsource this function to save money.
>
> **Example:** Following WWII, General Motors manufactured virtually every part of the typical automobile (i.e., engines, transmission, seats, etc.) with the exception of the tires. With the growing flood of Asian manufacturers with better quality, lower price cars, GM had to cut its costs in order to compete. It did so by subcontracting the manufacturing of various components to non-union facilities with lower costs.

2. Today, companies focus on providing those functions where they have a unique capability or distinctive competence. If another organization can provide a function at a lower price then there are growing pressures to subcontract.

> **Example:** "We used to believe that it was important that we control every aspect of our business. We grew our own hops and barley. We manufactured our own bottles. We brewed our own beer and distributed it through our own companies. We were determined that no external firm could have a major impact on our business. These days, we are taking a different approach. In order to compete, we have to. If another company can manufacture bottles to meet our standards but at a lower price ... then we will look at the economics.

3. Ultimately, many leading companies known for their design, manufacturing, marketing, and sales may end up a virtual company focusing on just one or two of the activities and subcontracting other functions to external specialist firms.

> **Example:** It has even been suggested that GM, could end up focusing on automobile design and outsourcing the manufacture of parts, the assembly process, the marketing and promotion, and the sales of its vehicles to external and independent firms.

CASE 8.5

FUNSTUFF TOYS

Funstuff Toys is a billion dollar a year company ... a major player in the toy industry. In its early years, it manufactured its own products in Massachusetts, as well as purchasing items from American-based companies. However, in the mid 70s, management was forced to look for cheaper overseas sources. By 1986, it had closed down its last American plant and all its products were manufactured in China, Taiwan and Thailand.

In 1988, it subcontracted its bookkeeping to a national chain and set up its human resource department as a separate company. These were primarily cost-cutting moves. That left the Funstuff Toys with 240 employees broken down into advertising and promotion, finance, marketing, product design, production control, sales and strategic planning.

In 2001, it handed over all responsibility for advertising and promotion to a local agency and the sales function to a large domestic sales organization. This cut their personnel numbers down to less than 100.

And, in early 2005, management was seriously considering contracting with a Hong Kong based company to take over production control, outsourcing product design to a California company, and handing over marketing to a company formed by two former Funstuff employees. That would leave the company (with $1.1 billion in sales) with a corporate staff of just 15 employees.

Question: Do you see this transition from a company with its own production facilities and a large workforce to a virtual company with little more than a coordinating management team as a positive step? Or a negative trend?

Question: What are the advantages and disadvantages of operating as a virtual corporation?

Question: To what extent can the concept of a virtual organization be applied to other industries and other companies?

SUMMARY

1. Organizations consist of people and one of the critical functions of a manager is to make the most of his/her human resources. This involves trying to get the right people in the right place.

2. Only rarely does a manager have the opportunity to build an organization starting with a blank sheet of paper. In most cases, he/she takes over an existing organization.

3. The organization planning process involves five key steps:

   - Determining (or reviewing) the actual goals and objectives of the organization.
   - Identifying the major tasks that need to be taken to develop the desired organization.
   - Breaking the major tasks down into a series of sub-tasks.
   - Allocating resources to each of the tasks.
   - Evaluating the performance of the organization against the goals and objectives of the organization.

4. Span of control reflects the number of employees that a person can effectively manage. It is normally thought to be between 6 and 10. However, it depends very much on (a) the manager and (b) the nature of the employee's tasks and the amount of supervision they require.

   Chain of command emphasizes (a) the importance of a person reporting to just one boss and (b) the need for a clear and unbroken line of authority running from the president to all employees.

5. Organizations go through a number of changes resulting from both growth and expansion and the changing needs of the customer.

   Most firms start with a very simple structure with all the employees reporting to the owner/president.

SIMPLE/FLAT ORGANIZATION

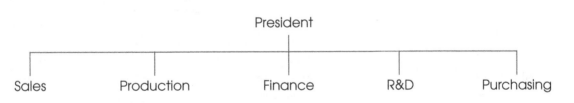

As the organization grows, we see the beginnings of specialization and the formation of departments. Individuals tend to focus increasingly on a specific set of tasks. As the departments grow, managers are appointed to coordinate and direct their activities.

DEPARTMENTAL ORGANIZATION

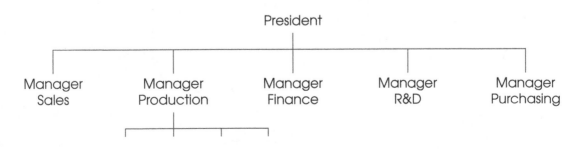

Further growth leads to further organizational change. However, the nature of this change depends on whether the growth relates to products, geography, or the customer.

If the growth involves the addition of new and different products then the organization will often set up a separate division for each of the products:

PRODUCT-BASED ORGANIZATION

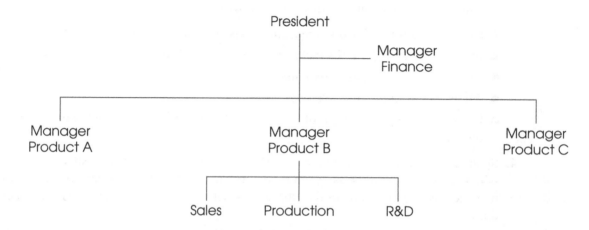

On the other hand, if the company moves overseas, then management will often utilize an organization based on geography:

GEOGRAPHICALLY-BASED ORGANIZATION

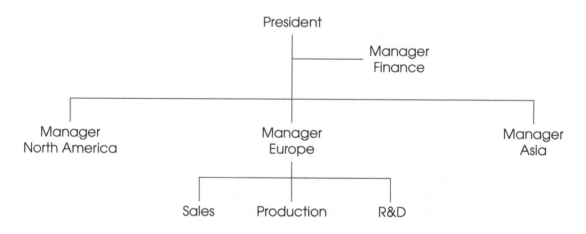

Finally, an organization may conclude that the important feature of its customers are their differences and may thus utilize an organization built around these differences:

CUSTOMER-BASED ORGANIZATION

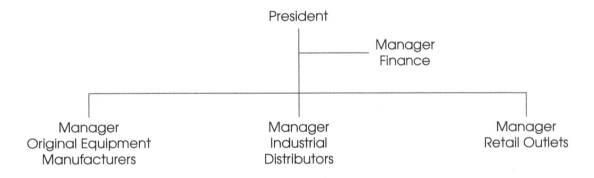

6. The matrix organization is one that attempts to achieve coordination by having managers responsible for different aspects of the business. The most common example of this is a two dimensional matrix in which an employee reports to both their immediate boss and to a product manager. Some firms utilize a three dimensional matrix in which they appoint a regional coordinator so that the employee now reports to their immediate boss, a product manager, and the regional coordinator.

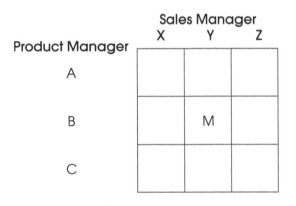

Employee M reports to both Sales Manager Y and Product Manager B.

7. Virtual organizations are those in which management outsources some (and ultimately all) the major functions to other organizations. The management of the company's main function is thus one of coordination and strategy.

CRITICAL THINKING QUESTIONS

1. Your company, Bartok Industries, has recently acquired one of its competitors, A&A Supply. A&A was once a very strong company with a great customer list. In recent years, however, it has slipped and is now in very bad shape. The president died and three key people retired. "Since I would like to continue to run A&A as a separate division," your boss says. "I want you to go in there and develop an organization that will restore it to its former position." What steps would you follow as part of an organization planning process?

   _____

   _____

   _____

2. Jim and Bob are having lunch together. Both have recently been appointed as managers. However, their experiences are very different. Jim has 3 people reporting to him and is being overwhelmed by the pressure. "They seem to spend most of their days in my office," he complained. "How do I do this? How do I do that? It is driving me crazy." Bob smiled. "Sorry to hear that. I have 17 people reporting to me and sometimes I only see one or two of them each day. In fact, I sometimes wish I saw more of them." Why the differences between Jim and Bob's experiences? What factors may contribute to Jim being swamped and Bob so relaxed?

   _____

   _____

   _____

3. The new owner of the Winston Paper Company completed his initial tour of the company and was appalled. A former senior officer in the Marine Corps, he was stunned by the informal way in which the company functioned. "In the Corps, we have a clear chain of command. Everybody reports to their superior officer and all communications flow up and down the organization," he commented. "You show me an organization chart that was created four years ago with numerous penciled-in changes and dotted line relationships. Now, that's not acceptable. Within a week, we will have a new organization chart with everybody clearly reporting to one individual and we will have posted rules and regulations with regard to the flow of information throughout the organization." How does the Marine Corps differ from Winston Paper? And what are the pros and cons of implementing a highly formalized and structured system?

   _____

   _____

   _____

4. In an interview with a reporter from a local newspaper, the president of Horton Products made the following statement. "We started with one product which we sold to businesses around the state. Since then we have grown to where, today, we have fifteen major product lines and we sell our products in every industrialized country in the world. We sell to governments, to universities, to large corporations, and to mom & pop stores." Impressed the reporter commented, "You must have gone through numerous organizational changes over the years?" The president smiled. "No, we have essentially the same organizational structure now as we did twenty years ago. Of course, it is much larger and has many more lay-

ers. However, everything is still run from this building." How is this possible? How can a company expand like Horton Products and maintain the same organizational structure? What are the pros and cons of doing so?

_____

_____

_____

5. Arlene and Terry had been secretaries for a property management firm for a number of years and were well regarded for their knowledge of the paper work and procedures. They were classified as senior secretaries and had reached their maximum level in the organization. Then, a consultant recommended a major organizational change. If they wished to do so, they could become assistant property managers working with one of the company's eighteen property managers. Both jumped at this opportunity. Within three months, they were both promoted to property manager (when their bosses resigned) and, within six months, they had both been fired. How would you evaluate the consultant's recommendations? What went wrong? What do you think the owner of a building wanted from his/her property manager?

_____

_____

_____

6. "As you know, Martin, we have plants in fifteen different countries around the world and sell our products in more than fifty. That's the good news. The bad news is that there is no coordination in terms of the individual products. So, you are going to be our guinea pig. I want you to become our point man for insecticides. As our first product manager, you will report to me and I want you to lay out a plan of action to ensure that it is a successful role. We need the role to work and we want you to provide a road map for future product managers." What would you do if you were Martin? What are the keys to making this new product manager role work?

_____

_____

_____

7. Alan and Carter Johnson worked together for ten years before a major disagreement caused them to break up their partnership and go their separate ways. Alan continued to run Johnson Manufacturing in the traditional manner. The company had more than 400 employees divided between the design group, the distribution facilities (warehouses and trucks), the four manufacturing plants, the marketing group, and a fifty strong sales force. Carter stayed in the same business. However, he had only one head designer who oversaw the activities of fifteen independent designers. He used a national warehousing and trucking company for all distribution. All manufacturing was done in China and he had one employee who lived in Hong Kong and controlled all production. Marketing was done by a firm in New York City. And he sold all his products through a network of five companies that sold to retailers. In total, CarterCo had a total of 7 employees (including Carter himself). What are the pros and cons of these two very different approaches to organization. What strengths does Alan's organization have? And what strengths does Carter's have?

_____

_____

_____

CASE
PROBLEM

BRAINTREE INDUSTRIES

After more than ten years of steady growth, Braintree Industries' sales had declined by 18% following a 10% decline the previous year.

"Last year, I didn't worry too much," Morton Hall the president commented. We were still profitable and the stockholders seemed perfectly happy with the dividend (65% of the company was owned by family members with a small number of local businessmen owning the remainder). However, looking at the final figures for this year, I am predicting a less than merry meeting this year. This is the first time we have suffered a loss in twenty years."

At a meeting of the management team a week before the board meeting, a number of possible reasons for the decline were suggested and discarded. "I don't think it is the product," one manager observed. "We added six new lines last year and they were all well received."

"And I don't think it is the competition," another manager added. "In fact, with Ableson going out of business, we're in better shape than we were a year ago. And I don't think it is pricing. We're still very competitive."

"We have lost quite a few senior managers in recent years and that may have hurt us," another commented. "True," Morton replied. "But we've hired and promoted some good people to replace them. My gut feeling is that it's the organization. The marketplace is changing rapidly and we still have the same basic structure we had when I took over eleven years ago."

"Well," the chairman observed. "If it is the organization then we had better have a game plan for the board meeting next week. We need to be able to tell our stockholders what we are going to do about it."

Question: As Morton Hall, what steps would you take to determine whether or not the organizational structure was at the heart of the company's rapid decline?

_____

_____

_____

_____

Question: What are some of the possible changes that may have occurred over the past few years that would have led to Braintree Industries' organization being out of step with the marketplace?

_____

_____

_____

_____

Question: *What are the pros and cons of making major changes to a well established organization?*

_____

_____

_____

_____

MAKING THE MOST OF PEOPLE

OVERVIEW

Many would argue that people are the most valuable resource of any organization. It is people who provide the creativity and get the job done. True, financial resources, equipment, facilities, etc., are extremely important. However, it is the skills and capabilities of the people who often differentiate a company from its competitors.

In this chapter, we focus on five key aspects dealing with the utilization of the personnel resource, namely:

- Personnel planning.
- The legal aspects of staffing.
- The hiring process.
- Orientation.
- Training and development.

PERSONNEL PLANNING

 Key Points:

1. In order to maximize the utilization of an organization's human resources, it is important to have a human resource plan which consists of a:

   - Human resource inventory.
   - Projection of the future personnel needs of the organization.
   - Replacement chart for senior personnel.
   - Training and development plan for all personnel.

2. A human resource inventory. The inventory should list the employees by name, their education, their prior employment, their skills and capabilities, the languages spoken, etc.

177

> **Example:** "It is really amazing the resources we have in this company. The sales people were having no success at all with a potential customer until somebody had the bright idea of checking the human resource inventory. We discovered that one of our production guys had worked for the client and knew many of the people very well ... including the one person we wanted to contact. From then on, everything went smoothly."

> **Example:** "We had potential customers visit the plant last week from the Ukraine. They didn't speak very good English and it wasn't a good visit. We couldn't communicate with them well enough to build up a rapport. This morning, I found that Bob Johnson speaks fluent Ukrainian. His mother came from Kiev. If we had had a human resource inventory, we could have used him."

3. A projection of the future personnel needs of the organization. This is (or should be) an annual analysis of the areas in which the organization needs to hire additional personnel. This need can result from growth and expansion and from the retirement and firing of existing personnel. Having a plan avoids hiring the wrong people at the wrong time ... and not being able to hire key people when needed.

> **Example:** "Our divisional plan called for a major expansion in the Fall ... specifically: adding at least fifteen people in a new Dallas office. When we informed top management that we are ready to begin the hirings, they tell us we can't. Why? Apparently management had imposed a hiring freeze because of the number of people hired by the other divisions. If the hirings had been coordinated, there would have been no problem."

> **Example:** "Tom Robinson has just announced that he is going to retire at the end of this month. That's three weeks from now. We have known for some time that he was looking to move to Florida. And yet we were apparently taken by surprise when he said he was leaving. We should have been planning for this so that we could find the best candidate, bring them on board, and have Tom train them. Now ... we are in a really awkward position."

4. A replacement chart for key personnel. Who is going to take over if a senior manager retires, resigns, or dies?

> **Example:** A number of years ago, the management of a major electronics company flew to Boston for a meeting with their most important client. The plane crashed killing all on board. There was no succession plan. Nobody had been trained to take over the positions of the managers who died. In the long run, the company survived. However, it went through a period of serious decline due to lack of leadership.

> **Example:** "I always assumed that Bob Anson would take over from me as president of this company. In effect, I have been training him for the position. Today, I find out that he is resigning to take over as president of another company. Now, I don't know who is going to take over from me or assume Bob's role."
>
> **Example:** "Mary DeCold has done a fantastic job as marketing manager and I am pleased to promote her to corporate vice president. Unfortunately, she has not identified and trained her replacement. There is nobody in her department who can take over her position."

5. A training and development plan for all personnel. Organizations usually have limited resources to spend on education, training and development. So it is critically important that management know what each individual requires (or would benefit from) in order to be able to allocate those resources in a manner that will maximize the corporate return.

> **Example:** "This year, in addition to doing an evaluation of the performance of the people in my department, I've been asked to complete a training and development plan for everybody. This will go to the human resources department who, in conjunction with the department heads, will make a decision on whether or not to fund the training. The instructions say we should focus on the situations where further training and education would have a substantial impact on the individual's productivity."
>
> **Example:** "I've just hired two new people and I want to send them to a conference in Milan. It is important that they go. However, I'm being told that there is no money in the budget. I'm not surprised. We sent eight people to Acapulco last month to a totally worthless meeting. They spent most of their time sitting on the beach. We need to spend money where it will do some good not where it will produce good suntans."

CASE
9.1

PEOPLE: OUR MOST IMPORTANT RESOURCE

"People are our most important resource. It is what makes the difference between us and our competitors." This was one of Mark McGuire's favorite statements. And, whenever he said it, his managers would mouth the same phrase. People generally respected the president of the company but this was a phrase that rubbed a number of people the wrong way.

Cecily Walker, head of purchasing, was one of those who found the statement irritating. "I have been asking for two new people for a year now. And each time I ask, Mark tells me we can't afford them. Personally, I think we would save two to three times their salaries if we had the people to ensure we always get the best price."

"Arthur Stone, head of manufacturing, was another who felt the statement was off target. "We spent $200,000 on new equipment last year and it has never been used because we don't have the people to operate it. It is easy enough to get Mark to o.k. equipment purchases because that is what he is interested in. But people . . . that's another issue."

Indira Sarik, head of advertising and public relations, had a different comment. "Mark comes back from a high power advertising meeting and says he has hired two new people for me. To be honest, I don't need more people. Chip Staley in sales does. We are hiring people . . . but for the wrong positions."

Thomas Lucas, head of engineering, commented that, "We have plans for everything: product plans . . . marketing plans . . . engineering plans . . . capital equipment plans . . . sales plans. We seem to be missing something!!"

Question: Do you agree with Mark McGuire that "people are [a company's] most important resource?*

Question: Why do you think there is an apparent "disconnect" between what Mark McGuire says and how the company functions?

Question: As a human resources consultant, what recommendations would you make to Mark McGuire with regard to the company's human resource planning process?

THE LEGAL ASPECTS OF STAFFING

⚷ Key Points:

1. In recent years, a growing number of laws have been passed that impact on the various aspects of staffing—not just the selection of employees. Managers need to be aware that such legislation exists and be familiar with the general provisions.

2. Among the main federal antidiscrimination acts are the following:
   - Title VII of the Civil Rights Act of 1964.
   - Employment Act of 1967.
   - Americans with Disabilities Act of 1990.

3. Title VII of the Civil Rights Act of 1964 ... prohibits discrimination in all employment decisions on the basis of race, sex, religion, color, or national origin.

> **Example:** Jane Harper applied for a position with a corporate executive search firm. She had more than ten years experience in this type of work but not in the industry for which the firm was hiring. They rejected her because she was an African-American and the industry was virtually 100% white. "We didn't feel there was a good fit between Ms. Harper and the typical candidates with whom we deal," the owner said. Ms. Harper complained that the company was discriminating against her on the basis of her race.
>
> **Example:** Brian Kelley applied for a position as salesman with a clothing company. Two weeks after having been turned down for the position, he had a chance encounter with the individual who was hired. It became clear from the discussion that the reason Brian had been turned down was that he was a gentile and not Jewish. He brought suit against the company on ground of discrimination on the basis of religion.

4. Employment Act of 1967 ... prohibits discrimination against people 40 years of age or older.

> **Example:** When Marvin Comstock lost his job at Hendrie Chemicals, he found it very difficult to obtain a new position. "Every time I go for a job interview, they tell me that I am over qualified. And, while I do have more experience than the average candidate, I think they are rejecting me because I'm 59 years old," Marvin commented. "My guess is that, if I were 39, they'd hire me."
>
> **Example:** "Look at that sign. It says 'Now Hiring' but if I go in and ask about a job, they will say they don't have any openings." Lisa Thurmond was complaining about a store in the local mall. "I am 48 years old and have spent much of my life in the retail business. I should be ideal for that store. But look at the staff. They are all young males. They don't want women of my age."

5. Americans with Disabilities Act of 1990 ... prohibits discrimination against disabled and chronically ill personnel.

> **Example:** Andrew Pannell was paralyzed from the waist down. While he possessed a wheel chair, he preferred to get around on crutches. "I am amazed at how well he maneuvers," one of the managers commented. "I know he can do the job. The problem is that I don't know how well he will do in the corridors. They are often very busy with people rushing back and forth. I'm concerned for him. However, if he accepts the job, we will have to do our best to accommodate him."
>
> **Example:** Maureen Scott suffered from narcolepsy (a chronic neurological order that causes people to fall asleep—normally for a few seconds or minutes). In fact, during the interview, she went to sleep for a couple of minutes. "I am not sure what we do in this case," the interviewer commented. "It's a strange experience when somebody goes to sleep in front of you. The question we have to address is: would this condition make it impossible for her to do the job?"

6. *Important note:* During the interview process (or on the application form), questions which might highlight age, sex, religion, marital status, etc. should be avoided.

> **Example:** "Are you married?" one of the interviewers asked the candidate. Immediately the chair of the committee stepped in. "Jim, you can't ask that. Next question?" Whether or not the candidate was married was irrelevant to their ability to do the job.
>
> **Example:** "I see you have your right arm in a cast. Is it broken?" The interviewer felt this was an appropriate question. "If I were hiring for a desk job, I wouldn't have asked. However, I was hiring for a position in the plant which requires the lifting of heavy objects. I felt I needed to know if the candidate could do the job."

CASE 9.2

A NASTY LEGAL MESS

"I made a mistake when I interviewed Tamara Boule. I knew that immediately when I asked her whether or not she was married. Before I had a chance to withdraw the question, she had launched into a long explanation of the relationship between herself and her husband. Then, she talked about her children and the problem the youngest was having. Each time I tried to jump in, she launched into another long description."

Ms. Boule was one of a group being interviewed for a position (advertised in the local newspaper) with the major hardware store in town. "We're very short of staff just at the moment and need to hire at least three people as soon as possible," the manager explained. "Having listened to Ms. Boule, I kept wondering how reliable she is. She clearly has some serious personal problems and we need people who'll turn up when they say they will."

"Viola Masterson poses a different problem. She is grossly overweight. I weigh 200 lbs and she must be well over 350. Now, look around. Everybody rushes here to help customers. Our informal motto is 'rush ... rush ... rush.' And I can't see Ms. Masterson rushing anywhere. She was a very nice woman but I don't think she will fit in with the other staff."

"Finally, there was Ms. Cara Yorke. "She's a very pleasant, older woman with no experience in this business. In her case, I saw her walking from her car to this office and it must have taken her ten or fifteen minutes. We don't have any physical test for employment but I wonder how fit she is. Then, when she was in my office, she had a coughing fit and I had to get her a glass of water."

The manager decided to reject all three applicants and place the advertisement again. However, as he was driving home that evening, there was a program on the radio about discrimination in hiring and he reviewed in his mind the interviews with Ms. Boule, Masterson and Yorke. Would any of all of them have grounds for a successful suit claiming discrimination?

Question: The manager admits he made a mistake in his interview with Ms. Boule. Should he offer her a job so that his mistake would never be questioned?

Question: Ms. Masterson suffers from a serious and incurable disease. Can the manager discriminate against her because of this affliction?

Question: Could Ms. Yorke be perfectly healthy and her slow walk a function of her being early for the interview? And the cough a momentary spasm? If so, is the manager guilty of discrimination?

THE HIRING PROCESS

🔑 Key Points:

1. The hiring process consists of a series of eleven (11) important steps:

   - Identifying the position to be filled.
   - Reviewing and updating the job analysis.
   - Preparing a job description.
   - Deciding whether or not to post the job opening internally.
   - Deciding whether or not to use an external search firm.
   - Advertising and promoting the position.
   - Reviewing the applicants' resumes.
   - Interviewing the better candidates.
   - The use of testing.
   - Deciding which candidate to offer the position.
   - Negotiating with the selected candidate.

2. Identifying the position to be filled. The hiring process generally begins with a manager identifying the need for an additional person in his/her department. This need can result from a retirement, illness, a resignation, or a firing.

   > **Example:** "I need two new accounts receivable clerks. Millie has been with us for fifteen years and is retiring. And Barbara is getting married and moving to Florida."

3. Reviewing and updating the job analysis. A job analysis is an assessment of the kind or skills, knowledge, and abilities needed to perform the job effectively.

   > **Example:** "Our man in Brussels has resigned and we need to replace him. However, I want to add a couple of new requirements to the job analysis. The next person should be fluent in both French and German and should have a working knowledge of Spanish. Also, they should have some knowledge of EU laws and procedures."

4. Preparing a job description. A job description is a statement of the minimum acceptable qualifications that a person must posses to perform the job effectively.

   > **Example:** "I don't have time to train the person for this position. So, at the very minimum, he/she should have at least five year's experience doing the job."

5. Deciding whether or not to post the position internally. Some firms normally post job opportunities internally before beginning an external search. They believe in promoting from within wherever possible. Other firms see the external search as an opportunity to bring in new ideas from outside the organization.

Example: "I have three people who are marginally qualified to move into the management slot. However, if I select one of them then I will probably lose the other two. So, I'm going to hire from the outside ... and give the three current employees more time to mature."

Example: "If I post the position internally, I know that Jim Boyer will apply. He did last time and that will cause problems. He thinks he is qualified and the man for the job ... and I don't think he is."

6. Deciding whether or not to use an external search firm. The search for external candidates can be done either in-house or through the use of an independent firm. The advantage of the latter is that most search firms specialize in one or two industries and thus have a better knowledge of who is well-regarded and who is available. They also protect the identity of the hiring firm (for a period of time). However, the disadvantage is that they charge a substantial fee for their services.

Generally speaking, the higher the position that a company is seeking to fill, the more likely they are to use an external search firm.

Example: "Last month we hired a financial analyst and a receptionist ... and we did it in-house. However, we also need a vice president for financial services and, although we have a couple of good people in house, we are going to use a search firm to see who they can come up with."

Example: "The Board has decided to fire one of our senior people. He doesn't know that yet. However, we want to start a search and have given the assignment to a firm that will represent us during the early stages."

7. Advertising and promoting the position. The level and nature of the advertising and promotional effort usually depends on (a) the importance of the position and (b) the length of time in which the position needs to be filled.

Example: "We hire maintenance personnel on a monthly basis. We put a small advertisement in the local newspaper and always get half a dozen responses from whom we make our selection. For a senior position, we run a much larger display advertisement in *The Wall Street Journal, The New York Times,* and five or six leading local newspapers."

Example: "Normally, our people give us six month's notice. They have been with us for years and this is one big happy family. Because of this, we have the time to place an advertisement in the trade magazines and conduct interviews at the various trade association meetings. We weren't under a great deal of pressure. However, when Andy had a heart attack last year, we had to move much more rapidly to replace him."

8. Reviewing the candidate's resumes.

> **Example:** "This pile of resumes came from one advertisement in *The Wall Street Journal.* I've counted them. There are 493. So, I have divided them into three piles: possible, doubtful, and no. The "possibles" are those who have an MBA, at least five year's experience in the industry, and have occupied a series of roles of increasing responsibility. There are 43 resumes in that pile and I am now going to go through them again and identify the 'highly possibles'. Hopefully, that will get the number down to 10 or 15."
>
> **Example:** I have a standard form against which I score all the candidates. And I focus on those with the highest score. In this way, I know why I turned down each candidate, which is very useful if one of them files a complaint."

9. Interviewing the better candidates. Different organizations follow different processes … depending on how many viable candidates there are and where they are located.

> **Example:** "When we were looking for a store manager last year, we found five candidates who really looked good. They all lived within 50 miles of here so we brought them all in for an interview.
>
> **Example:** "We needed to hire a manager of development and the advertising and promotion generated about twenty candidates who looked interesting. Some were local but the resumes came from all across the country. So, it would have been costly to have flown them here to our location. The solution was to conduct a telephone interview with each of them. Some of these lasted only 15 or 30 minutes, others lasted for an hour or more. At the end of the telephone phase, we had reduced the number to 5 … and we flew each of them in for a meeting.
>
> **Example:** When hiring new people, the accounting firm of Jason and Wise would bring in candidates for a full day. During this period they would meet with each of the members of the management team on an individual basis, go to lunch with the senior partner, and spend the afternoon with some of the junior personnel. Following these one-on-one interviews, the senior partner and management team would review the comments made with regard to the candidate (including those by the junior personnel) and make a decision.
>
> **Example:** The Chemistry Department at the state university local was going through the process of hiring an assistant professor. The interviews with the candidates were all conducted by an interview team as a whole. "We are very concerned that, in a one-on-one interview, a faculty member will make an inappropriate comment or ask a sensitive question. So, we always do group interviews."

10. The use of testing. There are two basic types of testing conducted in business today:

- Personality and aptitude testing.
- Drug and alcohol testing.

> **Example:** "When we are hiring a new paralegal, we give them a battery of tests which cover not only their knowledge of the subject matter but also their personality. Our goal is to get a better idea as to whether or not they will fit in with the firm."
>
> **Example:** "Our policies and procedures manual states that anybody either found with alcohol or drugs on a company site will be immediately suspended. In fact, there are a series of steps leading to firing. However, we don't test our candidates as part of the hiring process."
>
> **Example:** "The airline has a very strict policy with regard to drugs and alcohol. Pilots are not allowed to drink for twenty-four hours before a flight. If they do, they're immediately fired. And we test regularly for drug usage. Pilots know they are going to be tested on a random basis and, if they fail a test, we let them go."

11. **Negotiating with the selected candidate.** Having completed the interview process (which usually consists of two or three interviews for a senior position), the organization then makes its decision as to which of the various candidates it would like to hire … and begins the process of negotiating the terms under which that candidate will join the company.

> **Example:** "We ended up with three great candidates for the position. Making a final decision was difficult. In the end, we ended up making an offer to the individual who lived in the area and seemed the most enthusiastic about the opportunity."
>
> **Example:** "We decided that Phillip Manson was the best hire so we started talking about salary and terms of employment. Much to our surprise, we discovered that he wanted far more than we were prepared to offer. So, we went back and looked at our second candidate again."

12. **Making an offer.** The company makes an offer to the candidate and hopes he/she says "yes" to the offer.

> **Example:** "Michele Farragut was our number one choice. We discussed the terms of an offer when she last visited us and she seemed comfortable with it. So, we made a formal offer … and waited. After about a week, she called me and said she could not accept the position. Her stated reason was that her husband didn't want to move. However, I think it was because her current employer, when told of her impending departure, made a counter offer."
>
> **Example:** "The search ended with a number of acceptable candidates. We made an offer to A, he turned us down. So, we made an offer to B and she turned us down. Then, we made an offer to C … and, believe it or not, she turned us down. So, we had to start the search all over again."

CASE 9.3

LET'S HIRE MY BROTHER-IN-LAW

"The good news is that Pelham, a local supermarket chain, has accepted our bid for a study of customer attitudes. It is a little out of our field but it is a $50,000 project . . . and $50,000 is a nice piece of change. The bad news is that we don't really have anybody available to run the project. So . . . we need to get somebody on board . . . and quickly."

Hastings Research consists of ten employees who conduct marketing research projects for a variety of industrial, non-profit, and governmental agencies. This would be their first project in the supermarket area.

Back in her office, Theresa Calla pulled out the files of job applicants. Hastings received two or three each day and she generally kept them for three to six months. She then called those that looked interesting. Unfortunately, all had accepted other full-time positions. Then, it struck her that her brother-in-law, Alex Tandy, had recently retired after a long and successful career as director of human resources for a local brewery. Only this past weekend, he had commented that he was finding retirement rather boring and that he was looking for something to do. Theresa had always been impressed by Alex and she felt he could certainly do the job.

She called him and arranged for him to drop by the office and talk with her and the other members of the company. "I think I may have solved our problem," she commented to her assistant.

Question: Should Theresa hire her brother-in-law to handle this specific assignment? What are the pros and cons of doing so?

Question: How should Theresa regard the hiring of an individual to handle the supermarket project?

Question: What process would you recommend if you were a consultant advising Theresa on hiring an additional employee for Hastings?

ORIENTATION

 ## Key Points:

1. This is one of those areas of management where the "road to hell is paved with good intentions." Most managements see the advantage of having an orientation program for new employees. However, ensuring that new personnel go through the process is often a major challenge.

2. There are a number of advantages to having a comprehensive orientation and training program:

   - The new employees get a better overall sense of the company.
   - They gain a much better understanding of what each of the divisions does and, more importantly, the pressures they face.
   - They make contacts and establish friendships with people in the other areas.
   - When they have a problem, they can contact somebody they know and who can relate to them.

   > **Example:** "I had worked for another company for three years before joining Curtis. One of the things that had impressed me during the interview process was how friendly people were and how cooperative they seemed to be. I came from a company where each department was a separate empire and getting information or assistance was virtually impossible. The difference is that they have this program where you work with the other departments . . . and everybody gets to know everybody else."

3. While there are no major disadvantages to implementing this sort of program, there are some problems with ensuring that it is implemented:

   > **Example:** Henderson Products has a well-defined plan in which every new person spends time in different departments. Virtually nobody ever completes the rotation. Why? Because something comes up, a department needs a warm body . . . and the new employee is slotted in wherever there is a major problem.
   >
   > **Example:** The annual plan for the project management division states the goal of "having one person in training at all times." The company recognizes the benefit of allowing an individual time to work with a senior project manager (as a mentor) before having to take charge. There are two underlying problems. The first is that the "trainee" is often receiving a full salary at a time when every effort is being made to keep down costs. Second, if the company is awarded a new project, it needs somebody to take over . . . and an employee who has been with the company for two or three months is the obvious choice. The process is short circuited.

CASE 9.4

WELCOME TO THE NEW EMPLOYEE

"Michael, come on in. Nice to see you again. Welcome to Partridge Realty. I hope you will have a long and successful career with us."

This was Michael Lambourne's first day with one of the largest commercial real estate firms in town. Michael's goal was to become a successful leasing agent ... partly because it would enable him to develop an in-depth understanding of the industry and provide him with investment opportunities ... and partly because his brother was making a lot of money as a leasing agent with the same company.

"As I mentioned when you came for an interview, we have a six month orientation program. Normally, people start off with a month in accounting, another month in property management, and the third month in maintenance. Then, they spend a month in residential, a month in land sales, and then a month in leasing. The idea is to give them a sense of what our various divisions do. Our goal is to have at least one person in training at all times."

"We were planning to start you off in accounting. However, we have just hired a new manager and he is still getting his feet wet. And this morning, Jim Farley the head of leasing told me they needed some assistance on a project in the downtown area. So, I am going to start you out with them ... and pick up the other divisions later."

Accompanied by the president, Michael was again introduced to the head of leasing and immediately went into a meeting on the downtown project known as Carillon Towers. "Good to have you on board, Michael," Jim Farley said introducing him to the other members of the team. "I want to get you involved in assisting with the leasing of the retail space on the ground floor."

Two years later, Michael Lambourne was a seasoned leasing agent ... and had never completed the rest of the orientation program.

Question: What are the advantages of having an orientation program such as the one described by the president of Partridge Realty?

Question: Do you think Michael (and the company) has lost anything as a result of never having completed the orientation program?

Question: What are the pros and cons of having at least one person in the orientation program at all times?

TRAINING AND DEVELOPMENT

🔑 Key Points:

1. The goal of training and development is clear cut. It is to improve the skills and capabilities of the employees and thus, hopefully, improve the productivity of the company as a whole. In a perfect world, everybody would receive all the training, education, and personal development that they need. In reality, there are usually limits to the amount of money the organization can spend on such activities.

2. As indicated earlier in this chapter, the first step in any program should be to determine what education, training and development each employee needs or could benefit from.

> **Example:** "I have three people who really need training. Mindy needs to improve her software skills. At the moment, she is only using 30% of the capabilities of the program. Alec needs to broaden his view of the industry and should start attending seminars and trade shows. And Wilma. I can see her being president of this company some day ... and she really needs to complete her MBA."

3. The first criteria against which a manager should evaluate his/her personnel training needs is whether or not the education could be provided in house or whether the needed assistance is only available from external sources.

> **Example:** Bert Reinhart is a first rate manager ... with one exception. His time management is atrocious. He's never on time for meetings. His reports are always late. And so on. There are programs in time management and we were going to enroll him in one of them. It would cost a couple of thousand. However, somebody pointed out that Arthur Minzen, another manager, is extremely well organized. So, every morning Bert meets with Arthur and they plan out his activities. We didn't need to spend money. We had the needed resources in house."

4. The next criterion is undoubtedly the issue of cost. How much will the training or education cost?

> **Example:** "We would like to send Alan to Harvard or Stanford to do his MBA. He is going to be one of our stars and the money would be well spent. However, not only is it expensive but we would lose his services for the better part of two years. So, we have decided on a compromise. We will pay for his courses at the local university and then send him to one of the three month advanced management courses."
>
> **Example:** "In my department, there are six people who need a refresher course on our software and I was thinking of sending them to Chicago for a week long program. However, there is a local expert on this program and he's willing to coming in on five consecutive Saturdays at a quarter of the cost that it would take to send them to Chicago. With the money we will save, we can support a couple of other programs."

5. Finally, management needs to look at the potential return to the organization of the expenditure. Education, training and development can be divided into three categories: essential, desirable, and personal.

- Essential . . . training that needs to be provided in order for the employee to do their job effectively.
- Desirable . . . training that would be highly desirable for an employee in that it would enable him/her to do their job better and be more productive.
- Personal . . . training that would certainly benefit the individual (in terms of their career) and would probably benefit the company in the long term.

> **Example:** "Peter has the makings of a good salesman. However, he is not good when it comes to interacting with potential customers. He tends to be very sharp. I have gone on sales calls with him and tried to assist him. But he doesn't listen. So, we are going to invest a considerable amount of money in sending him to an extended training program. We think, or should I say hope, it will be a good investment."
>
> **Example:** The accounting department at Hooper Research has ten members. Most are specialists in one area of the business (such as accounts payable). The department runs smoothly except when two or three people are out sick or on vacation. The department head wants each of them to be cross-trained in at least one other area. She feels it is a desirable expenditure but not essential.
>
> **Example:** "A number of our employees have associate degrees and would like to complete their bachelor's degree. We have implemented a program with a local university to have their professors teach a range of courses in classrooms at our headquarters. We pay the student's fees. Is such a program essential? No, I don't think it improves our employees' performance at their job. But it is a benefit to our employees. They appreciate it. And I think it makes hiring entry-level personnel easier."

CASE 9.5

TOM, DICK, AND HARRY ... AND BETTY

"Fifty thousand dollars isn't a great deal of money to spread among more than 200 employees. However, I will just do my best to make sure the money is used effectively." The speaker was Pat Feeley who had just been appointed human resource manager for the company.

Ms. Feeley then sent out a memo to all employees announcing the availability of funding for training and development and inviting them to apply. The response was overwhelming. "So far, the requests for funding have exceeded one million dollars ... and the deadline for applying is not until the end of next week. Here are just four examples."

Tom (engineering). He wants to attend a course in New York on the usage of a software package. He said it would help him prepare to move up to a management position in a year or so. There are already two people on staff familiar with this particular program. The cost would be $1,500.

Dick (accounting). He has a B.A. in accounting and is a CPA. Now, he wants us to help him complete his MBA at the local university. His goal is to take two courses this year at a cost of $4,500. Dick's boss seems to think very highly of him.

Harry (manufacturing). His boss wants to send him to one week management training program provided by a company in Los Angeles. It will cost $5,000. According to his boss, "Harry is an assistant manager with potential. But he doesn't have any idea how to handle people. All he does is make them mad."

Betty (purchasing). She wants funding to attend a three day program offered by a trade association dealing with the purchasing of specialty steels. That will cost about $1,800. Her boss says we have had problems in this area in the past.

Question: Given that the $50,000 clearly isn't going to cover all the requests, what criteria would you use for awarding the available funding for training and development?

Question: How would you handle the specific requests from Tom, Dick, Harry and Betty?

Question: What should be the company's overall approach to training and education?

SUMMARY

1. People are a vital resource of every organization. They are also usually one of the major expenses and thus it is critically important that an organization have the right people with the right skills in the right position. Every effort must be made to maximize the productivity of the employees.

2. The human resource plan should consist of a:

   - Human resources inventory.
   - Projection of the future needs of the organization.
   - Replacement chart for senior personnel.
   - Training and development plan for all personnel.

3. Conducting a human resource inventory provides a summary of the skills and expertise that the company already has on board. This enables the organization to more effectively utilize its personnel and determine those areas in which it is weak and needs strengthening.

4. Human resource planning involves looking into the future and determining what personnel the company needs over the next year and even longer. What sorts of skills does it need to hire? How are changes in the marketplace going to affect the capability and skills requirements of the company?

5. Human resource planning also involves looking at the key people in the organization, identifying their successor, and providing them with appropriate training so that they are ready to step into their boss' shoes when the need arises.

6. One of the most important functions in the human resource area is the training and development of personnel. Their strengths and weaknesses are known (in comparison to hiring a relatively unknown person from outside the organization) and thus their potential for growth and development can be more readily determined. A regular analysis of personnel skills and capabilities provides the company with guidelines for future expenditures which will enhance the organization's ability to compete effectively.

7. Discrimination in terms of all aspects of employment is prohibited and organizations need to make sure that they are in compliance with Title VII of the Civil Rights Act of 1964, the Employment Act of 1967, and the Americans with Disabilities Act of 1990.

8. The hiring process consists of a number of important steps including:

   - Identifying the position to be filled.
   - Reviewing and updating the job analysis.
   - Preparing a job description.
   - Deciding whether or not to post the job opening internally.
   - Deciding whether or not to use an external search firm.
   - Advertising and promoting the position.
   - Reviewing the applicants' resumes.
   - Interviewing the better candidates.
   - The use of testing.
   - Deciding which candidate to offer the position.
   - Negotiating with the selected candidate.

9. It is highly desirable (although not always feasible) to allow a new employee time to get to know the company and its people. Ideally, he or she will spend one to three months with each of the major departments and divisions prior to taking up the position for which they were hired.

10. The business environment is a dynamic one. Every day brings changes and new challenges. It is extremely important, therefore, that employees continue to learn and develop their skills and capabilities—both from their own career perspective and that of the company. As a result, there needs to be an organizational training and development plan consistent with both the projected needs and the available financial resources.

CRITICAL THINKING QUESTIONS

1. "I need six people. And I need them now," your boss says. So, you go down to the local mall and grab the first six people you find. And your boss is delighted. Under what circumstance might this "hiring process" work? What is the reaction of your boss more likely to be?

   _____

   _____

   _____

2. It is the end of a unsuccessful season. With a 5-11 record, the NFL team fell way short of reaching the play-offs and Marty Scott, the head coach, is well aware of the fact that his days may be numbered if the team doesn't get off to a good start the following season. The annual draft is coming up. If you were Marty, what would you do in preparation for the draft?

   _____

   _____

   _____

3. The advertisement in the Health Care Job Market section of *The New York Times* indicated that a major hospital was looking for consulting physicians. "We are seeking Board Certified Internists for full time positions in a new medical-administrative initiative. You will lead interdisciplinary teams in optimizing care, resource utilization, and discharge planning. Requires a minimum of five years of experience in an in-patient hospital setting, a current NYS license, and American Board of Internal Medicine (ABIM) certification." The advertisement generates 265 responses. How would you proceed from this point?

   _____

   _____

   _____

4. "Are we all in agreement? We will offer the job to Paul Stedman on the terms I laid out in my memo." The president waited for comments. "I agree Paul is the best candidate. And he has great reference from the industry. A couple of people have said we have a winner if we can hire Paul." Paul Hoskins, from Human Resources, stopped for a moment. "Everybody liked his approach and personality. And we are offering him an increase of $15,000 per year with stock options. So, I know he is very interested. However, when I drove him out to the airport last Friday, he started talking about his wife and her activities, and his three teenage kids, and his house on ten acres looking out over a lake in rural Tennessee . . . and I began to wonder if he is going to accept the offer." What reasons can you suggest as to why Paul Stedman would decline the offer? After all he has spent a lot of time with the company and has gone through an exhaustive sequence of interviews and tests.

   _____

   _____

   _____

5. Wonderful Living Today is the name of a chain of retail stores stretching from Maine to California. They sell a wide range of household items; their niche being the better than average product for a slightly higher price. Historically, they hired their store managers from competitors. However, in recent years, they have tried to hire department managers (e.g., china, bedding, etc.) with the goal of training them for promotion to store manager. This hasn't been particularly successful. Many of the people hired as department managers have declined the opportunity saying they wanted to stay in their area of specialization. Others when pressured to move up have resigned and taken similar positions with other companies. So, management is looking at the idea of starting a management trainee program. "We are going to be looking for college graduates who are interested in a career in retailing," the vice president said. What should the advertisement for management trainees say? What career path would you lay out for those individuals hired under this program?

_____

_____

_____

6. "Each year, the university hires approximately 30 new faculty members. Most are doctoral candidates (ABD) or have just completed their dissertation. They join us as instructors or assistant professors with either very limited academic experience or experience in a totally different environment. They arrive on campus on the first day of class. We show them their office, give them a key, introduce them to any of their peers who are on campus that day, and wish them, 'good luck.' Basically, they are on their own. It has been suggested that we introduce a standard orientation program – either at the departmental level or university wide." What do you think of this suggestion? How long should the orientation program be? And what should it cover?

_____

_____

_____

7. Jenny Smith is very unhappy. She was a member of a team set up to establish a performance appraisal program for the service department consisting of 23 individuals who handle calls from customers. These calls are equally divided between product information calls and calls relating to problems with existing products. The team concluded that special bonuses should be paid on the basis of (a) the number of calls handled per hour and (b) the short satisfaction survey responses which were gathered at the end of the call. At the time, Jenny was a firm supporter of this new program.

   Her view has changed dramatically. "Product informaton calls tend to be short (5 minutes or less) and very pleasant. However, since I have the most experience, the supervisor passes the problem calls to me. I can spend 20 or 30 minutes on the phone with one client and they are not happy when I tell them what it will cost to fix their problem. At the end of the year, I had the lowest number of calls handled and the worst satisfaction rating." Is this system basically unfair? What is the company's objective in terms of this customer service department? What would you do to improve the system?

_____

_____

_____

CASE PROBLEM

REORGANIZATION–AGAIN!!

"Companies tend to go through cycles. About seven years back, we decided to change the ways we handled our marketing research activities. Prior to that, each of the seven divisions had its own research group. This worked quite well. However, the company was facing financial constraints and the consensus was that this arrangement wasn't cost effective. So, the company combined the researchers into a single corporate research department in an attempt to make the most of our available personnel."

"The problem with that organizational structure was that the divisional people felt that they had lost control of a vital piece of their business. They missed the close relationship and were always complaining about the poor service they were getting. So, now, top management has decided to split the function back to the divisions."

"My job," Lief Edmann explained, "is to come up with a game plan for the transition. There are currently a total of 25 people in the department—one department manager, two assistant managers, and twenty-two researchers ... and we now have eight major divisions. I am in the process of setting up meetings with the division heads and their key people but, beyond that, I haven't laid any real plan as to how to proceed. I need to present something to the Board at the end of the month. So, I have essentially three weeks to gather information and come up with a game plan."

Question: If you were Lief Edmann, what would be your first step in this reorganization process?

_____

_____

_____

_____

Question: What information would you aim to gather from the division heads and their staff?

_____

_____

_____

_____

Question: What specific plan of action would you present to the Board at the end of the month?

_____

_____

_____

_____

Question: *Which of the topics described in this chapter (i.e., human resource planning, hiring, orientation, training and development, and performance appraisal) would you expect to cover in your presentation to the Board?*

_____

_____

_____

_____

THE IMPORTANCE OF LEADERSHIP

OVERVIEW

There are numerous definitions of leadership. It has been described as:

Making things happen in an organization.

Others see leadership as:

Inspiring confidence and supporting people in their efforts to achieve organizational goals.

And yet others suggest that it is a process that:

Shapes the organization's goals and objectives, motivates the behavior of individuals to achieve those goals, and defines the corporate culture.

Leadership ability (like the ability to motivate) is a vitally important aspect of management and is one to which a large amount of time and effort has been devoted both in academia and business. The ability to determine whether or not an individual has leadership potential would be invaluable. It would be tremendously advantageous if there were some way of looking at a person and saying "that person is a leader."

In this chapter, we focus on the following topics:

- The difference between managing and leading.
- The characteristics (or traits) of successful leaders.
- The behavior of good leaders.
- Different situations—different leadership.
- Different types of leadership.

MANAGERS VERSUS LEADERS

Key Points:

1. There are major differences between a leader and a manager.

   - Managers are appointed and their authority (and hence their ability to reward and punish) is based on their position. In contrast, leaders can be appointed or emerge from within a group or organization. They can influence people to do much more than they might as a result of the formal position.

   - Managers emphasize getting things done through other people. It usually involves specific tools and techniques. Leadership places greater emphasis on assisting others to do the things necessary to achieve the organization's goals.

   > **Example:** The department ran very smoothly under Jim Fishbein. He knew the job and made sure that all the members of the department followed the rules and procedures he laid down. Failure to perform ultimately led to dismissal. When Jim resigned, his position was taken by Margaret Reid. She also knew the rules. However, she spent much more time with the employees exploring ideas that would lead to better performance. With her, failure to perform was merely an indication that the employee needed help and assistance. Over time, she totally revamped the department leading to both greater productivity and greater personnel satisfaction.

2. An outstanding leader is not necessarily a good manager ... and *vice versa.* An outstanding manager may not be an effective leader.

   > **Example:** Everybody loved working for and with Alan Carter. "If Alan makes a suggestion, you know everybody will jump on it. It is amazing. He can get you to do virtually anything. He's so enthusiastic and such a great salesman. Of course, he hasn't found time to do my annual review for three years now. And, if you ask him for the minutes of a meeting or a report ... good luck. He can't find it."

   > **Example:** Cara Jackson ran a tight ship. Her department always received one of the highest ratings in the company. She was always organized and reports were always on time. Her people liked Cara and they each performed their job effectively. The same systems and procedures had been in place for a number of years and Cara wasn't receptive to change. "If you suggest a new approach or something we could do for the customer, she isn't really supportive. I suggested we attend a seminar on a new software package and she said she'd look into it. But it just died ... none of us got to go."

3. Different people have different views on whether or not a specific individual is an effective leader. The meaning of the term "effective" (or "successful") is open to discussion and disagreement. The evaluation can depend on the person's perspectives and the time frame.

> **Example:** The Enron or WorldCom scandals are good examples. Some observers would say that the presidents of these two organizations were successful leaders. After all, for a number of years they were very highly regarded by business commentators. Others would say they were disastrous leaders because they committed illegal acts and acted in an unethical manner.
>
> **Example:** Throughout history, generals have led armies that, for a period of time, were extremely successful and they themselves were regarded as outstanding leaders. They then encountered a string of major defeats and their reputation as a leader (once so high) declined dramatically.

CASE 10.1

THE NEW PRODUCT DEVELOPMENT DIVISION

New product development was extremely important to B. J. Fanta & Co. A continual stream of new products was its life blood. Its ability to generate innovative ideas was what differentiated the company from its competition.

However, starting in the late 90s, the productivity of the division began to decline. A consultant, brought in to analyze the division, concluded that it needed new people and new leadership. So, in 1996, the division was revamped and Harry Stabler was brought in as the new division head. He lasted three years and did little for the divisional productivity.

The next manager to take over was Karl Haas. He suffered from serious and debilitating medical problems and paid very little attention to the division or to its people. The division essentially ran itself. During this period, the number of new products introduced increased dramatically. When Karl retired in 2004, the company looked outside the organization for his replacement and eventually hired Gary Loftus. According to those who knew Gary or had worked with him, he was one of the best managers in the industry.

Gary took up his position in mid-August and was appalled at what he found. "I walked into the building at 9:30 a.m. and there was hardly anybody there. A couple of people were sleeping on the floor. Others strolled in around noon looking as if they had come from the beach. Papers were strewn all over the place. The kitchen area was a mess. When I asked for copies of the monthly reports, I couldn't find anything later than May. In all, it was a disaster area."

Gary immediately set about righting the situation. "I immediately sent out a memo stating that the office hours were from 8:30 a.m. to 4:30 p.m. and that anybody who wasn't here during those hours, suitably attired, would be in trouble. I also made it clear that I wanted the monthly reports on my desk by noon on the first working days of the month. I made it clear that each group would hold a weekly staff meeting ... and that I would attend them."

By the end of the year, Gary had the division running smoothly. "Like a well oiled piece of clockwork," he commented.

Question: What would you predict happened to the productivity of the Division as a result of Gary's organization?

Question: Would you describe Gary as a manager or a leader?

Question: What would you have done if you were Gary and had just taken over the division?

THE TRAITS OR CHARACTERISTICS OF GOOD LEADERS

 Key Points:

1. Research has shown that leaders exhibit a number of traits or characteristics. Specifically:

   - Drive ... leaders usually have a high desire to achieve success.
   - Desire to lead ... leaders want to lead and influence others.
   - Honesty and integrity ... people trust leaders.
   - Self-confidence ... leaders tend to believe in their own views and positions.
   - Intelligence ... successful leaders need to have the intelligence in order to be able to create a vision, solve problems, etc.
   - Knowledge of the job ... effective leaders tend to know a lot about the company, its products, and its industries.

2. However, research has also shown that traits or characteristics alone do not explain leadership. Having the above traits may make it likely that the individual will be an effective leader. However, they do not guarantee that they will be successful.

Example: "Look out. Here's comes our fearless leader." That meant Sandra Hayes, the president of the company, was coming. When her father retired, she had taken over the leadership of the company and had immediately persuaded her two brothers that their future lay elsewhere. She wanted to be number one. And no one questioned her drive, her honesty and integrity, her self-confidence, and her knowledge of the business. "While she is intelligent, she doesn't know how to handle people. She makes people mad. And her rushing around makes people nervous. She would be a much better leader (and manager) if she focused on one thing at a time. And if she asked other people for their opinions more often ... and took notice of their views. I think the board will replace her in the next six months."

Example: Gus Pritchard was promoted from vice president—engineering in 2001. He took the position reluctantly and continued to focus primarily on the engineering division. He attended management meetings but rarely said anything of a strategic or dynamic nature. His knowledge of finance, marketing, and sales were limited. However, the company prospered dramatically because Gus had one great skill. He knew how to pick people and how to empower them. Some critics thought he was good at this because he was basically lazy. Gus would listen to a proposal, think about it, and then either give the go-ahead or suggest it be reworked. He rarely, if ever, said "no." And when you had Gus' approval for a project, you had his full support.

CASE 10.2

HOW DOES BOBBY DO IT?

"I was reading my son's management text last night and it talked about the six traits or characteristics that differentiate leaders from non-leaders. Quite fascinating."

"The first trait they mentioned was 'drive.' It said that leaders demonstrate a high effort level. Well that lets Bobby (the president) off the hook. He's the most laid back person I have ever met. 'A desire to lead' was the second factor … and nobody would accuse Bobby of wanting to run the company. The family had to force him to do so. A third factor is 'job-relevant knowledge' and Bobby didn't know anything about this business when he left his law practice … and he's certainly no expert even today. Also, it lists 'self-confidence' as an important trait … and he never comes across as being convinced of his own point of view."

"On the other hand, he certainly meets the "intelligence" requirement. He's very smart. And he has "honesty and integrity" in spades. Bobby is as honest as the day is long and you can always rely on him. If he says he will do something … he does it."

"Two out of six isn't that good. But we are the leading company in our field, sales and profits have increased dramatically for the past three years, and this is by far the best company I have ever worked for."

Question: What does this case say about the idea that one can identify leaders on the basis of their traits and characteristics?

Question: How can an individual who has limited drive, isn't particularly motivated to lead, isn't particularly self-confident, and doesn't have a great deal of job-relevant knowledge manage to run such a successful company?

Question: Which of the leadership traits or characteristics would you want your boss to have? And why?

DO GOOD LEADERS BEHAVE DIFFERENTLY?

 ## Key Points:

1. The fact that the traits or characteristics of people did not explain leadership led researchers to look at what effective leaders actually did. This research led to three main hypotheses:

   - Leadership style ... autocratic versus democratic versus *laissez faire*.
   - Initiating structure versus consideration ... focusing on roles rather than relationships.
   - Production versus people ... focus on getting the job done as opposed to satisfying the interests of the personnel.

2. Autocratic versus democratic versus *laissez faire*.

   - Autocratic ... this represented the leader who centralized the decision making. He/she makes unilateral decisions and does not involve employees to any great extent.
   - Democratic ... democratic leaders are those who involve employees in decision making, and delegate responsibility to their subordinates.
   - *Laissez faire* ... the leader using this style essentially allows employees complete freedom to make their own decisions. He/she delegates responsibility and authority to the subordinates.

   > **Example:** "We've had three department heads within twenty-four months. The first was Briana LeClerc. She was a very democratic manager. Every major issue that came up was discussed by the management team ... and she generally went along with whatever we decided. When she was promoted, Simon Langdon took over. He basically turned over the running of the department to the employees. As long as you didn't bother him, he didn't bother you. Our current department head is Wilma Ossening and she makes all the decisions. Our role is essentially to carry out orders."
   >
   > "Now, some people really liked Briana's style. I was one of them. However, a couple of my colleges preferred Simon's approach. And one or two like Wilma's style. Personally, I don't. I feel like a cog in a machine. I have no authority or responsibility. But then some people are more comfortable being told what to do."

3. Initiating structure versus consideration. Another research study suggested that the two key aspects of leadership style were the emphasis on:

   - Initiating structure ... the emphasis that the leader places on structuring his/her role and those of the employees in order to achieve the goals.
   - Consideration ... the extent to which a leader emphasizes the nature of the job relationships (i.e., the degree to which he/she respects the employees' ideas and takes into considerations their feelings).

> **Example:** "Max is an interesting manager. He spends most of his time planning and organizing. He seems to be fascinated by organization charts and job descriptions. He assigns group members to specific tasks. He expects workers to perform at a certain level and emphasizes the importance of meeting deadlines. His goal is to meet the company's targets for the year by making the organization work perfectly. If you don't like the plan . . . you are out of luck."
>
> "George, my former manager, was the exact opposite. He didn't really mind who did what so long as the tasks were completed. He spent very little time planning. He preferred to spend his time talking to employees and getting their opinion."

4. Production versus people. Yet another study focused on the emphasis that an individual places on:

   - Getting the job done . . . the individual emphasizes the technical or task aspects of the job. The people are essentially a way of getting the job done.
   - Focusing on the people . . . the individual works hard to build up a relationship with the employees . . . recognizing and satisfying the needs and goals of the employees.

> **Example:** Some leaders see the completion of the job as the critical aspect of their responsibility. The army is a good example. It has a well-structured hierarchy in order to ensure that orders are carried out and tasks are completed. There is relatively little emphasis on the needs and goals of the personnel.
>
> However, during peace time or when there is a shortage of recruits, the army is forced to place more emphasis on the needs and goals of its personnel and talks less about the task and more about the benefits to the individual.

5. As with the research into the traits or characteristics of effective leaders, the studies (and resulting models) into their behavior also failed to clearly predict whether or not an individual would be an effective or ineffective leader.

CASE 10.3

TWO BROTHERS—TWO STYLES

Even when they were very young children, people used to comment on how different they were ... despite the fact that they were born only minutes apart.

Andy was a very serious and reserved individual. Very methodical, he was always prepared and always on time. Kenyon, by contrast, was a happy-go-lucky, vaguely disorganized child. He did everything but nothing particularly well. Both went to college. Andy graduated in four years *summa cum laude*. Kenyon ... well, let's say he eventually graduated.

One of the few things the two brothers did have in common was a love of manufacturing and both enjoyed extremely successful careers becoming senior vice presidents of their respective *Fortune 500* firms.

Andy, as one would have expected, always had a firm idea of what needed to be done. A typical meeting consisted of him summarizing the situation and giving instructions. He demanded high standards of performance of his people and would roundly criticize any mistakes they made. However, he personally didn't take too kindly to criticism. His primary emphasis was on top quality production and he had limited interest in the company's customers. When something went wrong, he brooded on the matter for some time and then issued another set of instructions.

Kenyon also demanded a high level of performance from his subordinates but would rarely criticize them. He tended to work with them to come up with a better course of action. He spent much of his time asking questions and giving feedback to his people. Meetings tended to be animated and combative. He never took offense and only smiled when somebody pointed out that he had made a mistake. Unlike Andy, he also spent a lot of time with the company's customers. I have a great quality control guy ... and I leave the manufacturing to him. "Well fine," was Andy's response when anything went wrong. "Back to the drawing board" was his philosophy.

Question: Which do you think is the better of these two managers? Why?

Question: Would you prefer to work for Andy or Kenyon? Why?

Question: How had they both managed to be so successful ... given that they have very different leadership styles?

DIFFERENT SITUATIONS–DIFFERENT LEADERSHIP STYLES

⊙⟞ **Key Points:**

1. A number of factors determine the appropriate leadership style:

   - The nature of the task.
   - The skills and capabilities of the personnel.
   - The speed with which the marketplace is changing.
   - The individual preferences of the manager.

2. The nature of the task. The more complex the task, the greater the degree to which a leader may wish (and/or need) to maintain close control over his/her personnel. After all, things are more likely to go wrong if the task has numerous components and aspects. On the other hand, the simpler or more standardized the task, the more likely the leader will be less involved.

   > **Example:** "Historically, our stampings were very simple. You inserted the stock material and let it run. As a result, the manager of that department didn't have a major leadership role. He was more concerned with production scheduling. However, in recent years, we have had to produce a number of very sophisticated and complicated stampings. Now, the department manager is on the floor continuously because it is so important that he keep on top of product quality."

3. The skills and capabilities of the personnel. If you are a manager with a highly skilled and professional workforce then you can allow them to perform their roles with only limited leadership. However, if the employees are relatively unskilled then it may be necessary to provide aggressive hands-on leadership.

   > **Example:** As the manager of the Chicago office, Gordon Osterhuis spent most of his time meeting with potential clients. He held a weekly meeting with his five managers to discuss where they stood on specific projects and in terms of the company's budgets. "They are all first rate people and they don't need a great deal of leadership or management." However, when he took over the Seattle office, he found himself in a very different situation. "They had had a lot of turnover in that office and none of the managers was very experienced. As a result, I found myself being much more of a leader and mentor ... and spending much less time meeting with clients."

4. The speed with which the marketplace is changing. If the marketplace is a dynamic one (i.e., highly competitive and changing rapidly) then a manager may need to utilize an aggressive and involved leadership style. However, if it is relatively static then he/she may choose to play a less involved role.

> **Example:** The Anderson family owned an exclusive French restaurant and a bakery. Tim Anderson ran the bakery for a number of years. "It was very much a matter of deciding how many loaves of each type you needed to bake each day ... and ensuring that we had the necessary materials on hand. It was a very easy hands-off job. Taking over the restaurant was a real shock. The menu changed every day and I found I had to be there virtually all the time in order to watch the chefs and ensure that we were preparing the dishes correctly and maintaining the quality standards. I had never realized that the two jobs were so different."

5. The individual preferences of the manager. Some managers believe that employees need close supervision to ensure that they follow the rules and regulations. And that failure to provide this control will result in errors and mistakes. Others managers take exactly the opposite perspective. They believe that the company has hired the best people for the positions and thus should allow them to carry out their responsibilities without undue supervision and direction.

> **Example:** Tom Reinhold was a mathematician. He was interested in numbers and statistics. Exactly how he ended up as the manager of human resources for a *Fortune 500* company is unclear. He spent his days looking at total employment, changes in employment week by week, changes by department, etc. In fact, he rarely left the head office. His successor, Barbara Windall had very little interest in statistics. She was interested in people and their needs. She spent most of her time out visiting the divisions, talking with managers, and identifying ways in which she could more effectively support their interests.

CASE 10.4

THE BUSINESS HAS CHANGED

A number of years back, Max Lender inherited the family firm and was discussing what had happened in the industry and how it had affected him.

"My father opened one of the first gas stations in the area. Then, he opened a second and, over the years, he became one the largest independents in the region. As a result, we purchased a lot of gasoline. In those days, our buyers called the main suppliers on a daily basis asking for their best prices at various future dates. If they found an acceptable price on an acceptable date, you had a deal. The major task of the buyers was to get a sense of the trends and buy before prices started to go up. This was something of an art and we had a number of people who had been with the company for many, many years. My father's job was primarily to make sure that, in total, we had enough gasoline and that the employees were happy. It was quite a laid back time."

"Then the computer came along. For a number of years, we stuck with our traditional way of doing business. However, we suddenly realized that the market had totally changed. There were many more buyers who were speculating on gasoline futures. They would buy and sell many times a day. Whereas the prices had been reasonably steady, they now fluctuated wildly. Instead of dealing with suppliers by phone, you spend the whole time looking at the market on the screen."

"All the older people have long since retired and now we have a group of young Turks. We used to pay people a salary. Now it is all commission-based. It used to be very laid back. Now, it is intense. It is like a trading floor at a stock exchange and I'm in the middle of it all. We used to make money by buying gasoline and selling at the pump. Now, we make most of our profit by speculating. We don't take delivery of most of the gasoline we buy."

"I'm not at all sure I like this role. I'm just not comfortable with the business these days."

Question: What other industries can you think of where there has been a major change and thus the leadership needs have changed?

Question: Why do you think Max Lender feels uncomfortable with his new role?

Question: How would you suggest he respond to the changes in the industry and in his business?

DIFFERENT TYPES OF LEADERSHIP

 ## Key Points:

1. In recent years, there has been a growing emphasis placed on different leadership requirements for different types of business problems or situations.

   - Charismatic leadership.
   - Transformational leadership.
   - Strategic leadership.
   - Cross-Cultural leadership.
   - Ethical leadership.

2. Charismatic leadership. Charisma is defined as the ability to lead or influence others based on personal charm, magnetism, inspiration and emotion. Some of the characteristics enjoyed by charismatic leaders are:

   - Vision ... charismatic leaders provide an exciting vision of the future and where the organization is going.
   - Ability to communicate ... these leaders have the ability to communicate this vision in terms that are easily understood by their employees.
   - Ability to convey (through words and actions) a new set of values ... charismatic leaders set an example for their employees to follow.
   - A willingness to make self-sacrifices and engage in unconventional behavior ... leaders demonstrate conviction about the vision.

   > **Example:** "When she took over, Andrea inherited a dispirited organization. The first thing she did was to get everybody excited. She spent a lot of time talking to people to make sure they understood what she wanted to do. She even dressed up in a rabbit suit at Easter to get things going. Next, she went out and led the effort. That really impressed people. They had been used to a boss who delegated. The acquisitions she made were inspired but very high risk. She really put her career on the line.

3. Transformational leadership. While charismatic and transformational leaders share many of the same characteristics, namely: a vision and the ability to communicate that vision to employees, transformational leaders have:

   - High moral standards ... this provides them with a basis from which to get others involved in the transformation.
   - The ability to raise people's awareness of the importance and values associated with specific outcomes ... such leaders sell the benefits of achieving the vision.
   - The ability to get people to look beyond their self-interests for the good of the organization ... transformational leaders bring a broader perspective to the table.
   - An emphasis on questioning established views ... a transformational leader believes that nothing is sacred.

> **Example:** "I had worked for a charismatic leader at Teledata. However, the president here at Waterfield is somewhat different. He has his own vision and communicates it well. However, he emphasizes the benefits to not only the organization but also the individual employees. He's very big on teamwork. Also, he gets you thinking. Yesterday, he asked me if we should acquire our major competitor. They are three times our size. My immediate reaction was "no." But the more I think about it the more sense it makes. The entire culture is different here."

4. Strategic leadership. The primary skills of an effective strategic leader are that he/she has:

   ■ An in-depth understanding of the company, its history, and its culture as well as a knowledge of its strengths, weaknesses, opportunities and threats and a comprehensive understanding of the organization's environment ... strategic leaders have both the knowledge and the focus.

   ■ Has the insights and skills to maintain a close balance between the organization and its environment ... such leaders are fascinated by the company and its position in its environment.

> **Example:** "After a period of stability, the industry started changing dramatically. Foreign firms came into the marketplace and there were a number of mergers among American companies. We were in bad shape until David Green took over. He had been with the company for many years and really knew every detail about the company and the industry. We didn't need a charismatic or transformational leader. What we needed was somebody who really knew how to position the company to make the most of its opportunities. That's where David was so good. He laid out a sober and effective strategic plan and, by following it, we weathered the storm."

5. Cross-cultural leadership. This is a very different type of leadership but one which is becoming more and more important as firms expand into international markets and the nature of the U.S. workforce changes. The primary skills of an effective cross-cultural leader are that he/she:

   ■ Understands and appreciates the nature of the cultural differences in the countries in which they operate ... the effective leader has a specific sensitivity to such issues.

   ■ Is prepared to devote the necessary time to moderating interactions between the various cultures ... the cross-cultural leader recognizes the importance of these relationships.

   ■ Provide clear and comprehensive guidelines to the organization with regard to the handling of cultural issues ... thus setting the standard.

   ■ Ensures that all employees follow these guidelines ... enforcing the rules and allowing for no major infractions.

Example: "We were basically a domestic company for the first thirty years of our existence. We had small operations in Canada and the United Kingdom. But nothing major. Then, in 2000, we acquired Klimatrol. They were based in Zurich and had offices throughout Europe and the Middle East. As long as we left them alone, everything worked well. However, in 2004, the decision was made to integrate them with the parent company ... and it has been a nightmare ever since. Their culture is totally different from ours ... and management really doesn't know how to deal with the problem. We need somebody with experience in handling a multinational and multicultural organization.

Example: The Royce Company was established in 1946 in Birmingham, Alabama. The management team was exclusively white and almost 100% male. Over the years, the company grew and expanded. Race relations were never particularly good and the company faced a substantial number of sexual harassment suits. In 1985, Royce was acquired by a Chicago-based firm whose management had considerable experience in handling such problems. It immediately sent in a specialized team which implemented policies and procedures along with sensitivity training and a policy of strict enforcement. Many of the managers who were raised in the Deep South tradition were either fired or let go. Those that remained followed the company's cross-cultural guidelines to the letter.

6. Ethical leadership. While the early giants of industry in the United States acted in a manner that, by today's standards, would be unethical, most people have assumed that modern businesses (with their government oversight and boards of directors) were reasonably ethical. The recent scandals have raised serious questions about this proposition ... and firms are increasingly recognizing the need for ethical leadership. The primary skills of an effective ethical leader are that he/she:

- Has a firmly rooted appreciation and respect for ethical business practices ... so that he/she can lead by example.

- Recognizes that top management must be held to the highest ethical standards ... the effective ethical leader must be willing to hold personnel to a high level of accountability.

- Is willing to take immediate and forceful action whenever there is evidence that a member of the organization has acted in a manner that can be considered unethical ... he/she must be prepared to take action.

Example: Bob Hansen stopped the president as they were leaving the boardroom. "Jim, I think we have a problem. If you look at the sales figures for the South-West for the last three months, you will see a rapid increase in orders. That's wonderful if they are legitimate. However, I suspect the manager may be offering under the table discounts." The president immediately called the manager into his office where the latter argued that they were legitimate discounts not bribes. Phone calls to the customers convinced the president that questionable payments were being made. The manager was terminated the same day. "I'm not prepared to accept any action on the part of anybody associated with this company which has even the slightest hint of impropriety," the president explained.

Example: The name of Dennison & Faye was well known and respected on Wall Street as a trader of government bonds and securities. It came as a shock, therefore, when the company (and one of its brokers, Michael O'Flynn) was charged with fraud. Mr. O'Flynn had received commissions in excess of $10 million one year when the typical broker in the company made $260,000. Mr. Jim Dennison (the president of the company) pleaded not guilty to all charges and claimed he was totally unaware of Mr. O'Flynn's activities. "Weren't you ever curious?" he was asked. "You have an employee who is generating an income nearly forty times that of others in that group. Aren't you responsible?" Mr. Dennison denied any responsibility.

CASE 10.5

MORRIS CARSTEAD

"When I started my career, nobody really thought about different types of leadership. We just did our job to the best of our ability." The speaker was Morris J. Carstead being honored on his retirement after 40 years at Leicester & Perdue.

"My first position with L&C was as the manager of the transformer division. It wasn't doing well at all at the time ... and I knew nothing about transformers. So, I decided to bluff my way through. I exuded self-confidence and a firm conviction in my beliefs and ideals. I communicated high expectation to my people and I spent a lot of time talking to the employees congratulating them and expressing my confidence in them. I don't think I was a particularly good manager. But we turned that division around."

"Then, I took over the bearings group. That group was dying on its feet in a marketplace that was changing rapidly. So, I focused on creating a sense of mission. I set the group the goal of being one of the top three firms in the industry. I emphasized learning experiences and new ways of thinking. If it wasn't broken, I told them to break it. My goal was to change the way the group thought and did things."

"Most of my jobs involved taking over divisions that lacked a strong sense of direction. My responsibility was to conduct an in-depth analysis and lay out a three to five year game plan. Usually, I had to make changes in the organization and then maintain a close alignment between the organization and its environment. The trick was identifying the right organization for the marketplace."

"Handling the international division. That was a real challenge. It took a different approach to handle all the diverse groups and different cultures. When I started with the company, the workforce was almost exclusively white and male. Now women and minorities both make up a large percentage of our employees ... as do foreign nationals."

"Finally, there was our securities business. That place was an ethical nightmare. I had to go in and establish a code of ethics that we could be proud of and ensure that everybody followed it. I had to fire some of the most successful people and our profits suffered. Now, however, we have one of the best reputations in the industry and business is improving."

Question: How would you characterize the five different forms of leadership that Morris Carstead used during his career?

Question: Do you think Morris Carstead consciously tried to apply different types of leadership to the various organizations he ran? Or did he develop a style depending on the situation?

Question: Are the five types of leadership described by Morris Carstead really different? Or are they merely variations on a common theme?

SUMMARY

1. The ability to lead (and the ability to identify a potential leader) is an extremely important one. Organizations are always looking for individuals with leadership ability (i.e., people who can make things happen in an organization and achieve corporate goals).

2. As a result, academics and business managers have devoted a considerable amount of time trying to identify leaders and potential leaders.

3. There is a very real difference between a manager and a leader. Managers tend to focus on getting the job done by utilizing their subordinates. They tend to follow the rules and procedures. Leaders place more emphasis on developing a vision for the organization and helping their people achieve the vision.

4. A good manager can be a poor leader and *vice versa*. An outstanding leader can be a very ineffective manager. Ideally, of course, one finds an individual who is both a good leader and a good manager. At the other end of the spectrum are those individuals who can't lead or manage.

5. Characterizing a person as an effective or successful leader is not easy. One person may regard an individual as an outstanding leader while another person may regard them as mediocre. Furthermore, a person may be regarded as an outstanding leader for a period of time and then events overtake them and their reputation becomes tarnished.

6. One of the earliest approaches in trying to identify leaders was to focus on the traits or characteristics of people who were regarded as successful leaders. Although six factors (drive, desire to lead, honesty and integrity, self-confidence, intelligence, and knowledge of the job) were identified as important, these factors did not alone explain leadership ability.

7. Another approach to identifying leaders was to focus on how leaders behaved. Researchers looked at whether or not the individual was autocratic, democratic, or applied the principle of *laissez faire*. They studied whether or not the individual emphasized the structure for getting the job done or the job relationships. And they looked at whether or not they emphasized the job or the people. Again, these studies failed to clearly identify whether or not a person would be an effective manager.

8. More recent research has focused on the view that different situations call for different leadership styles (i.e., that the appropriate leadership style will depend on the characteristics of the situation). Four factors influencing the style of leadership are the nature of the task, the skills and capabilities of the personnel, the speed with which the marketplace is changing, and the individual preferences of the manager.

9. A number of terms have become popular in the area of leadership. Successful leaders have been described as charismatic leaders (i.e., individuals with personal charm, vision, magnetism, etc.) and as transformational leaders (i.e., those individuals who can communicate their vision for the organization and get people to question established views and look beyond themselves for the good of the organization.

10. Three other areas of leadership that have gained popularity in recent years are: strategic leadership (where the organization needs a detailed and comprehensive strategic plan for achieving its goals and objectives), cross-cultural leadership (where the major concern of the organization is to more effectively handle cultural issues—either domestic or international—to improve the working environment), and ethical leadership (where the organization faces ethical problems that need to be addressed by a person with strong ethical values and a commitment to implementing them).

CRITICAL THINKING QUESTIONS

1. The company's operation located in Cape Town, South Africa has a number of serious problems. Sales and profits are both down. New product introductions are running months behind schedule. Morale is extremely poor. A number of law suits have been filed complaining about sexual harassment and the mishandling of cultural issues. You have been asked to recommend somebody to go out to Cape Town and straighten out the operation. What sort of person would you recommend? And why? Do you need a manager or a leader?

_____

_____

_____

2. Porter Lang was known as "the corporate terminator." He was called in by companies that were close to bankruptcy with the mandate of turning the operation around. His approach was the same each time. He would spend a month studying the financials, evaluating the product lines, talking with the personnel, etc. And then the pink slips would begin to fly. In one company, he eliminated more than half the product lines, closed down 18 out of 32 plants, and terminated 62% of the workforce. The remaining part of the business was profitable and grew substantially over the next couple of years until Porter moved on to wield his axe elsewhere. Would you describe Porter Lang as manager or as a leader? Would you describe him as effective and/or successful? Would others describe him differently?

_____

_____

_____

3. "So, we are down to the final two candidates for the position. And we agree that we need somebody to provide leadership for the operation. Jim will stay on as number two and he can handle the day-to-day management. Now, Grierson looks good. He seems very motivated and has a desire to lead. And he's certainly very intelligent. Hamblin, on the other hand, has a strong reputation in the industry for honesty and integrity. He knows the industry much better than Grierson and is very self-confident. Between them they have all the right characteristics." Which candidate would you select for this position? And what other factors would you take into consideration in making your decision?

_____

_____

_____

4. Paper merchants are firms that buy paper from the large manufacturers and sell to local and regional users. Back in the 1960s, these firms had multiple locations and most of the managers had been in the business for many years and prided themselves on their knowledge of their marketplace. To them, it was a craft. Around that time, many paper merchants were acquired by the major manufacturers. Different companies followed different approaches in terms of managing these locations. Head Paper appointed a divisional vice president whose job was to visit all 26 paper merchants once every six weeks. He wined and dined them and tried to help in any way he could. The merchants continued to purchase paper from a variety of manufacturers. Barstow Paper also appointed a vice president. However, he took a very different approach. He immediately terminated the merchants' purchasing

from other suppliers, and informed them each week of which paper they were to purchase and in what amount. How would you describe the leadership behavior of these two vice presidents? Which would you predict would be the more successful?

_____

_____

_____

5. "I want to enjoy my job. I want to look forward to coming into work each morning. That means I like people to be friendly, cooperative, and enthusiastic. We are a family here. People have a coffee break together. They go out to lunch together. They go bowling together. I think that ensuring that the working environment is a pleasant one is the most important thing I do. When people have problems, we help them. If they are sick, we send them flowers and visit them. If they have money problems, we make them a loan. If they have car problems, we lend them a company car. Yesterday, I spent most of the afternoon talking with an employee whose husband is very ill." How would you characterize the leadership behavior of this manager? Would you want to work for this company? Do you see any problems with this style of management?

_____

_____

_____

6. Robert van Belen was the manager of a large chemical cracking plant. Reporting to him were a group of managers (all professional engineers) with whom he met once a week on Monday morning. He saw his main function as a planner, coordinator, and scheduler. When, one of the managers came to him with a problem, he would listen and then invariably tell the manager to do whatever he thought best. "Make a decision," he would say. "That's what we pay you the big bucks for." Very occasionally, he would leave the office and go into the plant with the manager. However, even if it were a serious problem, he avoided suggesting a solution. His only concern was that he kept losing managers. If somebody else in the plant wanted a skilled manager, they stole one of his. How would you describe van Belen as a manager? As a leader? Would you consider him to be effective? Successful?

_____

_____

_____

7. It is generally believed that charismatic leaders are born with personal charm and magnetism and that, if you don't have these characteristics, you can't take a course to become a charismatic leader. However, it is also believed that you can improve your image as charismatic by utilizing a variety of techniques. You have just been appointed head of a division that really needs shaking up and revitalizing. Unfortunately, you are a person who somebody once described as being "as charismatic as a dead fish." You start your position next month so what steps could you take to improve your image? How could you try to be the person this division seems to need?

_____

_____

_____

CASE PROBLEM

A CHANGE IN THE LEADERSHIP

Commonwealth Industries had been managed by the Hislop family for nearly sixty years. Four generations of Hislop had been in charge at one time or another. Now, however, the only remaining direct descendent was uninterested in taking over and the board of directors had hired a consultant to assist in the search for a new president. The family would continue to dominate the board.

The consultant started by interviewing the members of the management team and the heads of the various departments and divisions. His conclusion was that there was nobody in-house capable of moving into the top slot. He also kept hearing phrases such as "very conservative," "badly out of date," "way behind the times," "losing ground to the competition," and "stuck in a time warp."

Marlow Hislop, the president, wasn't too surprised by the feedback. "I admit we haven't done too well in training people to move up in the organization. However, I disagree with the company image that you paint. This is a very successful and profitable company. The job description for the president is perfectly clear and straight-forward. We just need somebody who can keep us going in the right direction."

The consultant went back to his office. There were certainly candidates available who would match the Hislop/Commonwealth leadership style and he could earn his commission by recommending one of them. However, he wasn't convinced that this was what the company needed.

Question: What sort of candidate do you think Marlow Hislop wants as the new president? What sort of leadership styles is he looking for?

_____

_____

_____

_____

Question: What sort of candidate (with what sort of leadership style) do you think the company needs?

_____

_____

_____

_____

Question: *Assuming that you are convinced that the company needs a charismatic/transformational leader, what would you do as the consultant? Would you rewrite the job description with a more aggressive or transformational slant? Or would you keep the current job description and try to identify candidates with charisma and vision?*

_____

_____

_____

_____

_____

CHAPTER 11

MOTIVATING THE TROOPS

OVERVIEW

Motivation is defined as:

> *The inner drive that results in an individual exerting maximum effort to achieve a specific goal or objective.*

In business, managers have to rely on their subordinates to achieve the company's goals and objectives since they cannot do everything themselves. This means that the greater the effort that others put into the task, the more likely the organization is to achieve its objectives.

This poses a critical question for a manager, namely: how do I motivate my people so that they will put forth the maximum effort? How do I encourage them to go the extra mile, put in the extra effort, etc? *Note:* there is a school of thought which argues that one person cannot motivate another. The only person who can motivate you is ... you!! However, from a manager's perspective, the question remains: what can I do that will result in my employees motivating themselves?

In this chapter, we look at:

- The connection between motivation and performance.
- Motivation through the satisfaction of needs.
- Motivation through setting goals.
- Motivation through behavior modification.
- The inner motivators—expectancy and equity.

THE CONNECTION BETWEEN MOTIVATION AND PERFORMANCE

🔑 Key Points:

1. There are a number of popular statements relating to motivation. Phrases such as:

> *You can do anything you want if you put your mind to it.*

and

> *Positive thinking leads to positive results.*

Without question, motivation is important precursor to performance.

> **Example:** Georgina Weiss was widely regarded as the best sales person in the company earning $75,000 to $80,000 each year. However, other sales people earned considerably more and Georgina rarely ranked higher than eighth or ninth in terms of earnings. "I could certainly earn a lot more," Georgina admitted. "However, I made a decision early on that I wanted to balance my job with my home life. I don't want to be away from home more than a couple of nights a week. And that limits my earnings potential.

2. However, ability also impacts on a person's performance.

> **Example:** Bob DeLuca was a very successful runner in high school and went to college on an athletic scholarship. While in college, he practiced virtually every day and was a star performer. As a result, he set himself the goal of making the 1996 Olympic team. In the trials, he finished fourth in the 1,500 meters and missed out on going to Atlanta. He was sixth in the trials for 2000 and was again fourth in the trials for Athens ... missing third place by less than a foot. Bob was an extremely motivated athlete and a very good athlete. But he wasn't quite fast enough.

3. Technology can also have an impact on a person's motivation and thus improve (or limit) their performance and commitment to the organization.

> **Example:** Lindsey Bracciale was employed to design the company's advertising and promotional materials. She was very good at her job. However, she was becoming increasingly frustrated by the technology with which she had to work. "I am a fan of Apple [computers]. For graphic design, I still think they're the best. However, I have to work on a Windows based unit because top management decided to standardize on this platform throughout the company. I sometimes think I am wasting my time here."

4. The availability of needed or essential resources can also have an impact on motivation and performance.

> **Example:** The dean of the college sent out a memo asking for suggestions as to programs that could be offered overseas. To his surprise he received not a single suggestion. So, at the next college-wide meeting, he asked if anybody was interested. When, again, he received no reply, he asked: why? The response from a number of faculty can be summed up as follows: on paper it sounds like an exciting idea. However, most of us have been down this path before. You put a lot of time and effort into developing a proposal, everybody likes it, and then you are told there is either no money to support it or there is money but it will cost you $10,000 out of your own pocket.

Day-to-Day Motivation (Reinforced Motivation)
↓
Long-term Motivation
↓
Loyalty and Commitment
↓
Dynamic Environment
↓
Corporate Competitive Advantage
↓
Increased Stock Price
↓
Increased Profits
↓
Greater Success

> **Example:** Jim O'Donnell worked in the quality control area of a large manufacturer. Whenever his boss came around, he was complimented on his performance and his commitment to the company remained high. When his boss resigned, his position was taken by another manager who rarely praised his subordinates. Jim's level of motivation went down. Yet another change in supervisors led to the appointment of a woman who saw Jim as having untapped potential. Her interest in him led, over time, to a rebuilding of his enthusiasm and commitment.
>
> **Example:** "When I first took over this department, we were number one in the industry. Then, all of a sudden, two new firms entered the business with new and better products. Our people tried hard but we began to lose market share. So, we began a series of programs designed to motivate them. Nothing worked. It was almost as if they were stuck in a losing mind-set. Then, last year, we decided to hold a two day, out of town retreat to discuss one question, namely: how do we get excited about this business again? It was slow going at the start but people warmed up and came up with some good ideas which we put into action. Today, we are gaining market share. The spirit in the department is electric. And the company is becoming much more profitable."

CASE 11.1

THE SOFTWARE DISASTER

The contract between TG Software (TGS) and Martin-Wohlson Corporation called for the software package to be developed, reviewed, installed, and completely tested by the end of January.

As the Martin-Wohlson representative explained, "we want the entire system up and running on February 1. If the software isn't one hundred on that date then we're in trouble ... and you, my friends ... you are also in trouble." The contract called for a substantial daily penalty if TGS failed to meet the January 31 deadline.

TGS's proposal was based on an estimate that development through testing would take 70 man-months of effort so the division head assigned nine individuals to the project for the next eight months. This would enable TGS to complete the project before the end of the year thus leaving an entire month to resolve any unforeseen problems or issues. The team selected for the project included some of the best programmers in the company and some of the highest paid salaried personnel. "I would say we put together a great team," the manager observed. The team was divided into three groups each focusing on a critical element. As soon as all three elements were complete then the team could move on to the remaining stages.

However, within months, the project was starting to fall behind schedule and by early September, management was starting to panic. "My guess is that we are two months behind schedule now," the manager commented. "It is the pricing sub-module that is causing the problem. The group working on that can't seem to solve some key problems. And the other groups are waiting for them to catch up."

By mid-November, the project was in deep, deep trouble. Management was projecting a half million dollar loss on the project which would have a dramatic impact on everybody's bonus. Furthermore, the completion date was now estimated to be May 1.

Question: Do you think the project team was appropriately motivated at the start of the project?

Question: What went wrong in this situation? Which of the factors influencing performance did the project team seem to be lacking?

Question: As a consultant, what, would you recommend to get this project back on track?

MOTIVATION THROUGH THE SATISFACTION OF NEEDS

🔑 **Key Points:**

1. Individuals have a number of basic needs. Abraham M. Maslow was the first to look at individual motivation from this perspective and he proposed the following diagram:

MASLOW'S HIERARCHY OF NEEDS

"Social Interactions" involve relationships and interactions with others while "Esteem" represents the recognition of a person's worth by others. "Self-Actualization" is the ultimate goal and reflects the maximization of a person's potential. "Be all that you can be" to quote Army commercials.

Maslow argued that individuals needed to move up the hierarchy ... satisfying the lower need before moving on to the next. As shown in the following examples, this makes sense in terms of overall existence.

Example: Simon Huntington was flying a small plane which crashed in the middle of a desert. His first concern, according to Maslow would be his physiological needs (i.e., air, water, food, shelter, rest and sleep). Of these, water soon became the critical factor. A human can last for days without food. Without water, a person can last for 24 to 36 hours ... and, without air, 3 to 5 minutes.

Example: In the movie, "Castaway," Tom Hank's character's first concern (after food) is shelter. He needs protection against the weather and against any deadly animals that may roam the island. Having satisfied this need, he then seeks companionship. Individuals have a need for love, belonging, and association ... thus leading to his "relationship" with the volleyball.

---

2. However, most people who work in any form of organization have already satisfied the basic needs of air, water, and food. They are more concerned with factors relating to their job and life in general. Clayton C. Alderfer essentially condensed Maslow's model into three basic categories of needs:

- Existence needs ... the need for water, food, shelter, etc.
- Relatedness needs ... the need for interactions with other people.
- Growth needs ... the need for continuing personal growth and development.

> **Example:** Mortimer Ryan came from a very poor background. For more than ten years, he lived on the streets where his main daily concern was survival. A period in the army provided him with his existence needs. For the first time in his life, he was more concerned with relationships with other soldiers, his superiors, etc. After leaving the army, he took a job delivering pizza. While he saw this as a dead end job, he did see opportunities in owning a pizza store. Within five years, he owned Mort's Pizza. And, within fifteen years, he had a chain of pizza restaurants statewide.
>
> **Example:** Carlos Laguna put in extremely long hours at the advertising agency where he worked. Starting as a copy writer, he rose to be the manager of the agency. He was now successful. He had enjoyed tremendous personal growth and development. At this point in his life, his focus changed. He married and started a family. He worked with local aid agencies. To him, relating was important.

3. Yet another way of looking at needs was proposed by David C. McClelland. He proposed that people had three fundamental needs ... a need for:

- Achievement (nAch) ... some people in business are driven to achieve their goals. People with a high nAch usually show initiative and set personal goals.
- Power (nPower) ... yet others are driven by a desire to influence and control others. These individuals are comfortable in a competitive environment and tend to seek advancement.
- Affiliation (nAff) ... people with a high nAff tend to have a very cooperative style and emphasize team effort. They need social approval and friendship.

> **Example:** Tom Corer was something of a loner. He preferred to work on his own and set his own schedule and goals. If you wanted something done (and done well), you went to Tom. When an opening for a management position opened up, Tom was passed over. "He's probably our best employee but he shows no desire to manage others and he certainly doesn't shine in a team situation (i.e., has a high nAch but a low nPower and nAff)."
>
> **Example:** Matty Lendine was the exact opposite. She was great when it came to taking charge and organizing others to get the job done (i.e., had a high nPower and nAff). However, if you waited for her to get herself organized to do something, she was only adequate (i.e., a low nAch).

CASE 11.2

PICKING THE RIGHT CANDIDATES

"Well, we are down to our final three candidates for the position (as director of product development). Bob, I know you favor Dennis Osloski. Dana, you favor Leonard Barber. And, you Max, seem to be leaning towards Cynthia Ruggiero. Personally, I think they are all good candidates. So, how do we decide which one to make the offer to? Shall we offer the job to the one who we think will accept the lowest salary? Or is there a better way of making a decision?"

"I certainly don't think we should go with the least expensive," Bob observed. "Let's go with the best. First of all, let's look at what we need. We need somebody who can come in and take charge of the department and really bring it together as a team. There are a number of good people in that area. The problem is that they don't work together towards a common goal."

"So, let's test them and see who looks to be the best," Max added. Let's give them the test that you gave me when I joined the company. The one that showed that I have a high need for achievement."

Dana laughed. "We've really paid a fortune for the mistake of hiring you. Just kidding, Max. But I'm not in favor of using any form of testing. Think back to the test results for the woman in San Antonio. She looked fantastic. And, according to the tests, she was exactly what we were looking for. She lasted three weeks and didn't sell a single thing. There are too many other factors that determine whether or not people will work out."

"So, you think we should just put the three names in a hat and draw out the winner," Max replied. "There has got to be a better way of making a decision."

Question: Does it make sense to ask the three candidates to take a test to determine their respective nAch, nPower, and nAff to determine who best matches the needs of the position?

Question: What other factors might be much more important in determining whether or not the selected candidate would be successful as the new director of product development?

Question: Do you think a candidate who had a good sense of what the company was looking for in terms of the position be able to modify his/her answers to match the company's needs?

MOTIVATION THROUGH GOAL SETTING

🔑 **Key Points:**

1. Underlying this approach is the belief that if you set a goal for an individual and they believe that this goal is both achievable and beneficial to them, then they will be motivated.

> **Example:** Two students were assigned the same paper. Student A saw the paper as very "doable" and likely to result in a high grade for the course. Student B saw the paper as involving a tremendous amount of work and, even if they did well, would not dramatically influence their final grade.

2. Research has shown that effective goal setting requires:

   - Joint goal setting by both parties.
   - Specific goals ... as opposed to generic or general goals.
   - Difficult but realistic goals ... as opposed to goals which are easily achieved.
   - Use of the goal as part of the evaluation of the individual ... with a linkage to feedback and rewards.

> **Example:** Each year Victor Lychenko sat down and established specific goals and objectives for each of the ten members of his department. They were widely known as "Lychenko's wish list." Nobody took very much notice of them. Why? Because Victor never involved any of his people in the goal-setting process. They had no commitment to the resulting goals.
>
> **Example:** Every year, on January 1, Mary and her sister Lynn would set their New Year's Resolutions. It was a fun activity which neither took too seriously. Last year, Mary's goal was to obtain a new position in the IT industry with more responsibility. Lynn's goal was to be "happy." Mary achieved her goal while Lynn never came close to achieving hers. In fact, at the end of the year, she couldn't even remember how she had defined "happiness."
>
> **Example:** "Last year, my boss set a goal for me of sales of $860,000. That was ridiculous since I did over a million the previous year. This year, he says my target is $1.9 million. That's equally ridiculous. It would mean that I would have to gain another $500,000 in sales and not lose one of my current customers. Impossible." As a result, neither goal was effective in terms of motivation.
>
> **Example:** "This year, each of you will be evaluated on the number of sales calls you make each day. At the last meeting, we set the target at three. So, if you average between 3 and 3.5, you will receive a 10% bonus. Between 3.5 and 4 ... 15% bonus and so on." "I thought the idea of having a bonus was a good one and I agreed that 3 was the right figure," one of the senior people commented. "However, the more I think about it, the more I think it will be counter-productive. I can make 5 calls per day if I am willing to limit my time with each customer. On the other hand, if I continue to spend a lot of time with them, I will be lucky to average 2.5."

CASE 11.3

MOTIVATE ME ... PLEASE!!

"It's that time of year again when I need to sit down with each of you and come up with some goals for the coming year. I want them to be goals that will motivate each of you to do your very best. I want them to be challenging but also 'doable.'"

This announcement by the department head, Tom Waddle, was greeted with little or no enthusiasm by the ten members present so he continued. "I want you to think about setting goals in terms of your total sales, your average profit margin, and the number of new customers you bring in during the year. Your bonus next year will be based on these three factors."

Alexa (34) had been with the department for less than a year and was just beginning to get a handle on her territory. "I should do well under this bonus plan since there is a good chance I will increase my total sales by 60% or more and that I will bring in quite a few new customers."

Marik (40) had been with the department for six years and knew his territory inside and out. "I call on every potential customer in my area and the chance of picking up a new one is pretty small. Also, my customers buy the specific products they need. They aren't interested when I try to sell them higher margin products. So, profit margin isn't something I can really control."

Angela (52) was the oldest and longest serving member of the department. "I know what our fearless leader is trying to do but ... My territory covers an area that is growing rapidly. I could certainly add three or four major customers and could increase sales by at least 30% to my existing clients. And, if I switched a couple of them over to the new polymer, my average profit margin would go up substantially. However, to be honest, I don't need the extra money so much as more time to spend with my grandchildren."

Question: What do you think of the proposed bonus plan? Is it a good idea to try to provide additional incentives to motivate them to work harder?

Question: What are the pros and cons of using the same bonus plan criteria for each of the members of the department?

Question: How would you motivate Marik and Angela?

MOTIVATION THROUGH BEHAVIOR MODIFICATION

Key Points:

1. The underlying concepts in behavior modification are that:

> *One should reward right behavior ... and punish or ignore bad behavior*

and

> *Continually reinforcing good behavior will lead to that behavior being repeated and behavior with negative consequences will be discontinued*

This is, of course, an approach much beloved by parents with small children. However, in more subtle ways, it also works with adults.

Example: "Johnny, if you hit your sister again, you'll go to your room with no dinner tonight." "Mary, if you clean up the bathroom, we can go shopping after dinner."

Example: "Congratulations. We're very pleased with your efforts this month and are delighted to present you with the 'employee of the month' award.

---

2. Within a business setting, a manager can utilize essentially four (4) basic strategies in an effort to achieve behavior modification:

- Positive reinforcement ... rewarding the desired performance.
- Punishment ... imposing a penalty (i.e., a negative factor) as a result of the action.
- Negative reinforcement ... removing a penalty to reward desired performance.
- Ignore ... close your eyes to the situation in the hope that it will change.

Example: The miners working on the Regis tunnel stepped out into the light at the end of the shift. They had set a record for the greatest distance achieved in one shift and management was there with a $100 bill for each of them. "Fantastic work," the manager exclaimed. "And here is something to help your memory of today."

Example: "The company's policies and procedures manual states that, if you are found sleeping on company property, the employee will be given a verbal reprimand. The second time, it will be a written reprimand. The third time this occurs, the employee is suspended for a week without pay. If it happens a fourth time then the employee is terminated. In your case, I am sorry to say that the rules give me no choice but to let you go."

> **Example:** Mrs. Jackson was talking to her daughter, Molly. "I know I grounded you for a month for not letting us know that you were going to an all night party. However, I think you have learned your lesson . . . and, therefore, I'm removing the last two weeks of the punishment."
>
> **Example:** "Just ignore Peter's jokes. If nobody laughs or takes any notice then, hopefully, he will realize that he is not being funny . . . and will change his behavior.

3. There is a basic rule of behavior modification:

> *Praise in public . . . criticize in private.*

Criticizing or reprimanding somebody in front of their peers may be both embarrassing for the individual and counter-productive. People do not like being shown up in public . . . and, if you do so, may be motivated to take revenge.

4. It should be noted that no behavior modification strategy guarantees success. It merely increases the probability that the individual will act in an appropriate manner.

> **Example:** "Last year, Ashton-Lyme changed its commission system. We wanted the sales people to spend more time trying to sell the specialty items (with a high profit margin) and less on selling the standard products (with only a small profit margin). So, we changed the commission program so that they would be paid not on the volume of sales but on the profitability of the sales. From the company's point of view it was a good idea. However, the sales people didn't like it at all. The standard products were their bread and butter and were relatively easy to sell. The specialty items took a lot of work." More importantly, the sales people could no longer easily determine how much they had earned since they didn't have information on the profit margins.
>
> **Example:** "We introduced a program designed to motivate and encourage our people to work harder. Each departmental manager would identify the best individual in his/her department. This person's name would then be combined with the winners in the other departments to give a divisional winner. And then the overall winner (who would receive a two-week vacation for two anywhere in the world) would be selected from the divisional winners. The prize was worth up to $20,000 so we thought it would really get our people excited. It didn't. True, it made quite a difference in a couple of departments. However, the majority ignored the program. Most people saw the competition as biased in favor of certain departments and saw their chances of winning as extremely small."

CASE 11.4

MODIFYING HASTY'S BEHAVIOR

The property management firm of Lewis & Abbott managed more than 30 large office buildings in the Los Angeles area. They enjoyed a reputation for being the best and most professional firm in the market. Much of this reputation stemmed from the efforts of one man, Hastings Sparrow whose nickname, Hasty, came from his belief in doing everything "now."

However, the current president, Thornton Abbott III, was concerned about Hasty's increasingly erratic behavior. Following the death of his daughter from cancer, he had had to place Mrs. Sparrow in a nursing home. Alone in the house, Hasty had sought consolation in whiskey, rum and other alcoholic beverages ... and had been known to turn up for meetings very far from sober. He had also been rude to a number of the company's more important clients. And his paperwork was increasingly delayed or forgotten.

"I don't want to have to fire Hasty," Abbott observed to his partner. "He's one of the main reasons we are where we are today. Furthermore, firing him could seriously undermine our credibility and reputation ... especially if one of the other firms in town immediately hired him."

"On the other hand, it is very clear that we have to do something ... and do it fast. Grant Michelson called this morning. He was very polite and friendly but I got his message. The question is: what can we do to change Hasty's behavior?"

Question: Would you adopt some form of punishment ... listing his recent infractions and warning Hasty of the consequences if he continues to behave in an unsatisfactory manner?

Question: What are the pros and cons of ignoring Hasty's behavior in the hope that he would pull out of this current state?

Question: Is there any way of using positive reinforcement in the case of Hasty Sparrow?

THE INNER MOTIVATORS—EXPECTANCY AND EQUITY

 ## Key Points:

1. While much of the emphasis (in terms of motivation) is placed on what a manager can do to improve the motivation of his/her personnel, there are important considerations in terms of the individual as the focus of these motivational efforts. Two, in particular are worthy of note:

   - Expectancy.
   - Equity.

2. According to the expectancy theory, employees will put the greatest effort into an activity if they believe that:

   - Their efforts will lead to a superior level of performance (expectancy).
   - This level of performance will be rewarded (instrumentality).
   - The reward will be meaningful (valence).

Example: A student may limit the amount of effort he/she puts into writing a paper because they don't believe they can produce a superior paper (i.e., a low level of expectancy).

Example: "One of the frustrations of teaching is that your compensation is established in negotiations between the university and the state. So, if you work really hard, you get a 3.5% increase. If you take it easy and do it as little as possible, you get a 3.5% increase (i.e., a low level of instrumentality).

Example: "My boss is forever trying to get us to put more effort into our work and he recently came up with the idea of offering a week in Las Vegas as an incentive. The prize would go to the person who made the most improvement. My friend Mickey got really excited by this and he is really working to win the prize. Now, I have no interest whatsoever in spending time in Las Vegas. I don't gamble and don't like shows. If Mickey wants to go, that's great but ... (i.e., a low level of valency).

---

3. According to the equity theory, an employee's level of motivation depends on whether or not they believe they are being fairly treated relative to their peers. If they feel that they are not being fairly treated then they may well:

■ Attempt to increase the benefits (e.g., negotiate a wage increase or a better schedule).

■ Reduce the amount of effort they put into the job … to more fairly balance what they see as the relationship between their efforts and their rewards.

■ Change their perceptions of the basis for differentiation (e.g., attribute skills to other employees that would justify their higher salary).

■ Change their reference group (e.g., measuring their benefits against not just the people with whom they work but with a far larger group of people in a similar position), and

■ Leave the position … and seek equity elsewhere.

Example: "I sat down with my boss last year and complained about my salary. I make $7,000 less per year than the other bookkeeper in the company and I work longer hours. My boss said he would look into it but nothing happened. So, I started taking longer lunch breaks and arriving and leaving earlier. Now, my boss is complaining about my attitude and lack of productivity. My only option now is to start job hunting in earnest."

Example: "I'm the lowest paid person in the department despite the fact that I have been with the company longer than anybody else. At times, I get really pissed off at this. However, I appreciate that I joined when there were a lot of people looking for employment and salaries were depressed. People who joined the company two or three years later when demand was up and supply was down got much better offers. Also, when I talk with people at other companies, I discover I'm doing pretty well. So, that makes me feel a little better."

CASE 11.5

LIFE JUST AIN'T FAIR!!

Regina Barlow and her sister, Victoria, were enjoying a latte and pastries at the local Starbucks while discussing their problems with their respective bosses and generally agreeing on the unfairness of life. Regina was the chief administrator for the local hospital and reported to Sister Maria Teresa while Victoria was an attorney with a *Fortune 500* company and reported to the head of the litigation division, Estelle Fortuna.

Regina commented that, "SMT (as she was known at the hospital) is a very pleasant and dedicated woman who has given her life to the hospital and thinks that everybody else should also do so. She has just given me the task of promoting computerization of all aspects of the hospital to the board of trustees and to the doctors. I don't have to worry about the nurses and the supporting staff. I know they are in favor of anything that will make their job easier."

"As you know, I'm no computer expert. So, I am going to have to put in many long hours to develop the knowledge and understanding to get on top of this job. Then, even if I work my buns off for the next three years, I don't know that the board will really recognize my contribution. They haven't in the past!! And, if they do, they will only give me an extra thousand or so. So, the question is: does it make sense for me to devote a great deal of time and effort to work on this issue?"

"I can relate to the problem," her sister replied. "For the past six months, I've been working on a major case for our largest client. It is going well. However, they have just announced that three of my colleagues are being made partners. I talked with Estelle about it and asked her why I wasn't on the partners list. She just gave me the run around. I don't know if it is discrimination against women or just against me. I am going to have a meeting next week with the people at Harper & Stanton ... and that will give me a better idea of where I stand. At the moment, my motivation has sunk to an all time low."

Question: What is the fundamental issue facing Regina? As a consultant, how would you suggest she respond to this situation?

Question: What are Victoria's options given the situation in which she finds herself? As a consultant, how would you suggest she respond?

Question: Assuming that the hospital and law firm would not wish to lose Regina and Victoria, what would you suggest SMT and Estelle do in the respective situations?

SUMMARY

1. Motivation is defined as:

   > *the inner drive that results in an individual exerting maximum effort to achieve a specific goal or objective.*

2. As a manager, one of your major functions is to motivate your personnel. The underlying assumption being that the more motivated a person is, the more likely they are to perform well.

3. Motivation, however, is not the only factor which leads to performance. Among the other factors that do have an impact are:

   - Ability ... can the person perform the assigned task?

   - Technology ... does the individual have the necessary technology to perform the task?

   - Resources and support ... does the person have the supporting staff to do the job and is the effort supported by top management.

4. Organizations are concerned about motivation because of the belief that motivating people on a day-to-day basis leads to long-term motivation which, in turn, leads to loyalty and commitment. This loyalty and commitment, in theory, leads to a more dynamic environment which leads to a competitive advantage and this, in turn, leads to increased profits and improved stock prices.

5. Each employee has his/her own personal needs ... and much of the early research focused on determining the nature of these needs and satisfying them. Three of the models in this area are:

   - Maslow ... with a pyramid of needs ranging from physiological needs (air, water, food, etc.) to self-actualization (i.e., achieving one's potential).

   - Alderfer ... condensed Maslow's pyramid into three basic needs: existence, relatedness, and growth.

   - McClelland ... who looked at individual's needs in terms of achievement, power, and affiliation.

6. Another broad area of research has been on the motivation of individuals by goal setting. Underlying this approach is the belief that, if an employee (with the guidance of his/her boss) (a) sets a goal that they believe is achievable and (b) recognizes that their rewards will be dependent on achieving this goal then (c) they will be motivated to work as hard as possible to achieve this goal.

7. Another fundamental concept in this field is that rewarding appropriate behavior and "punishing" inappropriate behavior will result in the desired behavior (i.e., that the individual will be motivated to do even better or to cease doing what they are doing. There are two primary strategies and two lesser strategies:

   - Positive reinforcement ... rewarding the desired behavior.

   - Punishment ... imposing a penalty on those who pursue undesirable behavior.

   - Negative reinforcement ... removing a penalty to reward desired performance.

   - Ignore ... close your eyes to the situation in the hope that it will change.

8. No strategy (i.e., needs satisfaction, goal setting, or behavior modification) guarantees success. They merely increase the probability that the individual will act in an appropriate manner.

9. Always remember to:

> *Praise in public ... criticize in private.*

10. Expectancy. For a person to be motivated, they have to believe that:
    - If they put in the necessary effort, the result will represent a superior level of performance.
    - This performance will be recognized and rewarded.
    - The reward will be sufficiently meaningful to justify the effort.

11. Equity. Generally speaking, people wish to be treated equitably. If they perceive themselves as being treated inequitably then their level of motivation will decline and they will consider using one of the following strategies:
    - Attempt to increase the benefits.
    - Reduce the amount of effort expended.
    - Change their perceptions.
    - Change their reference group.
    - Seek equity by leaving the position.

CRITICAL THINKING QUESTIONS

1. What other factors do you think might influence a person's performance besides their motivation and ability and the technology and support provided by the organization?

   _____

   _____

   _____

   _____

2. One of my people made an interesting comment to me the other day. He said, "You never praise people. You never give 'attaboys.' The only time you make any comment on the work I do is when I make a mistake." That really made me stop and think. Every quarter we award prizes to the people who have done an outstanding job. And, at the end of the year, we make a real fuss of them at the annual awards banquet. I thought we were doing a pretty good job in that area. What do you think the point was of the employee's comments? And what do you think the department head might do given this feedback?

   _____

   _____

   _____

   _____

3. As part of the hiring process, Paula Westin had been required to take a battery of tests. One of them showed that she had a relatively high need for achievement (nAch), a very high need for power (nPower), and a surprisingly high need for affiliation (nAff). The interviewer studying the scores was somewhat perplexed. "Your previous boss described you as a person who preferred to work on your own rather than as part of a team. He also commented on the fact, when you were a member of his team, you played a fairly minor and subordinate role and didn't complete the part of the project you were assigned." How do you think Paula might explain the marked differences between the test results and the views of her former boss?

   _____

   _____

   _____

   _____

4. In mid-December, the company chairman and the head of the office building development division (OBDD), Oscar Grange, sat down to establish goals for the division for the coming year. The chairman proposed that the division should set a goal of "one start" each year. "I want you to start one new project each year," he stated. He also suggested that Oscar and his people's bonuses be based on the profitability of the project when it was sold. "After all, until we sell the project, we don't have the cash flow to pay you your bonus." Oscar disagreed violently. "Starting a project just to meet the goal doesn't make sense. We may as well erect a tool shed on January 1 and get that requirement out of the way right up front. And paying the people only when the project is sold is ridiculous. If management places a high enough price on the building, it will never sell. The bonus needs to be based on the percentage completion for the building. The completion rate is something my team

and I can control ... the price is not." How would you resolve this disagreement? Is there a solution that would satisfy both parties and motivate the members of OBDD?

_____

_____

_____

_____

5. Martina Rosco watched as Bob Ungaro left her office. "Bob's one of our better people. However, that's the fifth time I've had him in my office over the past three months to reprimand him for not being polite to a customer. In retail, we are in the business of making customers feel welcome and ensuring that they come back. Now, I've watched Bob a number of times and, while he is not being rude, he's not following the store's policies. So, mindful of the "praise in public ... criticize in private" philosophy, I have brought him into my office. It clearly hasn't worked. So, at the next general staff meeting next week, I am going to criticize him in public ... and see what effect that has." What do you see as the pros and cons of this change in approach? How might Bob react?

_____

_____

_____

_____

6. "People are very different. Take Roscoe and Willa. If I say to Roscoe, 'this is very poor work. It is not up to your normal standard. I was very disappointed ... I expected better of you' then the next time he will work twice as hard and it will be great. However, if you say 'this is great. Well done,' the next project will be o.k. but nothing fantastic. On the other hand, if you say exactly the same thing to Willa, you get the opposite result. Tell her it is very poor and the next effort will be even worse. Tell her it is great and she will do even better." How would you explain this difference between Roscoe and Willa in terms of responding to criticism and praise?

_____

_____

_____

_____

7. Sven Bjornberg was talking to a good friend about his frustrations at the university. "I went for promotion again this year and, for the fourth time in a row, they turned me down. What really makes me mad is that they promote people over me whom I voted against hiring in the first place. The problem is that it's nothing more than a beauty contest. They don't know what they are doing. It is more a matter of who you know and who you suck up to than anything else!!" What are some of the ways in which Sven might react to this rejection? What might influence Sven's choice of game plan vis-à-vis promotion at the university?

_____

_____

_____

_____

CASE
PROBLEM

THE UNMOTIVATED DEPARTMENT

"I'd never seen anything like it. I gathered the members of the department together in the main conference room and told them I was taking the place of Alan Cartwright, the previous head, who had been promoted. I asked them to introduce themselves and tell me what they did ... and they did so. Then, I asked them if they had any questions for me ... and nobody said anything."

"So, the following day, I went around and spent between twenty and thirty minutes with each of them in turn. They were all very friendly. However, none of them seemed to have any great drive or enthusiasm. On a number of occasions, I asked them how they thought the department could do better and 'I don't know' seemed to be the most common answer. They seemed to do their job well enough but nobody seemed to have any real drive or any interest in changing anything."

My next call was to my predecessor. "Alan," I said. "The department I inherited from you seems to be running very well. Everybody seems to be doing their job. And yet I don't know how to motivate them. What do you suggest I do?"

Alan laughed. "I suggest you work on your golf game. That department will run perfectly smoothly whether you are there or not. How do you think I got promoted? Each of the members has their own task ... and they do it well. Over the past three years, all the younger people or the ones who wanted to change things have left. The people who are left as those who really appreciate having a job and are perfectly satisfied with the level of compensation. They don't have any interest in changing the situation. They want to be left alone to do their job."

Question: *How would you describe this department in terms of the needs analysis models of Maslow, Alderfer and McClelland?*

_____

_____

_____

_____

Question: *Would you try to use goal-settings and/or behavior modification to try to motivate the members of this department?*

_____

_____

_____

_____

Question: *What questions would you ask the members of this department if you were to administer a questionnaire to them to try and identify opportunities for motivation? And why?*

_____

_____

_____

_____

_____

CHAPTER 12

EFFECTIVE COMMUNICATIONS

OVERVIEW

In the previous chapters, we looked at leadership and motivation. Both of these activities (as do most elements of management) require communications between members of the organization. Thus, the ability to effectively communicate one's thoughts and ideas to others is critically important. Equally important is the ability of the recipient to accurately understand the meaning of the communication.

There are two other key factors in the communications process. The first is feedback. This is important not only because it indicates that he/she has received the message but also suggests how he/she interpreted the message. The second is noise. A number of factors can act as barriers to effective communication ranging from a jack hammer being used outside the window to a personal problem or concern that make it difficult to concentrate on the incoming message.

In this chapter, therefore, we focus on the following topics:

- The Communications Model
- Alternative Modes of Communication
- Barriers to Effective Communication
- Non-verbal Communications
- Formal versus Informal Channels of Communication

THE COMMUNICATIONS MODEL

Key Points:

1. The standard model for communications consists of seven (7) main elements, namely:

   - The sender of the message.
   - The translation of the idea into a message that can be sent (encoding).
   - The medium by which the message is to be communicated.
   - The translation of the message by the receiver (decoding).
   - The receiver of the message.
   - Feedback.
   - Noise.

COMMUNICATIONS MODEL

Sender ──→ Encoding ──→ Medium ──→ Docoding ──→ Receiver

Noise (above Medium)

Noise (below Medium)

Feedback ←──

2. For this communications process to occur there has to be a sender or originator of a message. Somebody has to develop a thought or idea in their mind that they wish to communicate to another person.

> **Example:** The meeting had been going badly. Nobody seemed to be able to get to the heart of the problem. The more she thought about it, the more Susan was convinced that they needed to take a very different approach. Having come to that conclusion, she was now ready to put her thoughts into words.

3. Until the human race learns how to communicate telepathically, the sender of the message has to convert the idea(s) in their brain into a message that can be communicated. This is called "encoding."

> **Example:** Jim Fisher was stopped at a traffic light waiting to turn right when another car crashed into him. This made him really, really mad since it was a brand new car. He climbed out of the car and walked back to the offending vehicle. He was already translating his anger into a collection of words which he would deliver to the other driver.

4. In order for a communication to be transmitted from the sender to the receiver, there has to be a medium or vehicle to carry the message.

> **Example:** Whenever a law firm sends out a contract, it sends it by registered mail to ensure that it is notified by the post office that the receiver has actually received the mailing. "It doesn't mean they have read it," the senior partner explained. "Just that they have received it and thus we have performed our fiduciary responsibilities."
>
> **Example:** "If I find out that the meeting has been moved forward from 4:00 p.m. to 2:00 p.m. today, it doesn't do any good to send out a letter. It will take two or three days to arrive. Sending an e-mail is quick but people don't always read their e-mail and, when they do, they don't pay attention to them. In this case, I telephone each member of the committee and track them down. I speak to them personally so that they know that the time of the meeting has been changed."

5. The message arrives (using some form of medium or vehicle) at the receiver. He/she then interprets the content of the message. This is known as "decoding" and different receivers will decode the message in totally different ways.

> **Example:** Two very good friends—one a Democrat and the other a Republican—were watching a televised debate between the two leading candidates. While they were both listening to the identical speech, one interpreted a pronouncement as being "dead on." "A clear and concise statement of the problem" while the other concluded that it "showed that the speaker was an idiot and had absolutely no idea what he was talking about."
>
> **Example:** The letter stated that the candidates could "meet with the members of the committee if they wished to do so (i.e., if they had something they really wanted to communicate to the committee)." Candidate A concluded that there was nothing he specifically wanted to discuss and thus declined the invitation. Candidate B read the same words and concluded that it was telling him that he was required to meet with the committee. Same words ... totally different interpretation.

6. For this communications process to occur there has to be a recipient or receiver of a message. Somebody has to be receptive to the message being communicated by another individual.

> **Example:** By the time Susan had gathered up the courage to make her views known to the committee, the chair person had decided to move on to the next issue. No communication occurred, therefore, because there was nobody who was receptive to her message.

7. Feedback ... this is the process whereby the receiver lets the sender know that they have received the message and provides an indication of their understanding of the message.

> **Example:** "I sent out the agenda for the meeting Monday to the seven members of the committee. Only one replied saying that he could not attend. So, I assumed that the remaining six would be there. I arrived ... and was the only person to turn up. I would have appreciated some feedback."
>
> **Example:** The memo stated that the next meeting would be at 9:00 on Tuesday, March 5. The only problem was that Tuesday was actually the 4th. March 5 was a Wednesday. All recipients of the memo queried the original date ... in order to clarify their understanding of the message.
>
> **Example:** "You want me to conduct this project," Jim Turner said for the third time. And for the third time, his boss said, "No ... I want you to oversee the project. I want one of the new people to actually do it. Are we in agreement on this?" Feedback was essential to clearing up a misunderstanding between Jim and his boss.

8. Noise ... these are the variety of factors which interfere with the reception and decoding of the message.

> **Example:** "I was talking by phone to one of my managers in the Middle East. The line was terrible. I thought he said he was going to be at headquarters later this month and I set up a series of meetings for him. It turned out that I had misheard him. He's going to Italy not coming here."
>
> **Example:** "The meeting started at nine thirty and I was fine until about eleven when I started to develop a splitting headache. As a result, I have no idea what was decided in the last hour or so. My mind wasn't functioning."

CASE 12.1

A HARD DECISION

Lance Randall was one of Louisa's best employees. In fact, he was probably the best employees in the design division. He was extremely creative and productive. His work was done on time and clients were generally delighted with his efforts. These factors made Louisa's decision even more difficult.

Offsetting his work performance was his attitude ... especially towards the five female members of the group. Lance seemed to take delight in teasing and making off-color jokes to them. He was forever inviting them to go out with him ... despite the fact that three of the women were married.

Initially, nobody took a great deal of notice. He was a young, attractive man with a quick sense of humor. However, the two single women had recently complained to Louisa that they were fed up with Lance's antics and that, if he didn't stop, they would file a sexual harassment suit against him and the company (for fostering an inappropriate atmosphere).

Louisa closed the door to her office and looked out of the window. She had to do something. Her predecessor had let a similar situation drift and had eventually been fired.

What should she say to Lance and how should she communicate with him? Then, there was the question of how Lance would interpret her communication and how he would respond.

Question: What is the first thing Louisa needs to do with these emotions? Can she communicate these emotions directly to Lance?

Question: Having reached a decision on the message, how should she communicate this message to Lance?

Question: What are some of the ways in which Lance might respond to her message?

ALTERNATIVE MODES OF COMMUNICATION

⊙⟶ **Key Points:**

1. There are a large number of ways one person can communicate with another. For example, a person could:

   - Set up a face-to-face meeting.
   - Send a letter, a fax, or a telegram.
   - Send an e-mail or use instant messaging.
   - Use the telephone or video conferencing.
   - Place a notice in a local newspaper, a magazine, or on a billboard.
   - Employ the services of a carrier pigeon.

   Each of these modes of communication has distinct advantages and disadvantages in terms of:

   - The richness of the medium (i.e., how much information can be included in the communication).
   - The speed of the medium (i.e., how rapidly the information moves from the sender to the receiver).
   - The impact of the medium (i.e., the degree to which the receiver pays attention to the communication).
   - The cost of utilizing the medium (i.e., the total cost of the communication).

2. A face-to-face meeting is the richest of all the media because it not only allows for interplay between two or more participants but also for immediate feedback (and thus the changing of views and positions). It is also the fastest of the media and the participants generally pay attention to the communication. The main negative is that of the cost. It is relatively expensive to bring people together in a single location.

   > **Example:** "We have representatives in all the major markets worldwide and, most of the time, we communicate with them by e-mail. However, once a year, we bite the bullet and bring them here to headquarters. It is amazing how much gets done. They get to know each other as people and ideas flow back and forth. It costs us a fortune but we think it is worthwhile."

3. Sending a letter, a fax or a telegram. All three media have the advantage of being relatively inexpensive. A letter, in particular, can include a tremendous amount of information and data. It may, however, take days to arrive and the recipient may not pay attention to it. A fax is far quicker but doesn't always carry the weight of a letter and may not be read. A telegram, by contrast, is generally carefully read (because most people associated a telegram with bad news). However, there is a limit to the amount of information that can be incorporated in text. On the negative side, none of these media allow for any immediate interplay between the sender and receiver.

> **Example:** "It was critically important that Jim Foster get the key points of the agreement. So, I sent him a letter detailing them. I didn't hear back from him so I faxed the same material to him. I still didn't hear anything so I sent him a telegram. That got his attention."

4. Send an e-mail or use instant messaging. The great advantage of using these technologies is the speed with which a message can be sent. And, in the case of e-mails, the message can be sent to multiple recipients. However, they have the disadvantage that they are casual communications. Unlike a letter, people don't devote a great deal of time to ensuring that the content is accurate and that it is presented in an appropriate manner. Coupled with the fact that they provide a permanent record and there is a serious potential problem.

> **Example:** "I sent off an e-mail to my boss last week. It was a spur of the moment composition and said exactly what I wanted to say. Since then, I have begun to have second thoughts and regret having sent it. Unfortunately, there is now a permanent record of my outburst and I have the feeling that may come back to haunt me."

5. Use the telephone or video conferencing. The major advantages of using the telephone as a means of communicating are that it is quick (assuming you manage to make contact with the recipient) and relatively inexpensive (at least in comparison with bringing all the participants to one location). However, it doesn't have the "richness" of a face-to-face discussion. You can't see the other party. You can't tell whether or not they are interested. It is hard to tell if they are lying. All you can do is to try to pick up signals from their voice and comments.

   Video conferencing overcomes this last problem by providing a visual component. However, both parties need to have compatible equipment . . . and it still doesn't have the same "richness" as the face-to-face meeting although recent innovations have improved the experience.

> **Example:** "Talking with my counterpart in Australia by phone was never very effective. It was better than sending a letter but nowhere near as effective as getting in a room and talking with them. Now, we have installed video conferencing and now you can see the faces when they are talking. It is not perfect but it is getting better.

6. Placing a notice in a local newspaper, a magazine, or on a billboard are all effective ways of communicating with an external audience. However, they all take a considerable period of time before the message reaches the intended audience. A job announcement in the local paper may not appear until a week after it is submitted. A magazine may take even longer and a billboard longer still.

Example: Herzog & Payne were advertising for two new positions. They put the announcement for a paralegal in the local newspaper since they needed to hire as soon as possible. The announcement of a position for a lawyer with expertise in the oil and gas industry was placed in the bar association publications. In this case, they wanted to get the best person available.

7. Pigeons . . . not a normal form of business communications. They have a tendency to go in the wrong direction and get lost.

CASE 12.2

"YOU'RE FIRED!!"

In May 2001, Mara Clay joined the firm of Pritzke and Associates. Pritzke consisted of five partners, each of whom had their own business. They joined together to share the overhead costs of the office in midtown New York.

Mara was hired by Kirk Mendizian and worked primarily for him. However, she also did work on occasions for the other partners and knew them all reasonably well. The vast majority of the employees (220 plus) worked for Richard Ugart who ran a small brokerage house specializing in small cap stocks.

Richard Ugart also made highly speculative investments for his own account. And in 2003, he had a run of disastrous situations. As a result, he decided to close down the brokerage firm. Pritzke and Associates was thus reduced to the five partners and three assistants (including Mara Clay). The company relocated to a much smaller office in the building across the street.

Mara could see the handwriting on the wall. Since Kirk was not doing well in his area and none of the others were generating substantial income, she decided it made sense to start looking for a new job.

One Friday evening, shortly after her first interview, Mara went to a party and didn't arrive home until about 3:30 a.m. The light on her answering machine was blinking. It was a message from Richard Ugart telling her that she had been fired and that she could pick up her personal belongings from the guard in the foyer.

Question: What's your reaction to the way this was done? What alternative ways of communication could Pritzke and Associates have used to fire Mara?

Question: What would have been the best way to communicate this negative information?

Question: Would it have made any difference (in terms of the medium of communication) if Pritzke and Associates had wanted to tell Mara that she was being promoted?

BARRIERS TO EFFECTIVE COMMUNICATION

Key Points:

1. The barriers to effective communication can be divided into two groups:

   - Individual barriers.
   - Structural barriers.

2. Individual barriers are those barriers which reflect on the receiver's ability to correctly interpret a message. These can include:

   - The source's view of the receiver.
   - The reviewer's view of the sender.
   - The experience and education of the receiver.
   - Noise.

Example: "Whenever I send a message to our office in Milan, I do a draft and then I hand it to my assistant and have him "translate" it into simple English in order to make sure they understand it. By contrast, when I am writing to the head of research in the United Kingdom, I throw in every long word I can think of in order to impress them with my knowledge of their language."

Example: "What did you think of Michele's proposal?" my boss asked. That put me in a bad position because I hadn't read it. Michele is forever sending out memos summarizing her crazy ideas. I sometimes suspect she tries to come across as a dizzy blonde. And, as a result, I dismiss her ideas without seriously considering them.

Example: Miles Tandy sent out a draft of an article to a publication and received two detailed responses. Reviewer #1 thought it was great. "Innovative and well written" was the conclusion. Reviewer #2 panned the article. "You make no reference to the early work of either Shelling or Mitwald. And you totally ignore the recent literature." The reviewers evaluated the article with reference to their own knowledge-base, interests, and experience. One loved it and the other hated it.

Example: Driving back from Tucson, Diane Hill received two calls on her cell phone. The first came as she was entering a long tunnel so she lost the first part of the message and then, when she exited the tunnel, she found herself in the middle of a very noisy construction site . . . and thus lost the end of that message. By the time she received the second call, she was less than half an hour from home. She was hungry. She felt rather sick (the result of a taco eaten some time earlier), and she was growing increasingly worried that she hadn't heard from her son yet. Thinking back on this second call, Diane was hard pressed to remember what the point was.

---

3. Structural barriers reflect the fact that:

- Business needs more and more increasingly complex information.
- The amount of time for communications has been reduced due to the constant need to learn new concepts and ideas.
- The globalization increasingly results in people coming into contact with individuals who do not speak English or speak it poorly.

Example: "I used to know this industry like the back of my hand. Nowadays, I open the trade magazine and find I can't understand some of the articles. They used to deal with the people aspect of the industry. Now, they are mathematical models that require a Ph.D. to understand."

Example: "When I was first appointed head of this division, I had four people reporting to me and I spent about half an hour with each of them every morning. Now, there are ten people who look to me for direction. The number of meetings has doubled. And the complexity of the problems has grown exponentially. It is not that I have trouble communicating with my staff so much as the problem of finding time to talk to them."

Example: In recent years, the art department had hired a number of instructors whose native language was not English. "We were understaffed. They had good academic qualifications. And they wanted to teach. Now, don't get me wrong. Technically, they are very good artists. The problem is that students keep complaining that they can't understand them. I have a lot of sympathy for the students. Three of our faculty argued, in English, for thirty minutes at the last meeting … and I really can't say I know what they were talking about."

CASE 12.3

I HEARD WHAT YOU SAID BUT ...

"Do you ever have occasions when somebody is talking to you ... giving you instructions. Then they walk away and you have absolutely no idea what they said?"

Melanie Tauber was shaking her head in disbelief. She had just had a five minute conversation with her boss outside the building and was now realizing that, apart from the fact that it was important; she couldn't remember any of the key points of the discussion.

"I remember leaving the restaurant. Something I ate wasn't sitting too well. And the sun was merciless. I drove back to the office and couldn't find a parking space. So, I had to park at the place on Archer Street, which is so damned expensive. Then, I had to walk all the way back to the office and, when I walked around the corner, there my boss was feet away from where they are digging up the sidewalk."

He said, "Melanie, do you have a minute before you go into the building. I talked with Payne Anderson this morning and he wants us to have the proposal completed by this afternoon. So what I want you to do is ... "

"And, at that point in time, my mind is blank ... I remember saying, 'No problem ... I'll get that done this afternoon' ... and that is it. Now I feel totally embarrassed."

Question: What are some of the factors that may well have influenced Melanie's lack of understanding of her boss's communication?

Question: What mistakes did her boss make ... given that this was an important communication?

Question: What should Melanie have done when her boss said he had an important communication?

NON-VERBAL COMMUNICATIONS

 Key Points:

1. Non-verbal communications are those "communications" or signals that a person transmits in ways other than the spoken or written words.

    Research studies have shown that a large percentage of the impact of a communication is carried by these non-verbal elements. The estimated percentages range from 50% to over 85%. And when the message is an emotional one then the non-verbal percentage is even higher.

2. The most common non-verbal factors are:

    ■ Gestures ... head movements, body language and hand movements.
    ■ Body language ... the posture of the listener.
    ■ Vocal tones ... the strength and intensity of the individual's voice.
    ■ Facial expressions ... the movement of the mouth and the eyes.

Example: In most countries of the world, shaking the head from side to side means "no" and up and down means "yes." Learning forward is generally viewed as showing interest while leaving back and crossing one's arms is taken to mean a lack of interest or resistance. A fist raised in the air can be regarded as reflecting anger and aggression while a finger pointed upwards is a sign of contempt.

Example: Think of the various ways a person could say "I hate you" to another person. The tone of their voice and the strengths of the utterance will clearly have a dramatic impact on how the recipient will decode the message.

Example: When the eyes or a person's mouth moves upwards, we interpret this to mean they are pleased or in agreement. When the mouth moves down, it implies sadness or disagreement. An open mouth implies shock while a tightly closed mouth will be taken to mean resistance.

---

3. Interpreting non-verbal communication is far from being a precise science. They have to be considered in context and in combination with other factors.

> **Example:** A tall person leaning backwards on a chair with their arms crossed may indeed mean that they are resisting the message. It may also mean that this is the most comfortable position to avoid falling off the seat. A person who doesn't look at you when they speak would be seen as somewhat shifty and questionable. However, they may have been brought up in an environment in which looking somebody in the eye was regarded as rude. Or they may be shy or have an eye complaint.

4. The same non-verbal communication can mean different things in various parts of the world with different cultures.

> **Example:** In the U.S., a person confronted by somebody standing two inches from them smelling strongly of garlic would probably step back. To the person used to standing close to another to show interest and respect would find the other's person's backing away both rude and insulting.

CASE 12.4

THE BEST CANDIDATE BUT ...

Following the end of the interview and the departure of the candidate, Tess Harmon wrote up her notes.

Jim Whistler has a degree in engineering and an MBA from Penn State and has worked in our industry for five years. For the past three years he has been doing the exact position that we are looking to hire. I would rank him number one (out of five candidates) for the position.

Mr. Whistler has a number of things going for him besides his experience:

- His references are outstanding. The one from Frank Pierson (who used to work here) is just great. He highly recommends him.
- He is active in various professional associations and knows a large number of our people.
- He and his wife live only about an hour from the office so we will not have to pay expensive moving costs.
- The salary we would be offering is considerably more than he is currently receiving so I think he would be very satisfied with that aspect.

On the negative side, he:

- Kept cleaning his glasses. Every couple of minutes he would take them off and clean them.
- Never leaned forward once during the interview. He leaned back in the chair all the time ... as if he was afraid of getting too close.
- Always looked away ... and when he did look straight at me, I had no idea what he was thinking. His face gave me no indication of whether or not he agreed or disagreed with my statements.
- Had a pulverizing handshake. My hand still feels as if it has been crushed in a vice.

Question: What do you make of this interview?

Question: How much importance would you give to the non-verbal communications?

Question: Jim Whistler is clearly the best candidate in terms of qualifications but would you hire him?

FORMAL VERSUS INFORMAL CHANNELS OF COMMUNICATION

Key Points:

1. Within any organization, there are two distinct patterns of communication:

   - Formal communications ... communications that follow the formal structure of the organization and are controlled by the company, and
   - Informal communications ... communications that arise as a result of individual contacts and relationships. An organization rarely has any means of controlling this channel.

   Furthermore, formal communications can be broken down into three categories:

   - Top-down communications ... communications flowing down from the chairman and president to the lowest employee or from any person to those individuals subordinate to them.
   - Side-to-side communications ... messages flowing between individuals with similar positions in the organization (e.g., senior vice president to senior vice president, manager to manager, etc.).
   - Bottom-up communications ... communications moving up the organization from individuals to their direct supervisors or other superiors within the organization.

Example: "Each month, I receive a number of communications from top management. Some of them are reports summarizing financial data. Others are announcements of changes and promotions within the company. And yet others are suggestions relating to the handling of a particular issue or problem."

Example: "I am one of four regional vice presidents and we work on similar and critical client problems. They have information I need (and *vice versa*) so there is a continuous flow of communications between us. We talk together daily and, whenever I come across something that will help them, I put it in the in-house mail."

Example: "We pride ourselves on getting our employees involved in the company. As you can see, we have suggestion boxes on every floor. Why? Because we get some very good ideas as to how things could be better handled. In addition, we require monthly reports from everybody. These are then summarized and passed on up the organization. These reports tell us what is going on in the field. Finally, top management has an "open door" policy which we enforce. Anybody at any level of the company can approach any member of top management with any issue with a guarantee of anonymity."

2. Informal channels of communication are very different. As indicated above, they are not controlled by the management of the organization and, as result, the content of the communication may range from being completely accurate to totally false. These informal channels occur because of people's interests and connections. They may be built around a car pool, a bridge club, a luncheon group, etc. People talk and are always looking for items of information that will be of interest to other members of the group. Thus "choice" information will jump rapidly from one informal group to another until the message has made its way to all corners of the organization.

> **Example:** "Last month I needed to inform all employees of a change to the health plan. It was a relatively major change and I wanted to let everybody know as rapidly as possible. As I was preparing the memo, I mentioned the change to my assistant and to another manager. Over lunch, three people came up and asked me what the impact of the change would be. The formal announcement probably won't go out until next week … and yet most of the people already know what is going to happen. The grapevine has triumphed again."
>
> **Example:** "For some time now, the board of directors has been considering making an offer for a competitor—T&M Industries. As of the meeting last week, no decision has been made. Yet that hasn't stopped the rumor mill. One of the guys in my car pool said he had heard that a deal had been finalized and that we were paying $42 million for them. My next door neighbor said she had heard the deal was dead. And my wife said a friend of hers had heard that T&M was going to buy us. All pure speculation."

CASE 12.5

I'M ALWAYS THE LAST TO KNOW

"I knew weeks back that top management was considering the sale of this division to Archer-Candy. Everybody knew that. Just as they knew that your boss was leaving at the end of the month. Top management is going to make both announcements in the next few days."

Tim Aston shook his head and wandered back to his office on the third floor. He had been talking with Santos Pascual in the cafeteria and had come to the conclusion that he was "always the last to know."

The memo from top management announcing the sale of the division had arrived in his in-basket that morning. It came as a tremendous shock and made him wonder about his career with the company. Then, the conversation with Santos and the revelation that his boss was leaving at the end of the month sent shivers down his spine. They had just bought a house and found a good school for the twins. Why was he always the last to know?

Picking up the phone, he called Santos and asked, "How did you know about the sale of the division weeks ago?" His colleague on the other end thought for a moment. "Well, Pete told me and he apparently got the information from Cicely. Now Cicely is in the same car pool as Glenda who used to date Rick Page who works for Archer-Candy. She apparently ran into him in our parking lot. He was coming in as she was leaving. They talked for a time and she asked him what he was doing. He said he was now heading up the acquisitions division and I gather that Glenda put two and two together."

"And the information that my boss was leaving?" Santos thought for a minute. "Bob Aspinall's wife plays golf with Debbie Swanson, who is a Realtor with a residential firm here in town. When Debbie's car broke down, Bob's wife drove her home. On the way, they passed a house on Mantingsale Road where Debbie had a sign on the lawn. Bob's wife had been there for a party and . . ."

Question: How is it that the official announcements take much longer to reach recipients than the informal network (known as the grapevine)?

Question: Why do you think Tim is always the last to know?

Question: Is a corporate grapevine a good thing or a bad thing?

SUMMARY

1. In order for a person to be able to manage, motivate and lead, they have to be able to communicate. This means that they have to transmit a message to others in a form that is appropriate and understandable.

2. The communications model consists of seven (7) key elements:

   - The individual who initiates the communication (i.e., the sender).
   - Encoding ... the "translation" of the individual's idea or thought into a form that can be communicated.
   - A medium ... a way of moving the message from the sender to the receiver.
   - Decoding ... the "translation" of the message by the receiver.
   - The receiver ... the intended target of the communication.
   - Feedback ... the response of the receiver to the sender indicating not only that he/she has received the message but also indicating how he/she interpreted the message.
   - Noise ... those factors (both individual and structural) that can interfere with or even block the reception and correct "translation" of the message.

3. Alternative modes of communication. A communication can be sent from one party to another via a number of different media. Each of these media has advantages and disadvantages.

   - A face-to-face meeting ... the richest of the media (in terms of content) but it can be expensive and time consuming.
   - Utilizing a letter, a fax, or a telegram ... less expensive but doesn't readily allow for back and forth interaction.
   - Sending an e-mail or instant messaging ... very quick and inexpensive. Hard to communicate depth of information (because the recipient only skims the document) and leaves a potentially dangerous paper trail.
   - Use of the telephone ... again quick (if you can catch the receiver) but with no hard copy of the conversation (his/her word against yours) and impossible to determine the non-verbal communications.
   - Use of video conferencing ... can be expensive and time consuming. However, it is probably the next best thing to being in the same room.
   - Placing a notice in a newspaper, magazine, or on a billboard ... a slow and often expensive process ... not suited for internal communications.

4. Barriers to effective communications ranged from the individual to structural barriers. Individual barriers can include:

   - The source's view of the receiver (e.g., an appreciation of their limited language skills).
   - The reviewer's view of the source (e.g., a lack of respect).
   - The level of education of the receiver (e.g., he/she may not be able to understand the message), and
   - Noise (e.g., somebody trying to talk to you, the sound of a baby crying or a television blaring, or the receiver feeling rushed, upset or depressed).

   Structural barriers can include:

   - The complexity and volume of communications may make it difficult for a person to get a handle on what is being communicated.

- The changing world of new ideas and new approaches leaves a limited amount of time for communications.

- The fact that a manager may have to deal with people who either do not speak English at all or do so only poorly.

5. Non-verbal communications are those that involve neither spoken nor written words. Research has shown that such communications can have a dramatic impact on the receiver's "translation" of a message ... and, in many cases, can be more important than the words spoken or written.

   The main types of non-verbal communications are:

- Gestures ... movements of various parts of the body.
- Body language ... the posture of the listener.
- Vocal tones ... how the words are spoken.
- Facial expressions ... the eyes, the mouth, the forehead, etc. can all give an indication of the receiver's true reaction to the message.

6. Formal communications are those initiated within the formal structure of the organization. Management controls this channel to a very large degree. Such communications can be divided into top-down, side-to-side, and bottom-up communications.

   Informal communications are those interchanges which result from informal structures and groups (such as a quality circle or a car pool group within the organization). Management has very little, if any, control over these informal channels (often called the "grapevine"). Information often flows very rapidly through this alternative network. The danger is that the content may be inaccurate, false or malicious.

CRITICAL THINKING QUESTIONS

1. "I purposely gave the students the materials without any specific questions or instructions. I saw the main issues as being the strategic decision as to what business the company should be in. The teams each submitted a written report and then made a thirty minute PowerPoint presentation. The three representatives from the company were quite impressed with the feedback. However, I was somewhat disappointed. All the teams focused on what I would call "operational" issues. None of them really tackled the underlying strategic issue." What went wrong with this communication? How could the communications process have been improved?

_____

_____

_____

2. "I look like a loaf of Wonder bread." The speaker was Brandon Smith and he was covered from head to foot with a mixture of red ink, blue paint and yellow egg yolks. "I guess an open meeting wasn't the best way of announcing that we are moving all production to Taiwan and are going to terminate one third of the workforce." The announcement followed an in-depth study by the board of directors working with a major consulting firm. The conclusion was that the company had to cut its costs to survive. Mr. Smith had explained the process to the gathered workers and then summarized the results of the study. However, when he announced the plants closings, he was pelted by the workers ... and forced to leave the stage. What went wrong here? Why do you think the reaction of the workers was so violent?—They also trashed his new BMW. And what could he have done to ensure a calmer environment?

_____

_____

_____

3. When one thinks of "noise," it is easy enough to think of it in terms of verbal communications (i.e., things that interfere with the reception of a verbal communication). However, consider the concept in terms of written communications. What type of noise could have an impact on an individual reading a three page letter? Or, at the other end of the spectrum, a three line advertisement in the local paper for a night shift foreman?

_____

_____

_____

4. Due to drought and famine, mothers in Central Africa often have problems breast feeding their babies and, as a result, many die of malnutrition. So, a major international corporation introduced a new line of baby formula to supplement their natural milk. The can stated that the milk should not be diluted and aid workers reinforced this point. However, in order to make the milk go further, mothers mixed the formula with water from the local river. Unfortunately, the river water was polluted from discharges up stream and thus contained cholera and typhoid. The babies, weakened by the diluted formula, died from these

diseases. What mistakes did the company make in terms of the communications process with respect to this product? What could/should the company have done to ensure that the product was used appropriately?

_____

_____

_____

5. "How did that guy get through the screening process?" the president of Northern Ohio Realty asked the consultant. They were interviewing candidates for the position of Director of Development. Compensation was in the $150,000 range with substantial benefits and upside potential. The consultant had screened each candidate ending up with an hour long telephone interview. On the phone, Candidate #5 (who came from California) sounded very sharp, knowledgeable, and excited by the opportunity. The company paid for his flight and transportation to the best hotel in the area. His appointment was for 9:00 a.m. and he eventually walked in about 10:15. He was wearing an open shirt, shorts and flip-flops (no socks). When asked to explain his ideas on project development, he spoke so quietly and slowly that the consultant (and others) became irritated with him. By noon, the candidate was on his way back to the hotel. He was not offered lunch. What happened here? Where did the communications process fall apart? How do you explain the candidate's behavior?

_____

_____

_____

6. Midland County Bank had received a bid from Western Banking Co. for the acquisition of their twenty-two branches. The two banking systems overlapped and, if Western could combine the deposit in their locations and eliminate the management and staff personnel that were no longer needed, they could enjoy substantial cost savings. While the formal announcement of the takeover occurred in August, rumors of the takeover had been circulating since late June. When Western's management sat down with the people at Midland to discuss which individuals should be offered positions with the combined company, they were dismayed to find that most of the better people (especially those in two key expansion departments) had already left or submitted their resignations. Were these departures inevitable? Could Western/Midland have taken steps to avoid this exodus? How would you have handled this acquisition if you were a senior manager for either of the banks?

_____

_____

_____

7. Can you think of any situations where it would be advantageous to "leak" an announcement of an organizational change (by hinting at the change in a conversation with somebody who was certain to pass it on) than to wait until one was in a position to make a formal announcement of the change? What are the risks inherent in doing this?

_____

_____

_____

CASE
PROBLEM

MIKE WELCOME—COMMUNICATIONS ISSUES

Mike Welcome looked down at his list of problems; each of which involved making a communications decision.

The first problem involved the West Coast office. On reviewing the records for the last quarter, he had decided to fire two sales people. Unfortunately, he wasn't scheduled to go back there for another seven weeks and the local manager was pressing him for permission to hire two new people ... despite the fact that they were short of office space.

Another problem was the Latin American office. When he had been down there, everybody sat around the conference table and agreed on a new discount schedule. However, it was clear from the last report that they weren't following the rules.

Then, there was the committee meeting scheduled for next Tuesday to discuss a proposed reorganization. The consultant has submitted a thick report and Mike wanted to make sure that (a) everybody knew of the meeting and planned to attend and (b) had read the report.

Finally, he had to decide how to announce the promotion of Kelly Liscombe to department head. He knew it would be a controversial appointment and would cause problems in the office ... especially among the three other strong candidates.

Question: How would you handle the firing of the two sales people in the West Coast office?

_____

_____

_____

_____

Question: How would you handle the promotion of Kelly Liscombe to department head?

_____

_____

_____

_____

Question: What would you do next to ensure that the Latin America office followed the agreed discount schedule?

_____

_____

_____

_____

Question: *How would you make sure that (a) everybody was planning to attend the meeting next Tuesday and (b) had read the report in advance?*

_____

_____

_____

_____

_____

CHAPTER

13

TEAMS AND TEAMWORK

OVERVIEW

All organizations consist of people. However, they function in terms of groups or teams. By definition, a team is:

> *A group consisting of members who have similar or complementary skills and competencies who work together to achieve a common goal or objective.*

In recent years, organizations have placed a growing emphasis on the importance of the use of teams and teamwork. Corporate recruiters are invariably interested to learn of a candidate's experience in working in teams and, equally importantly, their feelings about such activities.

In this chapter, we look at the:

- Reasons for the Growing Emphasis on Teams and Teamwork.
- Five Stages of Team Development.
- Characteristics of Effective Teams.
- Different Types of Teams.
- Approaches to Resolving Team Conflicts.

REASONS FOR THE GROWING EMPHASIS ON TEAMS AND TEAMWORK

 Key Points:

1. There have been five main reasons for this change in emphasis:
   - Downsizing.
   - Growth of technology.
   - Complexity of the environment.

- The diversity of the workforce.
- A growing belief in the value of teams and teamwork.

2. Downsizing (i.e., the reduction in the size of the staff and the elimination (often) of management levels in order to reduce their costs and compete in the worldwide marketplace) ... firms no longer have the personnel and the layers of management to which to delegate a project.

> **Example:** "When I first joined this company, we had assistant managers, managers, senior managers, regional managers, senior regional managers, vice presidents, and senior vice presidents. Many of them were little more than "paper shufflers." However, they were available when there was a need for somebody to handle a project. Today, the managers report directly to the vice presidents. All the other layers have been eliminated. 'Lean and mean' is the watchword today. We no longer have people sitting around with time on their hands."

3. Growth of technology ... the usage of the computer, e-mails, Wi-Fi, the cellular phone, etc. have made it much easier for people to communicate. Communications used to have to flow up and down the organizational chart (a slow process). Technology now allows more direct access to the data.

> **Example:** "I remember sitting in a customer's office and he asked me how much they had bought from us during the past 12 months. I said I didn't know but that I'd find out. That evening, I called my boss who said he'd look into it. He passed the enquiry on to his boss, who sent it over to bookkeeping. It took five weeks before I received an answer. Now, I just pull out my lap top, hit a few keys ... and there is the answer. We have so much more information available and we work directly with so many other people."

4. Complexity of the environment ... many of the problems facing a modern organization are extremely complex involving a wide variety of issues.

> **Example:** In 1929, Rexford introduced a new product line that went on to be a major component of their success. The then president went to a trade show where he saw something that sparked a great idea. Back at his office, he did a sketch which he gave to a designer. He then modified the design and gave it to the head of manufacturing. The final product was manufactured and samples were given to the sales force. In 2002, the company made another major, and successful, introduction. The product development team (for this product) consisted of two designers, the vice president of finance, two marketing managers, the head of the sales division, the head of manufacturing, the human resources manager, two attorneys, and the director of product. All worked long hours before the product was ready to be introduced to the marketplace.

5. The diversity of the workforce ... the growing diversity in the workforce (both domestically and globally) has made it critically important that people have the skills to work together in teams.

> **Example:** "We merged last year with one of our major competitors and my department was merged with their corresponding group. So, we went from a department of eight to one of fifteen. They turned out to be very different from us. They had three women ... we had none. They had four African-Americans ... and we had one. They had three Europeans and one Australian. We were all born and raised in the U.S. Their culture was very aggressive while we were relatively laid back. Their perspectives and attitudes were totally different. I was used to these differences both from college and working for another firm. However, some of our people have had serious problems working with the new people. It is a skill you need to have if you are going to be productive in the modern world."

6. A growing belief in the value of teams and teamwork. Because of the previous factors, managements increasingly recognize the advantage of bringing together individuals with different experiences and skills. While these teams can require more direction and coordination, the results are often far better and much more widely accepted than they would have been if the work had been done by one individual.

> **Example:** "There is an old saying that, 'the ideal committee is thee and me ... with thee absent.' And I always used to agree with that. It was easier to do things on one's own. One doesn't have to deal with other people and the problems they cause. However, the study I did regarding the reorganization proved me wrong. After a month on my own, I realized I didn't have the time or the knowledge to get it done. So, I asked the division heads to assign somebody (preferably one of their better people) to work with me. It worked reasonably well. I couldn't have done anything nearly so professional on my own.
>
> **Example:** For many years, Maggie Forlan had been in charge of organizing the holiday celebration at Reichert & Sons. She picked the restaurant, selected the dinner menu, organized the decorations, sent out the invitations, etc. 2003 was a disaster. In her rush to carry out all her responsibilities, she forgot to confirm the restaurant booking. So, at the last moment, she had to frantically search for a new location. Nobody was too happy with the result. So, in 2004, the president suggested to Maggie that she form a team to handle the arrangements. With three others members of the team, she was able to divide up the responsibilities ... and everybody agreed it was the best celebration in years.

CASE
13.1

CAN HE BE A TEAM PLAYER?

KMPB is a large, worldwide consulting firm whose clients are drawn largely from the list of the *Fortune 500.* For much of the past month, a committee within the real estate division has been interviewing candidates for a new tax position working with commercial real estate firms worldwide. The number one candidate for the position is Wilson Arbette.

The committee was split into three groups with regard to Arbette's candidacy. The first group felt that he was the best qualified candidate. This viewpoint was summarized by the following comment: "I was impressed by his knowledge of the subject. I don't think I have ever come across anybody who was so familiar with the relevant laws and tax implications in all the major markets. He would give us tremendous credibility in the field."

A second group, while admitting that he was well qualified was concerned by the fact that Arbette had always worked for himself. "He's been an independent consultant for the last twenty years. He works out of his own home. In fact, when I called him last week, he made a joke about still being in his pajamas. We pride ourselves on our team approach to all assignments. And I'm not at all sure, Arbette will fit in."

The chair of the committee had yet another perspective. "When I interviewed Wilson one-on-one, he was good. Very strong and positive. A couple of you made the same comment. Yet, when we put him through our case exercise, he seemed to flounder. We gave him the Anderman case well in advance along with background information on the five middle level managers. It should have been his group to control and run ... and he didn't. He deferred to others and let the discussion drift. He seemed particularly uncomfortable with Kristy Mariuku and Win Ban Gung. Compare his performance in this exercise with that of Pirelli ... and I'd go with Pirelli."

Question: How important is the ability to work in teams in this situation? Should KMBP hire Wilson Arbette?

Question: Why do you think Arbette did so well in the one-on-one interviews but wasn't impressive in a team situation? Why might he have had problems relating to Kristy Mariuki and Win Ban Gung?

Question: Do you think the capability to work well in teams can be taught? Can KMBP turn Arbette into a first rate team player?

FIVE STAGES OF TEAM DEVELOPMENT

 Key Points:

1. Research suggests that teams go through a series of five (5) distinct stages. These have been called:

   - Forming.
   - Storming.
   - Norming.
   - Performing.
   - Adjourning.

2. In the forming stage, the team comes together and meets for the first time. This meeting provides an opportunity for the members to:

   - Get to know each other.
   - See what sorts of people are on the team.
   - Identify possible sources of authority within the team.
   - Find out what is expected.

   In all probability, not all the members of the team will know each other. Furthermore, not all of them will be equally enthusiastic about being a member of this particular team.

   > **Example:** "I don't know how I came to be assigned to the Taurus Project. It was not something in which I was particularly interested. So, I wasn't wildly excited when I turned up for the first meeting. I was surprised (and pleased) to see that Heather Stockton was there. She's good. The only other person I knew was Eileen Brach, with whom I had worked a couple of time. We sat around for about an hour and a half. We introduced ourselves and what we did. And then a senior vice president explained the details of the projects and discussed what we would be doing. I came away from the meeting with a reasonable degree of enthusiasm. It might be an interesting project."

3. The next step is called "storming." This is the phase when the members of the team express their own views and interests. Disagreements and conflicts can arise during this phase due to different experiences and different perceptions as to the goals of the project. Individuals may see the team as a power struggle and may try to take charge. Others, seeing this, may fight against the authority.

> **Example:** "Unlike the first meeting, which had been extremely pleasant and enjoyable, the second meeting of the team was the exact opposite. While the instructions given to the team had seemed relatively straightforward, team members clearly had very different views on what the team was actually supposed to achieve. There was a lengthy argument over this. And then one of the senior people tried to make and implement a decision. That produced an uproar so very little was achieved. It took two or three more meetings (and the replacement of a couple of team members) before we finally agreed on what we were going to do and who was going to be the leader (at least initially)."

4. Phase three (called "norming") is the phase in which the team begins to agree on how it is going to function. It agrees on the rules and procedures i.e., (the "norms") the team will follow. It determines what will be acceptable behavior. Generally, any conflicts caused during the storming stage get resolved. In effect, things calm down and the team gets ready to focus on the project.

> **Example:** "We agreed what we were going to do and who was going to do that. And then we found ourselves arguing over relatively minor things. Some members wanted to start at 8:30 while others wanted to start at 9:30. Some wanted to limit the meetings to an hour and a half maximum while others felt we should keep going as long as we were being productive. One person wanted to designate somebody to keep and circulate the minutes of the meeting (for reasons of consistency) while most people wanted to rotate the responsibility. The biggest argument was over what we should do if people don't turn up. In the end, we agreed that, if a person missed three meetings, they were no longer part of the team."

5. This fourth phase (called "performing") is the one in which the team focuses on solving the problem which it has been assigned. By now, the members of the team should be familiar with their role and responsibilities and should know what they have to do to achieve the ultimate objectives.

> **Example:** "Once we had defined the rules and procedures, we really started to move ahead. Everybody seemed reasonably enthusiastic and was prepared with their materials at each meeting. Looking back, this was by far the longest phase."

6. The final phase in the stages of team development is "adjourning." The team has completed the task(s) for which it was assembled and is now approaching the point in time when it will disband. This is an important phase because it determines how the member of the team will feel about their involvement. Ideally, the team disbands on a high (i.e., with a positive feeling) rather than a down.

> **Example:** "I was on two teams last year. Both were successful in that they achieved the goals and objectives. However, I have very different feelings about the experiences. The first team held a meeting at which it presented its findings to top management ... and that was it. The meeting just ended. I walked away feeling very flat. The leader of the other team, however, announced that there would be a celebration luncheon the following week at a local restaurant. We all got together. The food was great. A few of us drank too much. And we had a great time. We all left with a warm feeling about the project."

7. The model implies that all teams have to go through these five phases in the sequence indicated. However, while most begin with the forming stage, many do not experience a storming phase. Everybody agrees on what needs to be done and how. Furthermore, the "norming" phase can be very short if everybody rapidly agrees to the rules and behavior that will be adopted. Finally, teams often go through each of these phases a number of times before they finally disband.

> **Example:** "I still remember the Solberg project. We sailed through the first three phases in two meetings. There was virtually no storming and everybody agreed as to how we would operate. About a month into the project, it becomes clear that things aren't working. So, we went back to phase two ('storming') and had four or five meetings before we resolve the basic problems. We replaced some of the team members and it looked as if we were in good shape. Another month passed and we found out that everybody was again dissatisfied with the way the team was working. So, we went back to "storming" again. Four team members walked out at this stage and management decided to start the project all over again. So ... next week, we will be 'forming' again."

CASE 13.2

THE TASK FORCE FROM HELL

In August 2004, the president of the Fireguard Corporation announced the formation of a task force to determine whether or not the manufacturing facilities in the U.S. should be closed down and production moved to the Far East. Over the next few days, people were asked to join the team and the eventual team consisted of senior and middle managers from each of the company's division.

The president attended the first meeting and explained the company's situation and the importance of the decision. When he left, there was absolute silence. Eventually, the most senior manager present suggests that everybody introduce themselves. This led to the observation that "that's a waste of time since everybody knows everybody else." Somebody else then told the speaker to "shut up and sit down" which, in turn, led to a heated discussion ... with the senior manager trying to regain order.

The second meeting didn't achieve much more than the first. It was clear from the start that the task force was divided into three parties. The first, consisting of the manufacturing personnel and their allies, were firmly against moving production overseas since it would mean the loss of more than 400 jobs. The second group, led by the marketing and sales managers, were in favor of the move since it would guarantee them cheaper products. Finally, the third group, consisting largely of staff personnel, were neutral and frustrated by the way the first two groups kept attacking each other.

In preparation for the third meeting, the senior manager formed a sub-group with the objective of identifying the alternative courses of action, the pros and cons of each, and a procedure by which the team could move forward. The chair of the sub-group presented their suggestions at the beginning of the third meeting. This led to complaints by the manufacturing group that the sub-group was stacked against them and that the decision has already been made by the board of directors and thus the team was a total waste of time. This group then packed up its materials and walked out.

Question: Was establishing a task force to investigate and make recommendations a sound move on the part of the president? Or a mistake?

Question: What could the president have done to make the team building process more effective?

Question: What would you have done if you were the senior manager present?

CHARACTERISTICS OF EFFECTIVE TEAMS

 ## Key Points:

1. Studies have shown that a number of key factors impact the effectiveness of teams. Specifically:

   - The right size of the team.
   - The appropriate mix of the personnel.
   - Organizational support for the team's efforts.
   - A belief in the value of the team's activities.
   - A feeling of empowerment.
   - Interdependence among the members of the team.

2. The right size of the team. The ideal size of the team depends, to a large degree, on the nature of the task or challenge. On the one hand, it needs to have enough members to be able to effectively complete its assignment. On the other hand, if the team is too large, it may experience confusion and lack of coordination. There has to be a degree of cohesion among the team members.

   > **Example:** When faced with the question of which schools to close (as a result of declining enrollment due to movements to the suburbs), a local board of education decided to establish a citizen's committee to look into the matter. It appointed fifty people to the committee. "That was far too large," the chairman commented. "Many people attended the initial meeting and were never seen again. Over time, the number of people involved declined so that, in the end, four people did 95% of the work. We went from far too large a team to one that was much too small."

3. The appropriate mix of personnel. If the team consists of bright people who are constructive and willing to work then the team is more likely to be effective. On the other hand, if the team consists of mediocre people who are not particularly constructive then the team is likely to fall short of its goals.

   > **Example:** "One of the problems we face is that we're not getting new products to market fast enough. Some people throughout the company seem to have a knack for speedy innovation. So, I'm going to establish a team consisting of the best people we have. Let's see if they can teach the rest of us how to do it." The resulting team of eight people worked extremely well together. Within months, the team has come up with protocols for rapid innovation. While they came from very different areas of the company, they all brought an awareness of the importance of rapid innovation and a knowledge of how they did.

> **Example:** After a year (and no apparent results), the president of Tabor & Associates disbanded the team looking into ways of increasing customer satisfaction. "I thought they would come up with some ideas but they didn't." One of the members of the team had the answer. "The team consisted of members who had been appointed by their department heads and weren't particularly interested in customer satisfaction. The people who were creative managed to avoid being on the team."

4. A belief in the value of the team's efforts. The effectiveness of a team is often impacted by the degree to which top management (or any sponsor of an activity) is enthusiastic about the potential results. If the team believes that what it is doing is important to the future of the company then it is more probable that it will be effective. If the team sees itself as wasting its time then the results will be of marginal value.

> **Example:** Under pressure from the board of directors, the management of Archer Glass set up a team to investigate alternative technologies. "A total waste of time," a couple of managers commented following the meeting. The team met a number of times but made no progress. Then, a new president was appointed who saw tremendous potential in the adoption of new technologies. His enthusiasm was infectious and members of the team experienced a growing sense that what they were doing was important.

5. Another factor that is important relative to the effectiveness of a team is the organization's support for its efforts. You often hear the phrase, "let me know what you need and I'll make sure you get it." That makes team members feel that top management is fully behind what they are doing.

> **Example:** "This time last year, I was absolutely exhausted. In addition to my regular full time job, I was working on a couple of teams looking into quality issues. I was getting home late and couldn't sleep. It all changed when a senior manager from headquarters came for a visit. He was impressed by what we were doing and amazed by how little support we had. Boy did things change. For the next six months, all the members of the team were relieved of their day-to-day operations. We were given a budget to attend trade shows and visit other firms. And he found us a couple of research assistants from the local university. The productivity of the group sky-rocketed."

6. A feeling of empowerment is also important. A team that is told exactly what to do will, in all probability, do exactly that . . . and nothing more. However, a team that is given overall responsibility for achieving specific goals is likely to be far more effective. Why? Because they are in charge and thus control their own destiny.

> **Example:** Jim Mason was the manager of a fast food franchise. At the end of each shift, he found himself arguing with the staff over the cleanliness of the facility. He would tell them to do this and that . . . and they either ignored him or did it badly. Criticism didn't seem to do any good. Then, during the two weeks he was on vacation, his brother-in-law, Peter, took over the franchise. When he returned, Jim was amazed to find the place spotless. Not only that but the staff really attacked cleaning the place. "What did you do?" he asked his brother-in-law. "Nothing at all," Peter said. "I just told them that they were the cleaning experts . . . and let them do it any way they wanted."

7. Interdependence among the team members also impacts the effectiveness of a team. A team by definition is a group whose members influence one another towards the accomplishment of the organization's objectives. If each member of the team can perform his/her function essentially independent of the others then, in reality, it isn't a team. It is merely a group of individuals functioning in a common space.

> **Example:** "At the first meeting, we divided the design tasks among the team members. Each week, we met for an hour but nothing really came out of these sessions. Then, after about ten weeks, I realized I needed to coordinate with Art on a key feature of the unit. So, he and I got together and then, at the next meeting, we started to reinforce each other. People were surprised by our enthusiasm. The meeting ran much longer than was typical. The next few weeks were completely different. Increasingly, members found that they needed others . . . and, all of a sudden, we were actually functioning as a team."

CASE 13.3

A DEAD END OR A NEW BEGINNING?

The first meeting of the new product development team went well. The atmosphere was friendly and cooperative. Consisting of middle- and upper-management representatives from each of the seven divisions, it seemed to have the makings of an effective team. Ashley Bloom, a regional vice president, took the lead in defining the task and laying out the ground rules. And virtually everybody had one or more ideas or suggestions.

The next few meetings also went well. There was general agreement on how to proceed and Ashley's efforts were generally appreciated by the other members. In early April (two months after the first meeting), the team submitted its first set of recommendations to top management.

By the end of July, the team had not heard anything back with regard to its suggestions and no meetings were held in August. Then in mid-September, the team received a memo indicating that their suggestions were being considered and thanking them for their efforts. At the next meeting, Taylor Rubens (marketing) exploded. "I don't know about you but I think this letter is insulting. We spend all this time on coming up with ideas and all they can say is 'thank you.' My suggestion is that we call it quits."

The team turned to Ashley for her insights. "I agree with Taylor. It is frustrating. However, we all agreed at our first meeting that the company needs to come up with a lot more new products ... and fast. So, I'm reluctant to walk away from the issue. Assuming we keep going, the question is: where do we go from here?"

Graham Stewart (production) agreed with Ashley commenting that, "what we need is an infusion of momentum." To which somebody added the observation that they should see if Wal-Mart was having a special on that this month.

Question: Do you agree with Taylor Rubens' suggestion that the team should be disbanded?

Question: What mistakes do you think top management made in setting up this committee?

Question: What would you do, as Ashley, if you felt that the team should try to continue ... if only because of the importance of the task?

DIFFERENT TYPES OF TEAMS

 Key Points:

1. There are a number of different types of teams ... each of which has specific advantages and disadvantages. Among the more important teams are:

   - Formal organizational groups.
   - Top management teams.
   - Self-managed work teams.
   - Project teams.
   - Cross-functional teams.
   - Virtual teams.

2. Formal organizational groups ... within any organizational structure, there are teams (i.e., groups of individuals) who either have similar skills or have a common ongoing responsibility.

   > **Example:** Initially, Astrol Components' organization was built around a department that handled both sales of the company's products and any post-sales service that was required. However, as the company grew and the products became more complex, the personnel found themselves spending more time supporting clients than selling the product. Management decided, therefore, to split the department into two separate teams (departments) namely: sales and service.
   >
   > **Example:** Each semester, the university's philosophy department received a number of complaints from students with regard to their grades. As a result, the department established a team (i.e., a committee) to handle these complaints. The committee continued from year to year as a permanent feature of the department with the membership changing annually.

3. Top management teams are essentially the same as committees except that membership of the team is limited to the senior personnel within the organization.

   > **Example:** The president of a *Fortune 500* company decided that he needed to get a better handle on the operations of the organization. To do so, he established a top management team (consisting of the senior vice presidents of all the divisions plus the corporate counsel) which met regularly every Monday morning.

4. Self-managed work teams (also called self-directed work teams, semi-autonomous teams, and production work teams) represent a growing trend in corporations today. The approach represents an expansion of the concept of empowerment (i.e., the process by which managers share power with group members). These formally recognized groups differ from committees in that they work together on an ongoing, day-to-day basis ... and they differ from departments in that they are responsible for a specific process or segment of the operation.

> **Example:** Kasse Motors established a production line for its new prestige brand of automobiles. While the brand received generally good reviews, a number of complaints were received with regard to its stability at high speeds. To focus on this problem, Kasse's management set up a self-managed work team. The team functioned independently of the overall production line and the members shared the management and leadership functions.

5. Project teams (sometimes called a task force) are groups of individuals brought together to work on a specific assignment. The unique feature of these teams is that, when the assignment is completed, they are normally disbanded.

> **Example:** In preparation for the construction of a new high rise office building, Hislop Construction established a project team consisting of the managers representing each of the major areas (i.e., structural, electrical, air conditioning and heating, plumbing, landscaping, etc.). As soon as the project was completed (i.e., had been turned over to the owner), the team was closed out and its members assigned to other projects being handled by the company.

6. Cross-functional teams are similar to project teams in that they consist of individuals (often at the same level of the organization) who come from very different functional areas (such as manufacturing, finance, marketing, computer science, human resources, etc.). The underlying concept is that, by bringing people from different specialties together, the company can generate a richer body of knowledge and creativity, move ahead more rapidly, and save money.

> **Example:** In the automobile industry, it used to take a number of years for the development of a new model. The process would go through a sequence of steps from design to engineering to production to marketing and, eventually to sales. If the final product did not sell then the process had to be repeated. These days, manufacturers put together "platform teams." These are teams that consist of representatives from each area of the company and thus, if a sales manager has a concern over a specific aspect of a vehicle, he/she can immediately suggest changes.

> **Example:** "I've been a member of a number of cross-functional teams. In general, they are a good idea. However, there is one key requirement, namely: that the members of the team have to be able to communicate effectively. We had a serious problem in the last team I was on because, although we met together regularly and got along well, two of the team members had serious problems communicating. One was from Korea and his English was minimal. And the other suffered from some psychological problem. As a result, the team was nowhere near as effective as it should have been.

7. Virtual teams. As the term suggests, a virtual team is one which exists in cyberspace rather than in the real world (although an actual meeting of the team members is not out of the question). A virtual team conducts almost all of its work through the use of e-mails, groupware, chat rooms, etc. As technology improves, this type of team becomes more prevalent especially in organizations where the members are located worldwide.

> **Example:** Each of Rondan International's operations had its own information technology teams that met every two or three months to discuss change in the industry and evaluate proposals for new programs, data bases, etc. However, top management was concerned that these teams were reinventing the wheel (i.e., that the Indian team had spent a lot of time covering issues that had already been studied by the U.S. team) and not communicating between them. As a result, it set up a virtual team (with representatives from each country) that "met" on-line on a bi-weekly basis.

CASE
13.4

WE DEFINITELY NEED SOME NEW IDEAS

Chetwynd Industries (CI) consisted of fourteen companies (ranging from manufacturing to retailing). Each company operated as a separate entity with its own unique management structure, a separate board of directors, its own legal staff, and its own finance, accounting, and human resource groups. All except one had operations worldwide.

By contrast, the headquarters staff consisted of the three founding partners, two senior accountants, three assistants with MBAs, and two lawyers. The three partners spent 90% of their time traveling from one company to another (accompanied by their assistants) meeting with the management, reviewing plans, laying out strategy, and generally discussing issues of concern.

In January 2005, the partners received an unsolicited offer for the purchase of CI. The offer was a very attractive one and they began negotiations with the potential buyer. From the initial discussions, it rapidly became clear that, if they sold CI, the company would cease to exist as currently structured. The boards of directors would be eliminated, the staff departments could be consolidated and top management at each of the companies would be replaced by a senior vice president. "We believe that this company could be much more profitable if we dramatically downsized the organization and concentrated management in one centralized location," one of the team commented.

While they were appalled by the thought that CI might be dismantled with a substantial number of employees losing their jobs, the partners were impressed by some of the ideas proposed for making the company more profitable. "I think we need to set up some teams to take a look at how we can bring this company together," one of the partners suggested.

Question: What would be the pros and cons of each of the six types of teams mentioned above as a means of exploring ways of integrating the company as a whole?

Question: How many teams would you establish of each type? And who would you assign to each of these teams?

Question: Who would you want to be on one of these teams? And who might see them as a waste of time?

APPROACHES TO RESOLVING TEAM CONFLICTS

 Key Points:

1. Just as in any department or division of an organization, teams experience conflicts arising from differences of attitudes, opinions, objectives, etc. But such conflicts are not necessarily bad. The right amount of conflict can lead to increased:

   ■ Creativity.

   ■ Effort.

   ■ Group cohesion.

   > **Example:** Bob and Roger were arguing over the focus of the company's upcoming advertising campaign. Bob felt it should be targeted to a specific group of users and should emphasize the primary benefit to the customer. Roger believed it was more important that the advertising describe all the features and be aimed at a broader spectrum of customers. The conflict led the two men to work hard to prove that the other was wrong. The net result of this increased effort was a totally new and more creative approach that brought the department together around what they felt was a winning idea.

2. On the other hand, too much conflict can result in:

   ■ Wasted resources.

   ■ Loss of focus on the organization's goals.

   ■ Increased self-interest.

   ■ Medical and health problems.

   > **Example:** "There are two groups in the department who are forever at each others throats. It is a very unhealthy atmosphere. We are not getting the job done (wasted resources). We aren't focusing on the company's long term objectives (loss of focus). There is no team spirit ... everybody is concerned only with their own position (increased self-interest). And I am having serious headaches and an upset stomach (medical and health problems).

3. There are five basic approaches to dealing with conflict:

   ■ Avoidance.

   ■ Forcing.

   ■ Accommodation.

   ■ Compromise.

   ■ "Win-Win."

4. Avoidance ... this strategy doesn't help resolve the problem. However, ignoring it or avoiding getting involved in the conflict does allow one to sleep at night.

> **Example:** "My mother used to say to me, 'just wait until your father gets home' and I would hide and try to avoid him. Now, I know my wife says the same thing to our kids and, quite frankly, I don't want to get home and find myself in the middle of a battle that occurred hours before. I'm quite happy to avoid the whole thing."

5. Forcing ... the conflict is resolved by a person in authority making a decision and then telling others what they will do ... or else.

> **Example:** The R&D Division was generally recognized as being overstaffed and under producing. So, on his first day in his new position, Frank Grillo asked the secretary for a listing of all 24,000 plus researchers ... and he fired every tenth name off the list. Productivity improved.

6. Accommodation ... this is sometimes called "appeasement" ... with one party essentially giving in to the other. While it solves the problem, it doesn't necessarily result in the optimal course of action.

> **Example:** "I think we should hold the meeting in San Francisco. However, if you think we would get a better attendance in Seattle ... go ahead. I am not wild about Seattle at this time of year but ... let's go with your choice."

7. Compromise ... sometimes called "splitting the difference" with the two parties agreeing to adopt a middle ground. Again, this solves the problem but it may not result in the optimal course of action. And neither party may be happy with the outcome.

> **Example:** "You're asking $24,000 for this car and I agree it has low mileage and is in first rate condition. I wasn't planning to go over $20,000 so why don't we settle on $22,000." Neither party is overly happy. One is not getting as much as he/she hoped for and the other is paying more than he/she wanted. But the problem is resolved.

8. "Win-win" ... this involves the parties working together to develop a solution which benefits all parties. This is probably the best solution since both parties walk away feeling they have won.

> **Example:** The union and management had been fighting over the issue of seniority and retraining for months without success. Management wanted to train only the younger employees (who would be with the company for many years) and the unions wanted training to be given first to the senior personnel (so that their position was not undermined). The two parties brought in an outside negotiator who focused on identifying the essential requirements of the two parties and then proposed a solution that would leave them both satisfied with the outcome.

CASE 13.5

SHALL I SHOOT MYSELF NOW OR LATER?

"I get to my office about seven o'clock every morning. I'm arriving earlier and earlier in order to get some work done before the other members of the department arrive and stand in a line outside my door. Furthermore, the phone doesn't normally start ringing until 8:30."

As head of engineering, Lea Prosudki, spent most of her day handling problems and trying to resolve conflicts. "The stress is killing me. I find myself snapping at my secretary, at the guy at the local deli, and at my husband when I get home. There are times when I think it would be simpler to just shoot myself."

"I attended a seminar on conflict resolution earlier this year but still haven't really been able to put what I learned into practice. I like the idea of ignoring the various conflicts that swirl around me. However, doing so will be bad for morale. I'm supposed to be the head of this department not a by-stander. I've also thought of simply telling the two parties to get out of my office and resolve their own problems. The problem with that approach is that there is a danger that they will go and do something stupid. The idea of telling them what to do doesn't appeal to me. After all, I'm supposed to be training these people to be managers. And playing the autocrat isn't going to help them develop."

"Another option is to look at both sides of the issue and come up with a compromise somewhere in the middle. However, if people realize that is all I am doing then, I lose control. And, in any case, I am paid for implementing the best solution not the easiest to implement. So, that leaves me the collaborative approach. I can work with the various parties to identify the actual problem and can then help develop alternatives, and then see if we can identify the best solution. Unfortunately, that's a time-consuming process and time is the one thing I don't have at the moment."

Question: Which of the five basic strategies do you think Lea should adopt for handling the conflicts that arise in her department?

Question: Do you think there is a single approach she can take? Or should she vary her conflict resolution approach according to the situation?

Question: What do you think of the idea of stepping back from a conflict and focusing on identifying the actual problem before moving on to developing alternatives and solutions?

SUMMARY

1. The ability to function as a member of a team has become increasingly important and valued in recent years. There are five main reasons for this:

   - Downsizing ... organizations no longer have the people available to take on tasks on their own.

   - Growth of technology ... making it far easier for individuals to communicate.

   - Complexity of the environment ... problems need people with different skills and experiences.

   - Diversity of the workforce.

   - A growing belief that a team can be more effective than an individual ... corporations have seen the advantage of cooperation and coordination among individuals.

2. Teams go through a series of five stages that have been given the following (rather cute) names:

   - Forming ... the members of the team get to know each other and learn about the project.

   - Storming ... different members of the team have widely varying views as to what should be done and how it should be done ... so you can have disagreements and conflicts.

   - Norming ... by this stage the team has overcome its disagreements and is defining the rules and procedures by which it will function.

   - Performing ... this is the stage when the team focuses on the conduct and completion of the project.

   - Adjourning ... the team has completed its task and, in this phase, begins to disband with team members going on to other projects.

3. Not all teams go through all of these stages. There is always a "forming" stage. However, if there is general agreement on the project, the team will rapidly move on to "norming" and "performing." Many projects have no formal "adjourning" phase although this can be critically important for both the client and the team members. Some teams don't progress past the "storming" phase while others go through a number of "storming" phases as they try to gain control of the project and ensure that it is successful.

4. Effective teams tend to be those which:

   - Are the right size ... not too small but overwhelmingly large.

   - Have the appropriate mix of people and skills ... they have the tools to get the job done.

   - Are strongly supported by the organization's management ... management is 100% behind the team and provides the personnel, financial, and emotional support that it needs.

   - Believe in the importance of the task ... the team members are convinced that what the team is trying to achieve is important to the organization and its employees.

   - Is given the authority to do the job ... management has empowered the team.

   - Requires that team members work together effectively to achieve the ultimate objective ... by definition a team is a group of individuals working together to achieve a common goal.

The existence of all these factors does not guarantee that the team will be effective. However, it does greatly increase the probability that it will.

5. There are a number of very different types of teams ... each with its specific advantages and disadvantages. Six of the more commonly used teams are:

- Formal organizational teams such as departments and committees ... these are groups of individuals working together on a permanent (or semi-permanent) basis.

- Top management teams ... these teams are similar to the formal organization except that they are made up of senior management personnel.

- Self-managed teams ... teams that are given a specific task and essentially given total control over its own operation and management.

- Project teams ... teams established to conduct and complete a specific project. As soon as the project is complete, the team is normally disbanded.

- Cross-functional teams ... teams consisting of individuals (often of the same level) from very different parts of the organization with very different functional skills.

- Virtual teams ... these are teams that function in cyberspace. They interact primarily through e-mails, groupware, chat rooms, etc.

6. Conflict. There are both advantages and disadvantages with regard to conflict within teams. While conflict can enhance creativity, the level of effort, and the group cohesion, too much conflict (or where the conflict becomes too intense) can cause the team to perform poorly and thus waste resources, lose sight of its goals, cause individuals to focus on their own interests and agenda (rather than on those of the team as a whole) and, in some cases, can cause team members to suffer from medical and health problems.

7. Individuals have their own points of view, their own attitudes, their own goals and objectives so it is inevitable that conflicts arise. This is especially true when dealing with teams since the individuals are brought together with a common objective. As a manager, there are five fundamental ways of dealing with such conflicts:

- Avoidance ... don't get mixed up with the conflict (not always a practical solution if you are in charge of the team).

- Forcing ... tell the team members to "shut up and do what you say."

- Accommodation ... persuading one party to give way to the other.

- Compromise ... finding some middle ground that will satisfy both parties without necessarily satisfying either.

- "Win-win" ... identify a solution that will ensure that both parties are satisfied and feel that they have gained from the decision.

CRITICAL THINKING QUESTIONS

1. Organizations have been increasingly enthusiastic about the use of teams and the concept of teamwork. If you were asked to give a short presentation on the disadvantages of using teams, what points would you emphasize?

   _____

   _____

   _____

   _____

2. What do you think happens to the level of enthusiasm of team members as it goes through each of the five stages of team development? Assuming that "high" means a high level of enthusiasm and "low" means the opposite, what would the diagram look like? How would this curve compare with the level of work performance (i.e., achieving the goals sets for the team)?

   _____

   _____

   _____

   _____

3. "Welcome to the team," somebody says to you ... and you take your place at the end of the table. This is the second meeting of a team established to propose changes to the company's policies and procedures manual. Your boss, the head of marketing, had planned to be on this team but, due to problems with one of the foreign operations, he has asked you to take his place. You sit quietly and observe the team and the way it is functioning. What factors might give you a sense of whether or not this team will be successful?

   _____

   _____

   _____

   _____

4. "Here is the assignment, ladies and gentlemen. I had intended to have Dick Allward (the executive vice president) chair this team. And I am sure he would have done a good job laying out a plan of action and assigning roles to each of you. Then, he broke his leg skiing and I decided that, rather than finding somebody else, I would leave it up to you." The president took a deep breath. "So, it is up to you. Make up your own minds as to how you want to organize and handle the project. Looking around the table, I see one or two intelligent people here. In any case, if there is anything I can do to help, let me know and I will provide all the resources within my ability." What do you think are the pros and cons of the president's decision to set this group up as a self-managed team as opposed to a project team led by the executive vice president?

   _____

   _____

   _____

   _____

5. Archer and Company, an American company headquartered in Kansas City, built a chemical plant in northern China in 1994. Three years later, under pressure from the Chinese government, administration was turned over to local managers. While the plant functioned reasonably well, the parent company was concerned over the quality of the maintenance programs. So, they sent out an engineering team from Kansas City which spent six weeks trying to improve the level of maintenance. The results were disappointing. The next year, a second team (this time from Houston) visited the plant with the same results. Then, in 2000, management sent out yet another team. This time the team consisted of representatives from various divisions other than engineering and none of the members of the team were American. This time, the team was extremely successful in upgrading the quality of the maintenance program. Why do you think this third team was so much more successful than the first two?

_____

_____

_____

_____

6. "One of the decisions made at the last board meeting was that we need to move toward uniform standards worldwide. I'd like you to set up a team with your counterparts worldwide and work on ensuring that our hiring and firing procedures are the same in every country in which we operate. If there are differences then we should support them by reference to local laws." You, as head of human resources for North America, have had some experience ensuring that policies and procedures are comparable in the U.S., Canada and Mexico. Now, you need to integrate that document with similar materials from twenty-three additional countries. That clearly means that it is going to be a virtual team and all work and interactions will have to be handled electronically. What special problems do you think you will experience in setting up this worldwide, virtual team?

_____

_____

_____

_____

7. "Moving on to the next item on the agenda ... establishing a worldwide price for Endophil. It currently sells for $125 per 100 tablets in the U.S. and for $55 in Canada. The people in Paris want us to introduce it there at the equivalent of $100. However, the German think that is way too low and want to set the price at $195. And when we go into Britain later this year, we are considering pricing it at $75 per 100 tablets. Now, I know you all feel passionately about this issue. And I understand why. I have heard your arguments. However, I have been asked to develop a standardized approach." Here you have five parties that are in conflict and your job is to resolve the conflict. What steps would you take to defuse the situation and resolve the conflict?

_____

_____

_____

_____

CASE
PROBLEM

THE FIRST MEETING

"Now we're all here, let's get started." The speaker was George Katlin (the head of engineering) and the most senior person present. "You all received the president's memo pointing out that we need to improve our overall profitability and that he wants us to look at ways of cutting costs. That's not going to be easy. We went through a major cost cutting three or four years back and cut out a lot of the fat. However, if we don't get back to profitability very soon we are going to the target for a takeover. And none of us want to face that possibility. So, who would like to start us off here? Andrew, will you take notes? Andrew Fisher (a marketing intern) agreed to do so."

"Don't everybody speak at once," George said with a smile after a rather embarrassing period of silence. Alan Goedler (a supervisor in the manufacturing department) then spoke up. "I think you should give us some direction, George. You've been with the company longer than anybody else." Others, including Thomasine Walker (head of the advertising department), Paxton Brown (a salesperson in the local region), Rodger Levine (the senior vice president for operations) and Bryan Gustafson (a lawyer with the firm's outside counsel), nodded their heads in agreement with this suggestion.

When George didn't pick up on this opportunity to take the lead, Clay Henderson (head of the accounting department) jumped in. "I think we should start with the financial data for the past four years for each department and see where costs have gone up since the last cost cutting venture." "Are you going to give us that data?" Marla Scott (the number two in the design department) asked. She, like others in the room, had little time for Clay. She thought he was an uncooperative and unpleasant individual with whom she had had many fights over the years.

"I don't think we should start by focusing on the departments. Let's first determine how much the company has to reduce its expenses in order to generate an acceptable level of profitability. Then, each of us can suggest ways in which that reduction might be achieved." The last person to participate was Prabhaker Kundra who had recently joined the company as an assistant to the president responsible for strategic planning.

Question: *How would you characterize the stage of development of this particular team?*

_____

_____

_____

_____

Question: *What, if any, mistakes have already been made in assembling this particular team?*

_____

_____

_____

_____

Question: *Assuming that the meeting ended without any real progress (other than scheduling another meeting for the following week), what would you do if you were (a) George Katlin, (b) Prabhaker Kundra, and (c) Paxton Brown?*

_____

_____

_____

_____

CONTROLLING— FINANCES

CHAPTER 14

OVERVIEW

The fourth and final function of a manager involves controlling the operation. In a business sense, "controlling" means:

> *The comparison of actual performance to predetermined goals and objectives to see whether the organization is on track and whether changes need to be made.*

Controlling is sometimes considered as the terminal managerial function (i.e., it comes after planning, organizing, and leading). However, more realistically, it can be considered as an integrating function which feeds back to planning, organizing, and leading.

In this chapter, we focus on:

- The financial control function.
- Budgets and budgetary controls.
- Key financial ratios.
- Managing cash flow.
- Activity-based costing.

THE FINANCIAL CONTROL FUNCTION

 Key Points:

1. The key to any financial control system (and this is equally true if you are dealing with people or production) are the answers to three key questions:

   - Where do we want to be?
   - Where are we now relative to where we want to be?
   - What can/should we now do to bring us to the point where we want to be?

295

In order to answer these three questions, a manager needs to:

- Establish appropriate financial standards.
- Measure the actual performance in dollars and cents.
- Compare actual performance to the established financial standards.
- Take corrective action.

> **Example:** The Henderson family went on vacation to Disney World. Having pre-paid the air fare and the hotel, all they needed to cover were their daily expenses and, for these, Mr. Henderson has brought $2,400 ... equivalent to $300 per day. At the end of day four, he counted his money and found he only had $800 left. The vacation was proving to be more expensive than he had anticipated. After a lengthy discussion, the family agreed that the best way to get back on track was to limit their expenditures to $150 for the next couple of days.

2. *Establish appropriate financial standards* ... these are units of measurement against which the actual performance will be compared. They can be total revenues, sales of a specific product, profitability, margins (i.e., profitability as a percentage of sales), return on investment, etc.

> **Example:** The new VB line was ready for introduction and the chief executive officer was discussing the goal for the coming year. "I'd like to see us generate sales of $2.1 million. Is that realistic?" The division manager shook his head. "That's equal to 42 units. And we estimate that the total market last year was between 120 and 140 units. So, in our first year of operations, we would need to obtain more than 30% of the market. So, no ... I don't think it is an appropriate or realistic standard."
>
> **Example:** When Andy Parsons graduated from college, he had a single goal in mind. As he explained to his friends, "I want to be fantastically wealthy." Asked what he meant by being 'fantastically wealthy,' he replied, "I want to have a million dollars in a bank account by the time I'm thirty." "Will you feel that you are a failure if you only have half a million in the account?" Andy thought for a moment and finally laughed. "No. Even $250,000 would be fine."

3. *Measure the actual performance* ... this is the step that answers the question: where are we now?

> **Example:** "According to this printout, there are 126 stores carrying our line. Between them, they sold $1.4 million of our items last month."
>
> **Example:** "We sold 8 copiers last month for a total revenue of $15,000." Our sales of paper, toner, and maintenance services generated another $18,000."

4. *Compare the actual performance with the standard* ... this is the step that brings together the standard and the actual performance and determines the deviation from the plan or standard.

> **Example:** It was Friday, December 17, and the Christmas tree lot on the corner of Albert and Conway still had more than two thousand trees unsold out of an original delivery of 3,800. "No, I am not concerned," the owner commented. We've had this site for a number of years now and know when people buy. The trees will start moving tomorrow. Now, if you come back Sunday night and I still have 1,500 left ... then I will start to worry."
>
> **Example:** "We projected that our dealers would sell 28,000 units during the first quarter generating total revenues of between $780 million and $800 million. In actual fact, total sales were less than 26,000 and total revenues were only $690 million."

5. *Take corrective action* ... the knowledge of where you stand financially relative to where you wanted to be enables you to take corrective action.

> **Example:** "We had expected to see sales increase dramatically in October when temperatures begin to fall. This year, they have stayed flat. Revenue in October was down 20% on last year so we have decided to run a major advertising campaign starting next week."
>
> **Example:** "Last quarter the company lost approximately $200,000 and the projection for the coming quarter doesn't look any better. So, we had to cut back. We let a couple of employees go and also cut back on travel expenses and attendance at conferences. Hopefully, that will bring us back into the black for this quarter."

CASE 14.1

THE R&D DEPARTMENT

"I say, let's get rid of all the people and cut our losses. We're wasting money having a research and development (R&D) operation." The fate of the R&D Department at Osceola Chemicals was the subject of the discussion and the speaker was Graham Sundell, the chief financial officer. "That department costs us $11.6 million last year and what did we get from it. Nothing. My vote is to get rid of it."

"I think you are being unfair," Martine Croxall, head of the sales division commented. "You are trying to measure an R&D activity in terms of dollar and cents. And I don't think that's appropriate. Their function is to develop new uses for our raw materials and to resolve problems encountered by our customers. And I think they are doing a good job."

"That's my whole point, Martine," Graham replied. "Are they doing a good job? Are we getting value for our $11.6 million? Our stockholders want us to use their money wisely and some of them think that this is a large chunk of change that is going down a rat hole."

At this point in time, Victor Olyrenko, the president, jumped into the discussion. "What about the development of the low temperature cement that they developed last year? That was a major breakthrough. And what about all the work they did for Resin Industries. RI thought the reformulation was a dramatic improvement. So, I don't think you can say they did nothing."

"Well, maybe nothing was the wrong word," Graham responded. "However, the fact remains that we are still waiting to make our first sale of the low temperature cement. And the people at RI haven't shown their appreciation yet by increasing their purchases from us."

Question: Is there an appropriate financial measure for the success or failure of an R&D operation such as the one at Osceola Chemicals?

Question: While the expenses associated with the R&D department are relatively easy to determine, how would you measure the "revenue" generated by this department?

Question: What time frame should one use to measure the value (or otherwise) for an R&D operation?

BUDGETS AND BUDGETARY CONTROL

 ## Key Points:

1. A budget is defined as:

> *A financial plan for a specific period of time that indicates how funds will be obtained and how they will be spent.*

Example: Louisa shared an apartment in New York City and, on January 1, sat down to prepare a monthly budget. "Assuming that I continue to work for Grace & Co., I will receive $1,450 per month after taxes, health insurance, and other deductions. My share of the rent is $800 and half the bill for gas and electricity is $120. My phone costs $55 per month. And the cat costs another $25 per month. So, that will leave me $450 for meals, clothing and entertainment. What I need is a rich boyfriend."

2. Two of the more typical financial budgets are the:

- Revenue and expense budget ... this represents a forecast of the company's projected revenues and expenses.
- Capital expenditure ... this is an estimate of expenditures on new equipment and buildings (i.e., capital items that need to be depreciated rather than expensed).

Example: "We are preparing a revenue and expense budget for the coming year. Now, we estimate our revenues will be $180,000 and the cost of goods sold at $80,000. That gives us a gross profit of $100,000. Salaries are estimated at $50,000. We will have to pay for rent on this building and utilities so that's another $20,000. I allow $1,000 for miscellaneous expenses. And maintenance on the equipment will probably be another $3,000. That gives us a net income before taxes of $26,000 ... and, allowing for taxes of 40%, our net income should be $15,600.

Example: "We need to build an extension on to this building. The best quote so far is $2 million. Breaking that down on a quarterly basis over two years means that we have to pay out $250,000 each quarter. Approximately $75,000 of that money will come from the reinvestment of profits from current operations and $50,000 for additional investments from the partners. Another $60,000 will come in the form of a loan from our bank. That just leaves us short $65,000 per quarter. Before we begin the construction, we need to know where that is coming from!!"

3. A budget is of little value unless actual financial performance is measured on a regular (i.e., weekly, monthly, or quarterly) basis . . . and compared with the expected values.

Example: "The budget for travel for this division for this year is $360,000. However, we hadn't allowed for two new and important conferences—one in Hong Kong and the other in Paris—that were held this year. We hadn't planned to attend and then decided that we really needed to be there. So, while our budget projected travel expenses of $170,000 in the first six months (and $190,000 in the second six months), we have already spent $245,000. That leaves us with only $115,000 for travel in the second half of the year. We're going to have to tighten our travel belts."

Example: The management team of a German manufacturer sat reviewing the financial data for the first six months of the year. "You can see the problem," the chief financial officer explained. "Worldwide sales are exactly as projected. And the cost of goods sold and the operating expenses are very close to budget. The problem is the weakness of the U.S. dollar. When we prepared this budget, the exchange rate between the dollar and the euro was close to 1:1. It is now 1.25 dollars to the euro. That means that, while our sales in the United States are on budget, the number of euro we are receiving is considerably less than expected. When we did the budget, we assumed $125 million would be equivalent to 125 million euros. But now it is only worth 100 million euros."

CASE 14.2

THE MAGIC OF THE ORIENT

Grace and Lyle Prothero have been talking about opening a small store selling imported furniture and other items for some time and, with Lyle's retirement, they now had the time to devote to the concept. Since neither of them had any real business experience, they were visiting the local Small Business Development Center (SBDC) location to talk with one of the consultants.

"We've registered the name "The Magic of the Orient" and have identified a location for the store in the Waterville Center" Lyle explained. "Also, we've arranged with a firm based in Hong Kong to provide us with our initial inventory. We are thinking of a store similar to Pier 1. Now, we are trying to put together a budget for the first year."

Following are some notes made by the consultant:

- Store ... 3,200 square feet (of which 1,400 can be used as storage).
- Rent—$4,800 per month.
- Gas and electricity ... projected to be $1,000 per month.
- Renovations to space (at tenant's expense) ... $9,000
- Inventory ... $200,000 (a bank loan backed by a mortgage on the Prothero's home).
- Salaries ... estimated at $800 per month.
- Signage ... $3,000.
- Advertising/promotion ... $5,000 in month one and then $1,000 per month.
- Insurance ... estimated at $800 per month.

"The realtor wants us to sign a three year contract starting on March 1," Lyle explained. "If we do so then, we can have the renovations completed in March and arrange for the inventory to arrive in mid-April. That would allow us to open the store on May 1."

Question: What other major expense items should Grace and Lyle include in their initial budget? What have they overlooked?

Question: What will Grace and Lyle's actual expenses be in March? April? May?

Question: What can you say about when the expenses will have to be paid? And when the revenue will come in?

FINANCIAL RATIOS

⌁ **Key Points:**

1. There are four (4) main categories of financial ratios that a manager can use to measure the "health" or otherwise of the organization:

   - Liquidity ratios ... these focus on how solvent the company is in the short-term (i.e., how able is it to pay its bills).

   - Leverage ratio ... the ratio between the equity that the founders put into the company (equity) and the amount of money they have borrowed (debt).

   - Profitability ratios ... how profitable is the company (i.e., how effectively it is using its assets).

   - Activity ratio ... the turnover of inventory or the efficiency of inventory management.

2. *Liquidity ratios* ... these compare what the organization has (i.e., its assets) against what it has to pay out (its debts). In general, the higher the ratio the better. The two measures most often used are the current ratio and the acid test.

   The current ratio compares the company's current assets (as defined on the balance sheet) with its current liabilities.

   > **Example:** "We ended the year with approximately $22 million in current assets. Our current liabilities were $16 million. So, if our creditors (vendors, etc.) had come to us and said, "pay up," we would have been able to do so ... with $6 million left over. Our current ratio as of December 31 was 1.38 (22 ÷ 16 = 1.38)."

   By contrast, the acid test ratio takes into account the fact that not all a company's assets can be realized immediately for their full value. So, the acid ratio (or test) compares the cash that the company has and the cash it could rapidly generate with the current debts.

   > **Example:** "While our current ratio is 1.38, the acid ratio shows that we are in a rather less favorable picture. Of the $22 million, only about $9 million is actually in cash or could be rapidly converted into cash. If our creditors said "pay up," we would only be able to cover slightly more than half of it (an acid ratio of only 0.56 (9 ÷ 16 = 0.56))."

3. *Leverage ratios* ... the primary ratio in this area is the one between the debt taken on by the company and its equity (i.e., the money put into the company by its owners and investors).

   The differences between these two sources of funding are that investors put in money with the hope and expectation that the company will grow in value over time. Somebody lending money to a company does so in the expectation that they will be paid interest on the loan in addition to receiving repayment of the investment. In general, the lower the debt to equity ratio the better.

> **Example:** "I met with the manager of the local bank last week. We need to purchase a new piece of equipment and I had all the necessary paperwork showing how cost-effective it would be. However, he wouldn't make us the loan. He looked at our balance sheet and concluded that our debt to equity ratio was too high. He didn't feel he could get it through the loan committee."

> **Example:** Max Tornquist was facing a key decision. The company needed a further $2 million to enable it to continue to expand. "I can either borrow the money and pay interest on it. A local company will loan us the money at 6% for five years so we would be paying out a little less than $4,000 per month on that. Or I can issue shares to one of my friends who has wanted to invest for some time. That will reduce my ownership from the current 85% down to approximately 58%."

4. *Profitability ratios* ... there are three ratios that managers use on a regular basis. The first two are the:

- Gross profit margin ... the sales minus the cost of goods sold divided by the sales,

and

- Profit margin ... the net income (i.e., the total income minus expenses) divided by the sales.

    The higher the gross profit margin and, more importantly, the profit margin the better.

> **Example:** "Last year, our total sales were $13.3 million. The cost of manufacturing these materials was $6.5 million. So, our gross profit was $6.8 million and our gross profit margin was 6.8 divided by 13.3 or 51.1%. In addition, we had operating expenses (salaries, travel, advertising, etc.) of $5.6 million. So, our net profit margin was 6.8 − 5.6 divided by 13.3 or 9.0%. Not bad!!"

> **Example:** Frencham Industries' sales in 2004 were $243 million. The cost of goods sold was $197 million giving the company a gross profit margin of $46 million or 19.0%. Due to abnormal charges, expenses for the year amounted to $61 million ... and thus the company incurred a loss of $15 million and had a negative profit margin.

The third measure of profitability is the:

- Return on investment or equity ... this is an indicator of how much money the company (or an individual) is earning on the investment.

    And, once again, the higher the ratio the better.

> **Example:** "When my uncle died last year, he left me about a hundred grand and I still haven't decided what to do with it. A friend of mine wants me to invest in his company. He's convinced that he has a product which will take the market by storm. I agree. It looks good. However, I could also put the money into a guaranteed account. The potential return would be much less but it would be much less risky."

> **Example:** "I bought two houses in 1999 paying $240,000 for one and $410,000 for the other. The cheaper of the two proved to be a great investment. It is now worth half a million. The other one has been a disappointment. I've had to put a lot of money into it and it still isn't worth much more than I paid for it."

5. *Activity ratios* … these are the two ratios that managers use to measure the effectiveness of their operation from a financial perspective:

- Inventory turnover … this is the value of the sales divided by the inventory and is an indicator of the efficiency with which the firm is using its inventory.

- Total asset turnover … this is the value of the sales divided by the total assets of the company and is a measure that indicates the efficiency with which the firm is using all its assets.

The higher the ratio the better. However, in those industries which have to have large inventories of expensive items (e.g., a high class jewelry store), the inventory turnover can be quite low.

> **Example:** "Sales last year were $65 million and our cost of goods sold was $48 million. Our inventory varies from month to month but it averages about $6 million. So, we turn over our inventory about eight times per year. That's pretty good in this industry."
>
> **Example:** "The total assets of the company are $150 million broken down into $30 million of equity and retained earnings and $120 million in debt. Last year, revenues were only $180 million so our total asset turnover ratio is only 1.2. That's not very good in this industry. We need to reduce our debt."

CASE
14.3

THE LANDEN JEWELRY STORE

"My brother-in-law has invited me to make an investment in his jewelry store in the Carlsburg Mall. He has sent me an income statement and a balance sheet as of the end of last year. However, I'm not sure how to read the data. How is this business doing?

The income statement was as follows:

Total Revenues	*$685,000*
Cost of goods sold	*375,000*
Operating expenses	
Salaries	246,000
Miscellaneous	93,500
Net income before taxes	*35,500*

The balance sheet—as of December 31, 2004 was:

Current assets		*Current liabilities*	
Cash	$48,500	Accounts payable	$435,500
Accounts receivable	124,000	Notes payable—bank	235,000
Inventory	1,600,000		
Fixed assets			
Furniture/fixtures	195,000	Long-term debt	1,364,500
Total assets	*$2,067,500*	*Total liabilities*	*$2,035,000*
		Equity	*$32,000*

Question: What are the current ratio and the acid test ratio for this company?

Question: How heavily leveraged is the Landen Jewelry Store?

Question: What is the return on the investment for this store?

Question: What additional information would you need to make an evaluation of the "health" of the Landen Jewelry Store?

MANAGING CASH FLOW

🗝️ Key Points:

1. There is a very real and important difference between profitability and cash flow. Profitability is the net profit *generated* during a specific period of time. Cash flow is the actual net cash *received* during that period of time.

> **Example:** Patrick & Lehigh were hired to assist a major financial institution with its strategic plan. "While it was an attractive contract, it caused us some financial problems," Wayne Patrick commented. "The contract called for four payments of $200,000—the first before we started, the second at the end of phase I, the third at the end of phase II, and the fourth at the end of phase III and submission of the final report. The first payment covered most of our initial expenditures but we've only just submitted the billing at the end of phase I. Unfortunately, phase I took much more effort than we had anticipated and bills are coming in well in excess of the money we will receive from the client ... and we may have to wait another 60 to 90 days before they pay that. In the end, the project will be profitable but the cash flow may kill us."
>
> **Example:** "One of our best people sold 24 CP-84 units to a government agency in December of last year and we have their signature on the contract. However, it is now April and we're ready to ship all 24 units. The problem is that they still haven't indicated when they want the first unit delivered so the units are just sitting there on the dock. The problem is that we don't get paid until 90 days after delivery and acceptance by them."

2. From a manager's point of view, both the income and expense statement and the cash flow statement are important tools in controlling the future of the organization. The fact that a company has extensive accounts receivable (i.e., a lot of customers owing them money) may look great on paper. However, the company may go out of business awaiting the arrival of those funds.

> **Example:** "We sold a large plating unit to Aberson Industries. It was delivered and installed and they agreed to make full payment within 90 days. We had done a lot of business with them in past and had always found them to be reliable customers. It didn't work out that way. At the end of sixty days, I called the president to ask when we could expect our money. He said they were experiencing a cash flow problem but would pay as soon as they could. Ninety days went by ... I called again to find they are no longer in business. Now, I am sure we will get our equipment back at some stage but the reality is we are now $2.3 million short."
>
> **Example:** "Whenever the economy is depressed, we run into the same problem. Customer slow down their payment to us. Firms which paid within 5 days start to take thirty days. Firms which took thirty days now take sixty. I understand their position but I have a staff that expects to be paid on Friday. I can't turn around to them and say, 'Sorry folks. I'll try to pay you next week.' As a result, I continuously monitor our cash flow position."

CASE
14.4

ALBRACA PET STORE

In mid-2003, three friends (Alec Taylor, Brad Epstein, and Carter Folkes) decided to open a pet shop in the small town of Mayfield. In preparation of approaching the local bank for a $100,000 line of credit, they prepared a business plan that they showed to a consultant.

The business plan showed revenues of $390,000 for the first 12 months of operations with total expenses of $340,000. "According to the plan, the store should make a profit by the end of the year," Alec explained. The consultant was far less positive on the planned venture than the three partners. "How did you come up with these figures?" he asked

"On the revenue side, we tried to be conservative. We started with sales of $5,000 in month 1, $10,000 in month 2, $15,000 in month 3 ... and so on up to $60,000 by month 12."

"Then, we are estimating that our cost of goods sold will be 50% of the monthly sales. The rent is $4,000 per month and we are estimating the utilities at $1,500 per month. I will be working full-time in the store at a salary of $3,000 per month and Brad and Carter will both receive $1,000 per month."

Question: Would you agree or disagree with the observation that a plan is only as good as the assumption underlying it?

Question: Given the limited data available, how much will the Albraca Pet Store have to borrow in months 1, 2 and 3 to pay its bills?

Question: What happens to the Albraca Pet Store if sales never reach more than $20,000 per month?

ACTIVITY-BASED COSTING

⊙━━ **Key Points:**

1. Activity-based costing is defined as:

> *A process that allocates all applicable costs to the specific product or service being produced.*

As previously indicated, a manager needs to know whether his/her division or department is profitable on a weekly, monthly, or quarterly basis. However, the fact that the division or department is profitable as a whole does not mean that all the elements are profitable. The idea behind activity-based costing is that the manager also needs to know whether or not the production of a particular product or service is generating a profit or a loss.

Example: "When I took over as head of this division, I was impressed by the fact that it had been profitable for many years. However, it seemed to me that we were selling essentially the same product to different industries and, when I asked which of them was the most profitable industry, nobody knew the answer. It tuned out that we were making a substantial profit on one industry, breaking even on the second, and losing our shirt on the third."

Example: At Bricker & Company, land sales were the most important and glamorous part of the business ... and the sales associates were the "stars." They flew back and forth in the company's jet showing clients the potential sites. By contrast, the company's property managers were at the bottom of the hierarchy. *Per se,* this did not worry the property managers. What did make them mad was that the company charged off the cost of the plane to the property management division which only handled properties in the downtown area. As the head of the property management division complained, "The president charges the plane to my division so that the sales division will look good and the associates will make high bonuses. My guess is that, if the company actually allocated expenses according to where they are incurred, my division would be the most profitable."

CASE 14.5

WHERE DO WE MAKE MONEY?

According to its annual report, Prater Template Company generated total revenues of $41.2 million. Cost of goods sold were $27.4 million and other expenses (general and administrative) were $10.8 million resulting in a net profit before taxes of $3.0 million.

The largest of the three divisions was the consumer products division which had sales of $19.7 million and direct costs of $11.4 million. The second largest division was the automotive group which had sales of $14.4 million and cost of goods sold of $9.2 million. The smallest division sold its products to the pool supplies industry. Its sales were $7.1 million with a cost of goods sold of $6.8 million.

Traditionally, the corporate overhead ($10.8 million) was allocated on the basis of the division's sales. As a result, the consumer products division covered 47.8% of the overhead ($5.2 million), the automotive group covered 35.0% of the overhead ($3.8 million) and the pool supplies division covered 17.2% of the overhead ($1.8 million).

"Based on these figures," the president observed, "we should shut down the pool supplies division. We are losing $1.5 million on that operation and making $3.1 million and $1.4 million on the other two. Instead of making a net profit before taxes of $3.0 million, we would make $4.5 million and that would make our stockholders happy."

At this point in time, the head of the pool supplies division jumped in. "The problem with that suggestion is that the allocation of the company's overhead is purely a mathematical calculation based on sales. It doesn't involve any allocation of the expenses (i.e., the corporate overhead) according to the division's usage. I had the company's accountant look at the figures and they estimate that we only benefit from 7.3% of the overhead. The consumer products division should be carrying 74.3% (because that is where top management spends its time and where most of the money is spent on advertising). And the automotive group should carry the remaining 18.4%."

Question: Why does the president's suggestion show a lack of understanding of basic accounting?

Question: Which is the most profitable division given the percentage derived by the company's accountant?

Question: What action, if any, would you take as a result of these activity-based calculations?

SUMMARY

1. Controlling, while often considered the terminal managerial function is actually the function that integrates those that have gone before (i.e., planning, organizing, and leading).

2. All controlling functions answer the same three questions:

   ■ Where do we want to be?

   ■ Where are we now relative to where we want to be?

   ■ What can/should we do now to bring us to the point where we want to be?

3. The four steps in the control of financial issues are:

   ■ Establishing appropriate financial standards.

   ■ Measuring the actual performance in dollar and cents.

   ■ Comparing the actual performance to the established financial standard.

   ■ Taking corrective action.

4. The key tool in financial control is the budget which is a financial plan for a specific period of time that indicates how funds will be spent and how they will be obtained.

5. The two most commonly used budgets are the:

   ■ Revenue and expense budget … this represents a forecast of the company's projected revenues and expenses.

   ■ Capital expenditures … an estimate of expenditures on new equipment and buildings (i.e., capital items that need to be depreciated rather than expensed).

6. In order to be able to determine the "health" (or otherwise) of an organization, one can use a number of financial ratios:

   ■ Liquidity ratios … the current ratio and acid ratio.

   ■ Leverage ratio … the ratio between the equity (the funds contributed by the owners and the business) and the debt (i.e., funds owed to others).

   ■ Profitability ratios … the gross profit margin (the sales minus the cost of goods sold divided by the sales), the profit margin (the total income minus expenses divided by the sales), and the return on equity or investment.

   ■ Activity ratios … inventory turnover and total asset turnover (i.e., the company's sales divided by either its inventory or its total assets).

7. It is important to differentiate between profitability and cash. Profitability is the net profit generated during a specific period. Cash flow is the actual net cash received during this period.

> *Important note:* A company may be doing very well and have large accounts receivable (i.e., funds owed to them) but be in a dire cash flow position. If the money arrived today, it can pay its bills. If it doesn't arrive until next month, the company may be out of business.

8. Activity-based costing is a process that allocates all applicable costs to the specific product or service being produced. The importance of this technique is that it identifies those products and services which are profitable (when carrying a full overhead) and those which are not.

CRITICAL THINKING QUESTIONS

1. It is suggested in this chapter that, rather than being a terminal function, controlling is, in fact, more of an integrating function. What examples can you think of which would show the integration between controlling and planning? Controlling and organizing? And controlling and leading?

   _____

   _____

   _____

   _____

2. Mr. Amos Johnson ran a small store where he sold newspapers, magazines, candies, etc. People used to stop by on their way to and from work. Without question, Uncle Amos was one of the characters of the neighborhood. His accounting system consisted of two boxes. "I put the cash into one box and the bills into the other." Then, once every two weeks, I take out the bills and pay them with the cash. Hopefully, there is still something left in the cash box when I have finished paying the bills." What problems do you see with Uncle Amos' financial control system?

   _____

   _____

   _____

   _____

3. PayTell is a large chain of convenience stores covering five mid-western states. In 1998, the company introduced a bonus program based on a store's annual sales per square foot. The higher the figure per square foot, the greater the bonus. Each year, Max Lombard complained to top management that the system was unfair. "I run a relatively small store in a depressed area of town. I don't have space to inventory many of the higher margin items. Anyway, the people living around here can't afford them. I'm never going to get a bonus irrespective of how well I do." Do you think the financial standard established by top management is appropriate? How would you suggest they change it?

   _____

   _____

   _____

   _____

4. Each year, Lisa Osborne sat down with her staff to prepare a budget for the coming year and, each year, she had the same argument with Charles Findlay, the sales manager for the Western region. The total amount available for advertising was $840,000 and she had proposed $210,000 be allocated to each of the four quarters. "It makes sense to spread the funding throughout the year," she commented. "Then, each quarter, we know where we stand relative to the budget." Charles disagreed. "All the budget does is to encourage people to spend the money in the quarter to which it is allocated. Last year, we spent $200,000 in the third quarter on a program that was a waste of money. And then, in the fourth quarter when I wanted to spend $450,000 on a program that would have had a dramatic impact,

I was told there was no money available!!" What does this say about the value (or otherwise) of budgeting?

_____

_____

_____

_____

5. The owner of Paragon Tool and Die Company, Clint Maier, was talking with a loan officer at the local bank about establishing a line of credit. "There are a couple of things that worry me about your financials," the loan officer observed. You have $17,500 in cash and $126,000 in accounts receivable and your current liabilities are $88,000. That gives you a current ratio of 1.63 which is reasonable. However, your acid test ratio is only 0.20. Secondly, if I divide your gross profit by your total sales for the last two years, the figure has dropped from 0.67 to 0.61. Why would a loan officer be concerned about these two factors? What would they show about the health of Paragon Tool and Die?

_____

_____

_____

_____

6. Maxine Thomson had just returned from a very successful trip to the East Coast where she had called on three potential clients: Vickers-Wright in Boston, Parton & Sons in Norfolk, Virginia, and Lewis-Templeton in Atlanta. Maxine was one of the leading consultants in her field and she worked for herself out of her home. The good news is that Vickers-Wright has signed a contract for work to begin later this year, Lewis-Templeton is 99.9% certain to hire me. And Parton & Sons is a solid "maybe." So, I'm looking at income of not less than $90,000 and, quite possibly, $140,000. The bad news is that I have just returned from a trip that cost me approximately $5,200 and my checking account has $102.50 in it." What fundamental problem is Ms. Thomson facing? And what could she do about it?

_____

_____

_____

_____

7. "Can you give us a better price than $72 on this model?" the purchasing manager asked. Uncertain, the salesman agreed to discuss the situation with the general manager. "Well, it is produced on line 7 along with two other products. So, in addition to the raw material cost of $35.25, we have one third of the line cost ... another $12.45 for a total of $47.70 to which we add 45% ... giving us $69.20 per unit. However, last month, only 10% of the production on line 7 was of this model. So, if we allocated just 10% of the line cost as opposed to 33.3%, we could reduce the line cost to $3.74 for a total cost of $39.00 per unit. Does reducing the price make sense? Or is it merely financial sleight of hand?

_____

_____

_____

_____

CASE PROBLEM

ANSON-RAND SUPPLY CO.

The Anson-Rand Company's main business was metal stampings. They had ten large 20 and 40 ton presses that produced metal washers and small parts (made from various grades of steel) that they sold to half a dozen large customers in the automotive industry. According to Tom Anson, the president, the company enjoyed 80-85% of the worldwide market for these types of stampings.

"When the company first started making stampings for the automobile industry, they were relatively simple," Tom explained. "They went through the machines two or three times and that was it. And quality control wasn't too important. From a management perspective, the important thing was the monthly volume. If we sold 5 million stampings per month, we were profitable. That was our bench mark. Our pricing was based on the raw material costs per unit plus an allocation of the total cost of the factory divided by five million. For years, we were competitive."

Despite having such a large share of the market, Anson-Rand struggled to make a profit. "We face two problems," Tom explained. "First, the nature of the business has changed. Products that used to involve three stampings now require eight or ten ... and they have to be produced to much finer tolerances. Second, our customers are large firms who are under pressure to cut their costs. We say that a stamping will cost 90 cents and they say they will only pay 85 cents. If we don't go along with them then they say they will manufacture the part themselves. So, we are between a rock and a hard place—rising production costs and declining sales prices."

Question: *Does Tom Anson know what it costs to manufacture a particular stamping for his customers?*

_____

_____

_____

_____

Question: *What financial control system would you suggest Anson-Rand Supply Company implement?*

_____

_____

_____

_____

Question: *How should Tom Anson handle the continual pressure from his major automotive customers for price reductions?*

_____

_____

_____

_____

CONTROLLING— PRODUCTION AND PERSONNEL

CHAPTER

15

OVERVIEW

This chapter looks at control as applied to both production and personnel (i.e., the human resources). We begin by focusing on the production aspects:

- The production control function.
- The time element in production control.
- Total quality management (TQM).

Then, we move on to two key aspects of control as it applies to the human resources, namely, maximization of the:

- Productivity of individuals.
- Overall effectiveness of the organization.

THE PRODUCTION CONTROL FUNCTION

Key Points:

1. There are two key elements of a production that need to be controlled:

- Quantity ... the number of units produced during a specific period of time, and
- Quality ... the percentage of these units that meet or surpass the specifications required by the customer.

There is often a trade-off between quantity and quality.

315

> **Example:** "Take this piece of equipment here," Bryan Pickering commented. "At the current rate of production, virtually all the units meet the quality standards. However, if we increase the production rate to the point where it should be to complete the order on time, the quality drops dramatically. It is a serious trade-off."

2. *Quantity* ... the number of units produced in a specified period of time.

> **Example:** "According to the manufacturer, this equipment is rated at 18,000 units per hour. However, we have never managed to produce more than 13,000. So, we talked with the manufacturer and they sent an engineer out to take a look at it. He concluded that the problem was caused by variations in the thickness of the raw materials. So, we are trying to find a better source of supply. If we can't, we will have to lower the standard to 13,000.

> **Example:** "We run three shifts here at Harrison. The day shift produces 120 plus units per shift. The evening shift produces 110 units plus. And the night shift produces 90 to 95 units. So, one of the things we have to do is to study why there are the differences. Do we have better people on the day and evening shift? I don't know. All I know is that there is a difference."

3. *Quality* ... the extent to which the units produced meets or surpass the standards established by the customer.

> **Example:** Avicor is a telephone service company that supports the products for a number of companies. "Customer satisfaction is important in this business. So, at the end of each call, we use a short questionnaire to rate the performance of the representative. An average score of 4.5 or above (out of 5) gives them a "superior" rating. Between 4.0 and 4.49 results in an "above standard" rating. And so on. Our people are required to maintain a rating of at least 3.5."

> **Example:** Harriet Levine purchased a new car. She went for a top of the line model with all the bells and whistles. When asked by the manufacturer to rate the quality of the vehicle, she went to town. "The driver's door doesn't shut ... the rear windshield wiper is broken, and the heater doesn't heat. I'd rank the quality of this car somewhere between 'poor' and 'very poor'."

4. *Important note:* Not too many years back, the emphasis was on quantity. As long as the quality was satisfactory, the product was acceptable. However, due to intense worldwide competition, the quality of the product has become much more important.

Example: For many years the automobile industry produced cars that had serious failings. The power windows didn't work. The turn signals were defective. The car rattled badly. However, while customers complained about these cars, they still bought them because there wasn't anything better. Then, the Japanese companies entered the market. They built cars which worked and didn't rattle. The marketplace changed and quality became increasingly important.

Example: "Look at these washers. The hole in the middle is supposed to be exactly 2.2 mm. I have just measured a hundred of them. Five of them are 2.0 mm or less. I can't use this lot. If I do so, our equipment will jam. So, I am going to have to return them to the manufacturer. They don't seem to know what quality is. The net result is that I am going to have to delay production until they can replace them."

CASE 15.1

BRYANT MANUFACTURING

"Let's move on to the next item on the agenda ... the new line. Does anybody have any comments at this stage?" Bryant Manufacturing's general manager looked around at his management team.

The sales manager, Lyle Tossi, was the first to respond. "In the past, we emphasized the production capacity of new equipment. However, increasingly, our customers are saying that they are seeing products from a couple of the Chinese suppliers that are better quality and cheaper. I know we have somewhat limited financial resources but, whatever system we purchase, I think we need to really emphasize quality."

The discussion then ranged back and forth as to whether Bryant should purchase the Alston-Hall equipment or the rather less expensive Fiedler equipment. When the group voted to go with Fiedler, Lyle Tossi again jumped in with his comment about quality. "It seems to me that we are cutting our own throats. We are focusing on price and speed. In the long run, we need to have the best quality product on the market to be able to compete."

"You're really serious about quality, aren't you?" the head of manufacturing commented with a smile. "Let's say we buy your argument that we need to be producing a top quality product, what steps would you like to see us take? What can we do to make you happy?"

Lyle thought for a moment and then said, "Here's what we should do to make sure that we achieve the required quality standards."

Question: Who determines the acceptability (or otherwise) of a product (i.e., who determines the quality)?

Question: Put yourself in Lyle Tossi's shoes, what steps would you suggest Bryant Manufacturing take before it makes a decision on whether or not to purchase the Aston-Hall or Fiedler equipment?

Question: Ashton-Hall's equipment costs $1.5 million and is guaranteed to generate not more than 3 defects per 100,000 units. By contrast, the Fiedler equipment cost $1.2 million with no more than 5 defects per 100,000. Which equipment would you choose?

THE TIME ELEMENT IN PRODUCTION CONTROL

 ## Key Points:

1. Control of a production line can be conducted at one of three points in time:

   - Preventive control.
   - Concurrent control.
   - Feedback control.

2. *Preventive control* … sometimes called "feedforward control," this is the control implemented before the process or production occurs.

> **Example:** Archer & Company purchased a new technology which promised that it could be used to produce a wide range of organic chemicals. "The technology was just what we needed … and, when we visited the manufacturer's plant, they showed us a 1/10th size facility that worked very well. In the end, the purchase was a disaster. We should have waited until the manufacturer had worked out how to 'scale up' their technology."
>
> **Example:** "A couple of years back, we obtained a large and very important contract with the air force that required the purchase and installation of new equipment. It was a very successful contract. Why? Before we produced the first item for the air force, we did a lot of work. One of the things we did was to establish high quality standards for all purchased parts. We also tested all the stages of the production process and worked out the problems. In fact, it took us longer to get the machinery ready for production than it did to actually produce the product."

3. *Concurrent control* … this is the control applied during the running of the process.

> **Example:** A brewery filling bottles will have both optical and human controls. A bottle only half filled will be removed from the line … as would one with a crack or chipped lip.
>
> **Example:** "We sort our fruit by quality. The goal on this line is to identify the best quality. If there are marks or molds on the fruit, one of the employees will pick it out and toss it into a bin. These rejects aren't thrown out. They will be used for other purposes."

4. *Feedback control* ... this is control following completion of the process.

> **Example:** "The toys come off the production line and fall into a large hopper. Then, when the hopper is full, we take a random sample of five items and test them to make sure that they meet the specifications. We fill up four or five large containers per shift so it means we look at 20 or 25 items per day. We are looking for basic things such as making sure they have eyes and tails."
>
> **Example:** "It is critically important that the thickness of this washer be between 1.25 and 1.50 centimeters. If they are too thin they will not hold the screws tightly enough. If they are too thick, they will jam the customer's machines. So, we pass them under a series of bars which are set to sort out any that do not fall within the range."

5. *Important note:* The earlier one implements control, the better. It is far more cost effective to focus on preventive or feedforward control than on concurrent control. And concurrent control is far better than feedback control.

> **Example:** A major manufacturer of printers emphasized feedback control in that it had a staff of quality control managers who tested each product as it came off the production line. Unfortunately, the resulting quality was very poor. So, they eliminated all but one of the quality control managers and passed responsibility for quality to the assemblers (i.e., they emphasized concurrent control).
>
> **Example:** Gale Henson took his VHS player into the local electronics store and explained that it didn't work. "Can you fix it?" he asked. "Yes," the store owner replied. "But it would be a waste of my time and your money. It will cost you $60 for me to take a look at it and find out what's wrong. It takes longer to pull one of these units apart than it does to build them in the first place. Buy a new one!!"

CASE 15.2

THORSEN COMPUTERS

Thorsen Computers is an assembler of computers. All the parts are manufactured in Taiwan and, because of the rapidly changing nature of the market, the company tries to minimize its local inventory. The parts are stored at one end of a building and then proceed through ten stages before the final product is packaged and shipped. Thorsen's products are sold through its web site and each computer is made to the customer's specifications.

Historically, Thorsen enjoyed a solid reputation. Its products were reliable, included many attractive features, and were highly price competitive. The products were shipped to the customer and, if problems arose, were supported by a small technical staff.

In August 2004, the company began to see an alarming rise in the number of complaints from customers. A number of units wouldn't boot and others would boot but then died. The technical staff concluded that the problem was related to the motherboards used in the PCs built between August 9 and 13. They immediately shipped out replacement boards and, if necessary, Thorsen paid for the cost of the service call to switch the motherboards.

Between January 10 and 14, the company experienced another burst of defective computers (due to a cracked capacitor) ... and, again, the company was forced to provide replacement boards. The head of quality control was asked to leave and was replaced by an individual, Lan Win, with a reputation for never being satisfied with respect to quality.

On his first day in his new position, Lan Win addressed a gathering of all the company's employees. "We are going to go back to basics," he said. "I know most of you are very experienced. However, Thorsen's reputation is on the line and we need to be the best we can. So, we are going to throw out the old quality manual and write a new one."

Question: What quality control procedures would you expect Lan Win to implement with regard to all incoming parts?

Question: What other quality control procedures would you expect Lan Win to implement?

Question: Five out of 940 computers shipped between August 9 and 13 and 7 out of 855 computers shipped between January 10 and 14 were defective. Does the company have a problem that justifies a major revamping of its quality control procedures or are these defects just a minor irritation?

TOTAL QUALITY MANAGEMENT

🗝 **Key Points:**

1. Total Quality Management (TQM) is defined as:

> *A system for improving performance in all areas of a business by encouraging employees to make continuous improvements and maximizing customer satisfaction.*

    In the last twenty years, there has been a growing emphasis on total quality management as a means of competing in the world economy. The key word in the above definition is "continuous." Firms that are committed to TQM are continually seeking better and more effective ways of performing all aspects of its business.

2. The five key elements of a TQM program are:

- Top management commitment ... the strategic commitment to building an organization that is focused on quality.

- Employee involvement ... TQM requires that all employees be committed to the same quality goals.

- Improved materials ... the continued emphasis on identifying and improving the quality of the materials that the organization uses.

- Utilization of cutting edge technologies ... one of the keys to a TQM program is the use of technology.

- Continuous improvement in the methods used by the organization.

Example: "We were being killed by better quality imports at a cheaper price. We either had to compete or go out of business. Management put together a team and made the commitment to support the very real cost of focusing on quality. Then, we had to sell the personnel on the benefits of the approach. We set up quality circles to focus on how everything we did could be done better. The net result is that we are still in business and competing effectively."

Example: The Hawkins Engine Company had focused on quality for a number of years but was still not competitive. In 2004, top management realized that they needed to go outside the company to generate increased savings and quality. "We approached our suppliers and worked with them to ensure that we were using the best materials. We also worked closely with the technology firms to develop new techniques and approaches. It has been expensive but it has been worth it."

---

3. *Important note:* There are a number of key terms associated with TQM:

- *Value-added analysis* ... this is a comprehensive analysis of all work activities, material flows, and paperwork to determine what value they add for customers.

- *Benchmarking* ... this is the process of comparing an organization with one or more of the leading firms in the market in an effort to answer the question: what do they do? And how do they do it?

- *Outsourcing* ... the subcontracting of services and production to other (external) firms that can perform the job either better or more cheaply.

- *ISO 9000 and ISO 14000* ... these are a set of standards created by the Internal Organization for Standardization. ISO 9000 covers areas such as employee training, record keeping, product testing, supplier relations, etc. while ISO 14000 covers environmental performance.

- *Six sigma* ... this is an approach which aims at improving quality and achieving fewer than 3.4 errors per million (the figure is derived from the area under a normal curve) where an error is anything outside a customer's specifications.

Example: "When I first joined the company, our main competition came from other American firms ... located largely in this area. However, now we are competing with firms from all around the world ... especially China that have much lower labor rates. It is tough to compete. So, we started by doing an internal value added analysis. We looked at every aspect of our business. We redesigned our forms. We upgraded the telephone system. We revamped our web site ... anything that could be made more effective."

Example: "We looked at what our competitors do and purchased competitive products and pulled them apart to determine how they were made ... and we changed our manufacturing processes. Finally, in those areas where we couldn't compete, we found foreign suppliers who could manufacture the quality we needed at a price that would make us competitive."

Example: "Quality has become the watchword around here. We didn't take ISO 9000 and ISO 14000 too seriously when the standards were first introduced. Then, our customers started telling us that they were only going to deal with firms that had these certifications. Top management decided we didn't have a choice ... we had to go for it. Now we are certified and are determined to maintain our certification. We are committed to six sigma and continuous improvement."

CASE 15.3

WALKERDEAN EQUIPMENT

"ISO 9001 certification. Thayer down the road is now certified and Pace-Farmhall expects to gain certification within the next six months. So, let's revisit whether or not we should go for it. Bob, I know you're in favor of it."

Bob Henderson, head of marketing, nodded. "I think we have to go for it. Some of our customers are starting to ask whether or not we are certified. And there is a rumor that Otis Industries (one of Walkerdean's main customers) may make it a requirement. I'm sure they will do so at some point in time."

"I disagree," Mike Pannell, head of manufacturing responded. "Our systems work well and we have very few preventable errors. Our quality is improving and the last survey of our customers indicated that they were very satisfied with our performance. I don't see what we would gain."

Simone Valle, head of human resources added. "We still have less than 200 employees and we struggle to manufacture and market our products. Who is going to do all the work? We would have to develop a quality manual, establish measurable quality objectives, design preventive action systems, generate procedure documents, plan and implement quality audits, train our people and ... the list goes on. I don't think we have the people to do the job."

The president thought for a moment. "Certification isn't something we have to achieve overnight. We can take our time. I pulled an action planning checklist off the internet this morning. So, why don't we implement these first four steps and see where we stand:

- Make a senior person responsible for the process and have them trained.
- Form a task force of a cross-section of the company's people.
- Look into the hiring of an advisor.
- Conduct an in-house audit to see where we stand relative to the standards.

Who would like to volunteer to spearhead our ISO certification team?" There was a distinct silence in the room!!

Question: Based on the above information, should Walkerdean Engineering aim to obtain ISO 9001 certification?

Question: What do you think of the president's proposed plan of action?

Question: Who should be responsible for spearheading Walkerdean's efforts in this area?

MAXIMIZING THE PRODUCTIVITY OF INDIVIDUALS

 ## Key Points:

1. The word "control" takes on a rather different meaning when applied to human beings. Unlike finance and production which are inanimate, one is dealing with individuals who, as we saw earlier, have their own personalities, their own goals and objectives, etc.

2. There are two key elements to maximizing the productivity of individuals:

   ■ Observation.
   ■ Performance Appraisal.

3. *Observation* ... the concept of managing by wandering around (sometimes called MBWA) to determine what is actually occurring within the organization. It is a vital managerial activity because it enables the manager to get to know and understand people. Also, as indicated in the section on motivation, people respond when an interest is shown in them.

Example: "I had a call from one of our clients asking, very politely, where his order was. I had to admit I didn't know, so I decided to go down to the shipping dock and find out. After all, we had never had any problems in the past. It turns out that one of the trucks was out of commission and the loading bay was blocked by another order which wasn't due to go out for a couple of days."

Example: "Once every six months, I visit each of the branches. I call it 'showing the flag.' I also learn a lot from these visits. I used to just sit down with the management team. However, I now wander around the store watching what is going on and talking with the employees. All of a sudden, I realized I was getting a very different picture from the one presented by the managers."

Example: Top management of the Revere Group was located on the 26th floor of the Revere Tower. As a result, people on the first three floors rarely saw any of the senior personnel. "They even have their own elevator so that they don't have to ride up and down with the peasants," one employee complained. "They may as well be on the moon. They certainly don't know what is going on down here," observed another.

---

4. *Performance appraisal* ... this is a formal process that enables a manager to evaluate his/her subordinates against specific criteria of importance to the employee's position.

> **Example:** "I evaluate all of my people once a year. It is essentially an open-ended discussion during which we discuss the job they are doing. I like to focus on whether or not they are ready for promotion. Whether or not they need further training and development. And, on occasions, we have to discuss their termination."
>
> **Example:** "My boss criticized me on the way I handle telephone inquiries. Now, I think that was very unfair. First of all, I am not supposed to answer the phone. It is not part of my job description. Second, I have never received any training on how to handle phone calls. Furthermore, he didn't comment on the reports I prepare each month and yet that is what I spend most of my time doing."

5. *Important note:* Managers, as a generalization, do not like doing performance appraisals ... and tend to put off doing them if they can.

> **Example:** "I hate doing performance appraisals ... especially when I know that the employee is likely to be upset and angry. It makes me uncomfortable."
>
> **Example:** "When I joined the company, I was told that I would be on probation for six months and then I would be evaluated by my boss. That was eighteen months ago. I still haven't received an appraisal. I assume I am doing a good job but each time I ask my boss when it is going to be, he says he is too busy."

6. *Important note:* While the evaluation of an employee by his/her boss alone remains the most common form of evaluation, a recent approach called the 360° feedback evaluation has enjoyed growing popularity. In this approach, the individual is evaluated by his/her supervisor, by his/her peers, by the people who report directly to him/her, and by internal and external customers.

> **Example:** "The reason I like this 360° process is that it gives the employee an evaluation by all the people who come in contact with them. And thus it is much more difficult for them to brush off criticism if it comes from multiple sources."
>
> **Example:** "I don't like this new approach. I don't mind being evaluated by my boss and by my internal and external customers. However, I am not too sure my peers know enough about my performance to provide useful feedback. And I feel being evaluated by your subordinates becomes something of a 'beauty contest.' If I say good things about them then they will say good things about me."

CASE 15.4

REWARDING SUPERIOR PERFORMANCE

The Leonard Tool Company employed an outside force of eight that called on existing and potential customers and an in-house sales force of five (located in the main office) which took orders called in by customers.

Traditionally, all employees were paid a salary because the founder, John J. Leonard, did not approve of paying commissions. However, his son, Richard, believed that sales people were more effective if superior performance were rewarded ... and thus had decided to implement an annual performance appraisal program and adjust the compensation system accordingly.

"I'm going to evaluate the outside sales people on two things: their total annual sales and the number of sales calls they make on new customers. The in-house people will be evaluated on the basis of the number of orders they handle each day and the way they deal with their customers. My plan is to reduce their salaries by $500 per month and pay them a commission or bonus based on a quarterly evaluation. My best guess is that most people will either break-even or make more money."

Almost immediately, both groups began to complain about the new system. "I don't like it," Shirley Hauser (outside sales) commented. "It is not fair to compare my sales volume with that of Brian Hicks. He has three large very steady customers in a relatively small geographic area. My territory is three times as large as his and the market is much more competitive. I have to work much harder to make a sale."

Peter Loman (in-house sales) was also upset by the new system. "I have no control over who calls and any one call can take a few minutes or an hour. Also, I don't control the person on the other end. Some are very friendly and some are quite unpleasant. Finally, who is going to evaluate how I deal with my customers? I only see Richard once every couple of weeks. And Ralph, my boss, doesn't have time to do it."

Question: Do you agree with Richard Leonard that a performance appraisal process is needed?

Question: What mistakes did Richard Leonard make in implementing this new evaluation and compensation system?

Question: How would you evaluate the external and internal sales personnel ... and how would you reward them for superior performance?

MAXIMIZING ORGANIZATIONAL EFFECTIVENESS

🗝 Key Points:

1. This is an area that is often overlooked by managers. They have a tendency to accept the organization as it is. However, the key question to be asked in terms of "controlling" the organization as a whole is: does our organization match the needs of the customer?

   Organizations (groups, departments, divisions, etc.) grow over time by the addition and loss of personnel. Often, there is a built-in inertia (i.e., a resistance to change) so that the organization no longer matches the needs of its customers.

2. There are two key types of customers:

   - Internal.
   - External.

3. *Internal customers* . . . these are the members of the organization itself who rely on information, services and support from others within the same organization.

   > **Example:** "If I want to obtain accounting data, I have to call up somebody in that department and ask them to pull the data for me. Some of the people are very good. They will do it while I wait. Others are much less cooperative."

   > **Example:** "We are totally dependent on the service personnel. They are the ones who follow up on the orders and have the close relationships with the actual users of the product. I just call on the purchasing agent. So, if the Service Department doesn't tell us about the problem, I don't know about it."

4. *External customers* . . . those individuals and organizations that purchase from the organization.

   > **Example:** "The reason we buy from Hazletine Industries is that they have a representative who lives a mile or so from our office. If we need something in a rush or have a problem, we call him and he's out here in minutes. Jenson Suppliers, on the other hand, carry a better line of products but their nearest representative is in Chicago."

   > **Example:** Blakeley Scientific has what they call their Ph.D. team. In order to be one of their representatives, you have to have completed a doctorate in a scientific discipline. "Without question, they are the most knowledgeable people in the industry," one customer commented. "However. I joined my father's company immediately after high school . . . and I don't understand them. I prefer to work with the people from Knightley. They aren't as knowledgeable . . . but I understand what they are talking about."

5. Organizational analysis and change ... this is a process by which a manager evaluates whether or not his/her organization is consistent with the needs of both internal and external customers. Again, the process involves:

- Setting standards ... identifying the needs of the customers.
- Measuring actual performance ... determining how well the current organization meets the needs of the customers.
- Comparing the actual performance with the needs and implementing appropriate changes.

Example: Partenza Photo is a web-based firm that supplies cameras and electronics and, as the general manager explained, "When our customers call up to check on the status of their order, they talk to our sales department. At that time, we generally try to sell them additional features as a way of boosting the value of the order. Unfortunately, many customers object to the sales pitch. In fact, a number of them cancel the order altogether."

Example: "When calling on customers, our sales people often come back with ideas for new products or modifications of existing products. They then pass on the idea to the design group which, they complain, very rarely does anything with it. Last month, a combined group sat down to see why the current organization wasn't working. The answer was quite simple. The sales people were merely e-mailing a brief description of the idea. The people in the design group wanted the name and telephone number of the person making the suggestion so that they could follow up and gather more information."

Example: Hapwell Truss and Door Company makes wooden trusses that are used to build houses and small commercial buildings. The trusses are manufactured and trucked to the building site. "We conducted a telephone survey and found that our customers weren't very happy. We assumed it was the quality or price of the trusses. However, it had nothing to do with either issue. They wanted the trusses delivered at a specific time ... not the day before or the day after. By merely reorganizing our trucking group we were able to satisfy the customer's need."

CASE 15.5

VALPARAISO CHEMICALS

"Organizational efficiency has always been our biggest problem," Max Welbourne explained. "We manufacture four different raw materials: polystyrene, polyethylene, polypropylene, and polyvinyl chloride. Each of these materials has its own distinct properties and they are sold to different customers who convert them into their end products."

"Initially we sold only polystyrene. However, as we added other products, we set up separate divisions. So, by 1995, we had four divisions each with its own personnel. The customers began to complain. The purchasing agents complained that we had four sales people in their offices at one time. And the plant manager complained that they had to call four different departments to get an answer to their questions."

"In 1998, we combined the four divisions into four regional groups. Now, the sales people sold all four products (which made the purchasing agents happy) and the plant manager now had just the one regional number to call. Also, unhappy were the engineers. They had liked working with specialists and now our people were generalists. They knew a lot about one or two of the plastics but not all four. We tried a training program but that didn't seem to solve the problem."

"Then, in 2000, we reorganized again. We organized within the region by customer. Our Class A customers had their own team of experts. The Class B customers could contact one of two people. And the Class C customers were serviced by the one generalist. The people who weren't happy about this arrangement were our people. In order to make this arrangement work, we had to shift them around and that meant they were no longer dealing with the same clients."

"Now, we are seriously considering a further reorganization although I don't know what arrangement we will come up with this time."

Question: Why has Valparaiso Chemicals gone through so many organizational changes? What is the company trying to achieve?

Question: What are the disadvantages associated with changing the organization many times within a relatively short time period?

Question: A consultant has suggested that the company conduct a survey of its customers to determine exactly what they want? Do you see this as a good or bad idea?

SUMMARY

1. In addition to financial controls, a manager needs to control two other aspects of the business, namely: production and human resources.

2. There are two key elements to the production control function:

   - Quantity ... the number of units produced during a specific period of time.

   - Quality ... the percentage of these units that meet or surpass the specifications required by the customer.

3. While the quantity produced is always a critically important factor, quality has become increasingly important in recent years.

4. Production can be controlled at three distinct points in time:

   - Preventive or feedforward control ... control implemented before the process occurs.

   - Concurrent control ... control implemented during the process.

   - Feedback control ... control implemented following the completion of the process.

5. The earlier one can implement control the better. It is far more cost effective to prevent a problem from arising than having to control it during the process. And both these are better than attempting to apply control methods after the process is complete.

6. Total Quality Management (TQM) is an important concept which emphasizes the continuous improvement in all areas of the company's operations with the goal of maximizing the customer's satisfaction.

7. For a TQM program to be effective, it must have:

   - Top management commitment.

   - Employee involvement.

   - Optimal materials.

   - Utilization of cutting edge technologies.

   - Continuous improvement in the methods used by the organization.

8. There are also two elements to the human resource control function, namely:

   - Personnel.

   - Organizational effectiveness.

9. "Control" as applied to people has a somewhat different application. It involves determining whether or not the human resources are being applied as effectively as possible. This can be achieved by:

   - Observation ... seeing how employees are performing their roles.

   - Performance appraisal ... the evaluation of the individual's performance against standard or measure deemed critical for that position.

10. Organizational effectiveness is another key aspect of control which involves determining how effectively the organization is structured to meet the needs of its customers—both internal and external.

CRITICAL THINKING QUESTIONS

1. A machine produces 1,000 parts per hour and the quality is perfectly satisfactory. Yet, when the rate of production is increased to 1,500 parts per hour, the quality starts to decline. More and more of the units are defective. Why would the quality of a product decrease with the speed of production?

   _____

   _____

   _____

   _____

2. Once a month, Curtin Industries ran off the same order for Pace Assembly: 10,000 parts. It was an ongoing contract. So, when Mitch Fernald (who was in a very good mood) picked up the phone he found himself talking to Jim Ebersole of Pace, who was in a thoroughly foul mood. "We are having problems with batch 23-75. My engineer estimates that twenty-five out of every hundred parts are defective. Our entire production line is down while we decide what to do. So, I suggest you find out what is wrong at your end." Mitch was mystified. Over the past five years, no lot had ever had a defective rate of more than two per thousand. What could be causing this unexpected problem? And what should Mitch do about it?

   _____

   _____

   _____

   _____

3. Truax Raingear was founded in the 1870s to manufacture functional raingear for fishermen, firemen, etc. As of 2002, the company was still run by a family member, Jim Truax, although the company's shares were publicly listed on the New York Stock Exchange. Manufacturing was still conducted at more than a dozen plants across the United States. On a recent trip to the Far East, Jim had met with two Chinese companies that offered to deliver better quality products at essentially the same price. Jim is just about to go into a meeting with a task force (consisting of representatives from all areas and levels of the company) looking into the question of the company's long-term competitiveness. To-date, Truax has chosen not to follow the path adopted by many of its competitors, namely: closing domestic plants and outsourcing production overseas. How should Jim present this Chinese offer to the task force?

   _____

   _____

   _____

   _____

4. In late 1999, Hairston Industries decided to implement a program aimed at obtaining ISO 9000 certification. The president was very enthusiastic and he appointed Mark Overmeyer to take charge of the program. As a first step, Mark conducted a value-added analysis and launched a detailed benchmarking analysis of competitive products. After nine months of work, he sat down with the president. "This is a fine piece of work, Mark," the president observed. However, the board and I have decided that this really isn't the time to move ahead with ISO 9000 certification." What went wrong here? After all, the program had the support of the president.

_____

_____

_____

_____

5. A search of the internet indicates that there are a number of disadvantages of ISO certification. As a consultant in the field observed, "It is costly to obtain and maintain, it takes quite a lengthy time to obtain certification, and it is difficult to implement. And there is no question that it results in much more paperwork. Also, many organizations are resistant to change and it is hard to maintain enthusiasm." In fact, a number of companies have gone through all the steps necessary for obtaining ISO certification and then, after a number of years, have dropped the certification. Under what circumstances do you think it would be worthwhile for a firm to invest in ISO 9000 certification?

_____

_____

_____

_____

6. "One of the things I'd like to see us do this year at this hospital is to expand the performance appraisal program. It has worked reasonably well for the doctors (where the hospital had extensive data on the number of patients, operation success rates, test and prescription records, etc.) and I'd like to include the research personnel (a group of fifteen Ph.D.s who were conducting research into ways of slowing down the growth of Alzheimer's) and the more than one hundred and twenty members of the nursing staff. How easy do you think it will be to extend the performance appraisal to the research and nursing personnel? What measurements would you use?

_____

_____

_____

_____

7. Many management "experts" believe that "organization follows strategy." They would say, "Tell me what your goals and objectives are for the organization and I will tell you how it should be structured." Does this statement make sense? Can you think of examples where it would clearly be untrue?

_____

_____

_____

_____

CASE
PROBLEM

A FUNDAMENTAL DIFFERENCE OF OPINION

Marius Gronholm had been the president and chief executive officer of the Gronholm Group for many years. However, at the age of seventy, he decided to move up to chairman and allow somebody else to handle the day-to-day operations. After discussions with the senior management team, Marius decided to conduct an external search for a suitable candidate which led to the hiring of Viktor Bannin.

However, it wasn't long before conflicts arose between Mr. Bannin and Marius Gronholm. In terms of strategy, they were in agreement. It was when it came to the controlling of the organization that they had very different approaches.

"I have always relied on my people," Mr. Gronholm commented. "You set up an organization, hire the best people you can find, and then let them function. I look at the broad picture and let my employees handle the details. I don't think it makes sense to try to micromanage the details."

Micro-managing seemed to be the primary approach that Mr. Bannin had adopted to run the company. "I need to know what is going on in the company," he explained. "I found this company to be very sloppy. Go down into the plant and there are no written policies or procedures, no quality standards, no quality records, etc. It is all in the heads of the people themselves. Immediately after I arrived, I started pushing for ISO certification. At my last company (Azkar Industries), it was the cornerstone of how we did business. Here I have met with resistance to the idea at all levels of the organization."

"Also, at Azkar, we had a standardized personnel performance evaluation system that was implemented every six months. If you failed to make the grade twice in a row, you were fired. Every year, the management team spent three days reviewing the performance of each division. We conducted an organizational audit, went through the financial data line by line, and discussed every one of the personnel evaluations. Here, performance appraisals are left up to the managers ... some do them and others don't. And the annual review is a joke. We meet down at the local country club and play golf."

Question: Put yourself in Marius Gronholm's shoes. What would you do? Would you fire Mr. Bannin? Or would you see Mr. Bannin as the type of manager that the Gronholm Group needs to compete in the modern world?

_____

_____

_____

_____

Question: *Would your evaluation of this situation be any different if the case had stated that the Gronholm Group (a) was extremely successful and profitable or (b) had been losing money and market share for the past three years?*

_____

_____

_____

_____

Question: *Is there a middle ground between the perspectives of Marius Gronholm and Viktor Bannin? If so, what would it look like?*

_____

_____

_____

_____

SOME FINAL THOUGHTS

OVERVIEW

The extent to which material is covered in a typical Introduction to Management course is largely a function of two factors:

- How often classes are canceled due to inclement weather and other acts of nature.
- The speed with which the instructor plows on through the chapters.

Invariably, the final chapter covered by the instructor is of the same "value" as those that preceded it (i.e., it introduces new material). At best, the instructor devotes a class to attempting to review the mass of material in those chapters that have been covered. With luck, the instructor has reached Chapter 12 (out of 18 or 20) before time elapses.

My goal in this chapter is to summarize the key points or insights of the previous fifteen chapters . . . and provide a sense of direction as to where this introductory material (the building blocks) takes a student in terms of subsequent upper level courses.

TWENTY KEY INSIGHTS

1. A manager is:

An individual who is responsible for the performance of the employees who report directly to him/her.

Associated with the title or position of being a manager (or a supervisor) go the responsibilities for the activities (and successes) of others. As a subordinate, your tasks are generally identified for you . . . and you are responsible for completing that specific task to the best of your ability.

What makes the role of manager so difficult, so challenging, and so interesting is that you have to rely, in large part, on others for your success . . . and, as we all know too well, people don't necessarily do what we want them to do or do it as well as we would like them to do.

A manager can be compared to a conductor of an orchestra. As a manager, you are responsible for ensuring that each element of the orchestra works together effectively. The violins, the clarinets, the trumpets, and the tympani have to be in tune and in concert. If they aren't then the conductor has to make changes. The same is true of a manager.

2. To be a successful manager, you need to appreciate that the role consists of four different, yet inter-related, functions, and that you need to be able to:

> *Plan ... determining the future direction and goals of the organization.*
>
> *Organize ... utilizing personnel (human resources) in the most effective manner.*
>
> *Lead ... motivating and inspiring the personnel to achieve the organizational goals, and*
>
> *Control ... monitoring the performance of the organization and, when appropriate, implementing changes.*

The importance of each of these functions will vary depending on the situation in which the organization (and, by this, I mean any unit ranging from the entity as a whole to a division, department, or group) finds itself.

Planning may be critically important when the organization is experiencing strong competitive pressures or serious financial problems. Organizing may become the most important function when starting a new business or responding to changes in the marketplace. Leading can be the critically important function when the organization is experiencing serious problems and morale is low. Finally, controlling can become the number one function when a specific project is in trouble or the organization's performance is way below the level expected.

3. How can an individual perform these four functions effectively? They can do so by developing the following skills, namely:

> *Technical ... the ability to do a specific task well.*
>
> *Interpersonal ... an individual's ability to communicate and work with other people and develop an effective team.*
>
> *Conceptual ... the ability to see the organization as a whole and visualize its future.*
>
> *Diagnostic ... an individual's ability to look at a problem and develop a solution, and*
>
> *Political ... the ability to pull together allies and supporters to achieve the organization's goals.*

Not all managers are skilled in all areas. In fact, most have their strengths and their weaknesses. The important point is, therefore, that you need to recognize the areas in which you are weak and either obtain training to improve your performance or work closely with somebody who has the skills you lack.

4. Contingency. This is a key word for the modern manager. It means that the individual recognizes that:

> *No book exists that will give the right answer. The successful manager must base his/her actions on the unique characteristics of the situation.*

Management would be relatively easy if there were a book that said, when faced with the following situation, you should do x, y and z. The reality is that all situations have unique characteristics that need to be taken into consideration.

5. A manager does not operate in a vacuum ... or in an external world that they control. They have to deal with five main general or macro environments, namely:

> ■ *Economic ... the general economy that influences the overall demand for products and services.*
>
> ■ *Social-cultural ... the characteristics of the population and the influence of these factors on the marketplace.*
>
> ■ *Political and legal ... the laws and regulations passed by government designed to promote and protect the well-being of society*
>
> ■ *Technological ... the output of research and development activities that are introduced to the marketplace as new products and improvements.*
>
>   *and*
>
> ■ *International ... the unique features or characteristics encountered in overseas markets.*

Even a senior manager of a very large organization has virtually no ability to directly influence the economic or socio-cultural aspects of the United States ... or, for that matter, the economic or socio-cultural characteristics of other countries (the international environment). They can (and must), however, respond to them.

Large organizations can certainly lobby for legislation favorable to them but their influence is legally limited to this lobbying activity. And the forces of technology are so widely spread that a large organization's influence is limited to its internal R&D and the acquisition of technology from external developers.

6. The operating or micro environment. This is the immediate environment in which the organization operates on a day-to-day basis and consists of:

> *Competitors.*
>
> *Customers.*
>
> *Suppliers*
>
> *and*
>
> *Labor.*

Can a manager control his competitors? Not to any great extent. They are separate organizations following their own game plan. A manager can, and often has to, react to his/her competitors. However, if the competitor decides to introduce a new product, reduce prices, conduct an advertising campaign, open a new office, etc., there is nothing a manager can do other than watch ... and then determine how to respond.

Customers can be controlled to the degree that it is in their best interest to be "controlled." They respond to opportunities that a supplier provides. They may adopt a new product, accept a long term deal, and enter into an alliance, etc. if they believe it is in their best interest.

A manager has rather greater control over his/her suppliers since it is their decision as to whether to use one supplier or another. Finally, as far as labor is concerned, a manager can control whom he/she hires ... and thus is generally in control. However, since a manager's financial resources are often limited, he/she may not be able to obtain the quantity and quality of labor that they need.

7. The internal environment consists of the divisions, departments, and groups within the organization which include:

> *Planning.*
>
> *Marketing.*
>
> *R&D.*
>
> *Finance.*
>
> *Sales.*
>
> *Engineering.*
>
> *Manufacturing, etc.*

Overall, this is an environment that a manager (such as the president of the organization) can control. He/she can determine the direction of the organization and thus its needs and requirements. A middle level manager (responsible for one of these divisions, departments, or groups) has a large degree of control but only over his/her specific area of the company.

8. One of the key areas that a modern manager has to focus on is technology ... specifically the different:

> *Ways of doing business.*
>
> *Means of communicating.*
>
> *Ways of collecting and analyzing data*
>
> *and*
>
> *Means of accessing information.*

The problem facing a manager today is that technology is changing so rapidly. As a result, virtually anything one writes on any of these subjects is very soon out-of-date.

What does this mean with respect to being a successful manager? It means that the manager has to be:

> *Aware of trends in those technologies relevant to his organization*
>
> *and*
>
> *Open to new ideas ... always willing to explore new ways of conducting business.*

This doesn't mean that the manager has to adopt every new idea that crosses his/her desk ... but they need to look at the pros and cons of adopting the approach.

9. The modern manager has to function in a very diverse and complex world and thus, to be successful, he/she has to be attuned to the cultural and demographic factors reflected around them. Specifically, they have to be aware of the:

- *Impact of diversity.*
- *Legal environment surrounding issues of diversity.*
- *Responsibilities of a manager to deal with issues that arise from diversity.*
- *Importance of diversity training.*

In recent years, society (especially in the United States) has become much more concerned about the rights of different types of groups and types of individuals ... aided, in many cases, by legislation enacted at the federal and state levels.

10. As indicated in Chapter 5, ethics are:

The rules or principles that define whether conduct is deemed right or wrong.

Each individual develops their own set of rules or principles depending on their:

- *Values (from parents, siblings, and peers).*
- *Personality.*
- *Life experiences, etc.*

But what are the ethics of a successful manager? In recent years, a number of senior executives have stepped over the ethical (and legal) line and have paid a substantial price (in terms of jail time, peer respect, etc.) as a result. As a general rule, a manager needs to ask themself whether or not a specific action is ethical and, if there is any question in their mind, step back from that action.

A successful manager, however, goes even further in that they take responsibility for the ethics of the organization for which they work. They take action to ensure that their peers and subordinates act in a manner that they deem ethical.

11. Social responsibility. While not everybody agrees that an organization has a responsibility to society (other than to maximize its profits), there is a school of thought that argues that, because a manager is part of society and enjoys the benefits of society, he/she has a responsibility to that society. Thus, social responsibility is defined as:

The responsibility of an organization to take action to protect, and even promote, the welfare of the society in which it functions.

Society is a very broad term. In reality, every manager interacts with a number of different "stakeholders" (i.e., organizations, groups and individuals) often with very different interests and goals. In evaluating the "social responsibility" of an action, a manager needs to consider the likely impact of that action on the various parties that will be impacted by it.

12. Planning ... the first of the four functions of a manager and, as an individual moves up an organization, he/she usually spends an increasing amount of time on this activity. The elements of a business plan are the:

Vision or mission of the organization ... what are its ultimate goals?

Baseline study ... where does the organization currently stand (in terms of its strengths, weaknesses, opportunities, and threats—the SWOT analysis).

Overall strategies ... the broad approaches that the organization will take to achieve its goals and objectives.

Action plan ... who is going to do what and when ... and what resources are needed?

Monitor ... who is assigned the responsibility for ensuring that action is taken according to the schedule?

Supporters of planning argue that it:

Forces the organization to focus on its future directions.

Emphasizes priorities and thus the allocation of resources.

Provides an opportunity for all employees to be involved in the organization's future.

Leads to the development of operational plans.

Those who argue against planning state that it:

Can be very time-consuming.

Can frustrate employees with reports and meetings.

Emphasizes planning rather than the implementation of the actions.

Can sit on the shelves for much of the year ... essentially unused.

Isn't used by the organization to review actual progress against the plan.

Can result in a false sense of security.

13. One of the key elements of both planning and operations is decision-making. Invariably, managers are faced with the need to make decisions—either individually or as a member of a team. Only very rarely do they have perfect information (i.e., all the accurate information they need) and an infinite time frame in which to make the decision. In most cases, decisions are made with limited (or often inaccurate) information when faced with a deadline.

The key steps in decision-making are:

- *Determine the nature of the problem or the focus of the decision.*

- *Identify the alternative solutions.*

- *Evaluate the pros and cons of the alternative solutions.*

- *Make and implement the decision*

  and

- *Review the effectiveness of the decision.*

There are a large number of tools and techniques used to assist in decision making. Some of the more basic that a student should be able to understand and use are:

> *Forecasting (based on historical data).*
>
> *Gantt charts.*
>
> *PERT/CPM charts*
>
> *and*
>
> *Break-even analysis.*

14. Organizing … the second of the key functions of a manager. Again, this is a function that increases with importance as the manager moves up the organization. It primarily consists of:

> *Deciding how the human resources of the organization can be most effectively deployed.*

Three important elements of organizing are:

> *Developing an organizational plan … the steps taken to ensure that the organizational structure is consistent with its goals and objectives.*
>
> *Span of control … the number of individuals that a manager can direct and control*
>
> *and*
>
> *Chain of command … consisting of the unity of command (i.e., the concept that a person should report to just one boss) and the line authority (running clearly from the president down to the lowest employee).*

However, equally important, are the main organizational types, namely the:

> *Basic organizational structures ... functional (i.e., organized by function), product (i.e., organized by product), geographic (i.e., organized geographically), or by customer (i.e., according to the size and needs of the customer).*
>
> *Matrix organization ... where one individual reports to two or more superiors with different responsibilities (such as to a regional sales manager and a product manager)*
>
> *and*
>
> *Virtual organization ... where most, if not all, functions are outsourced to other organizations.*

15. All organizations consist of people. Hiring and training people is, therefore, one of the most important functions of a manager. The opportunity to hire an individual represents a chance to both add new skills and resources to the organization and reinforce the strengths that it already has. However, rarely are there unlimited funds ... and thus the critical steps in his process are:

> *The development of a personnel plan.*
>
> *Understanding the legal aspects of staffing.*

The hiring process itself consists of the following eleven steps:

> - *Identifying the position to be filled.*
> - *Reviewing and updating the job analysis.*
> - *Preparing a job description.*
> - *Deciding whether or not to post the job opening internally.*
> - *Deciding whether or not to use an external search firm.*
>
> - *Advertising and promoting the position.*
> - *Reviewing the applicants' resumes.*
> - *Interviewing the better candidates.*
> - *The use of testing.*
> - *Deciding which candidate to offer the position.*
>
> - *Negotiating with the selected candidate.*

Ideally, the selected candidate then enjoys:

> *An orientation program ... giving them an understanding of the organization, the key personnel, and the way it functions.*
>
> *Training and development ... to maximize the individual's performance.*

16. Leadership ... the third of the four important managerial functions. As indicated in Chapter 10, leadership can be defined in many ways. However, one of the simpler definitions is:

> *Making things happen in an organization.*

A manager is the captain of a team and, irrespective of how good the individual players are, they need somebody to motivate, guide, and direct them. The successful manager is also somebody who can provide leadership.

> *Not all managers are leaders and not all leaders are managers. And, unfortunately, some are neither!!*

Identifying which person is a leader and which is not is (or would be) a very valuable ability. As a result, much research has gone into this area. Basically, the research has focused on:

> *The characteristics (or traits) of successful managers ... factors such as drive, enthusiasm, honesty, intelligence, etc.*
>
> *The behavior of successful managers ... what they do.*
>
> *The impact of the situation on the leadership needs, and*
>
> *Different types of leadership ... charismatic, transformational, strategic, cross-cultural, and ethical leadership ... which are appropriate to organizations faced with different challenges.*

17. Motivation is defined as:

> *The inner drive that results in an individual exerting maximum effort to achieve a specific goal or objective.*

Again, this is an area in which there has been a lot of research. Why? Because it would be extremely valuable to be able to identify ways of motivating ones employees.

The definition suggests that it is the "inner drive" that is critical ... and there is a school of thought that argues that the only person who can motivate someone is themselves. However, it is generally agreed that there is a definite connection between:

> *Motivation and performance.*
>
> *Expectations and behavior.*

Furthermore, there are a number of techniques which can help motivate people, namely:

> *Identification and satisfaction of the person's needs.*
>
> *Goal setting.*
>
> *Rewarding superior performance.*

18. The ability to communicate is an important managerial skill. It doesn't matter how brilliant a manager is if he/she cannot effectively communicate their ideas, plans, and recommendations.

In any communication, there are seven key elements:

- *The sender.*

- *The encoding process ... during which the sender converts (or encodes) their message into a format which facilitates transmission.*

- *The medium ... the sender then has to identify a medium through which the message can be communicated.*

- *The decoding process ... during which the recipient translates (or decodes) the message.*

- *The receiver.*

- *The feedback ... the mechanism by which the receiver of the message communicates their understanding of the message back to the sender.*

- *Noise ... a variety of factors (ranging from the noise caused by a jackhammer to the rumbling of the recipient's stomach) which can interfere with the way in which the message is decoded.*

Among the numerous media which facilitate the communications process are:

Face-to-face discussions ... very rich in content and allows for immediate responses.

Video-conference ... not quite so rich in content but does allow for an immediate response.

Telephone conversations ... limited richness of content but still allows for an immediate response.

E-mail and instant messaging ... very quick but limited in content and open to misinterpretation.

Letter ... slow but potentially rich in detail.

Fax ... quicker than a letter but normally containing limited detail.

Telegram ... quick but with very limited detail.

Newspaper, magazine or billboard ... slow and limited to a general audience.

Finally, it is important to note that a very large percentage of the information transferred from the sender to the receiver is non-verbal consisting of:

Gestures.

Body language.

Facial expressions.

Vocal tones.

19. Teams and teamwork have become extremely important in terms of management of modern business organizations and successful managers are those that are able to effectively manage them. A team is:

> *A group consisting of members who have similar or complementary skills and competencies who work together to achieve a common goal or objective.*

Emphasis has been placed on the use of teams for five basic reasons:

> *Downsizing ... the reduction in the number of people and the elimination of management levels in order to become more competitive.*
>
> *Growth of technology ... enabling people much easier access to data and information irrespective of their location.*
>
> *Complexity of the environment ... in order to handle the complexity, organizations need to bring together people with different knowledge and abilities ...*
>
> *The diversity of the workforce ... and the requirement that people of different backgrounds and experience be able to work together.*
>
> *A growing belief in the value of teams and teamwork ... a growing appreciation that this is the way to get things done.*

Conceptually, teams go through a series of stages:

> *Forming ... the initial interactions and indication of expectations.*
>
> *Storming ... the stage where friction may occur as team members express their own personal views and opinions.*
>
> *Norming ... the team settles down and begins to agree on the rules and procedure that it will adopt.*
>
> *Performing ... the actual performance of the task.*
>
> *Adjourning ... the team has completed the task assigned and now breaks up to move on to other activities.*

Successful teams are those that have:

> *The right size of the team.*
>
> *The appropriate mix of the personnel.*
>
> *Organizational support for the team's efforts.*
>
> *A belief in the value of the team's activities.*
>
> *A feeling of empowerment.*
>
> *Interdependence among the members of the team.*

Finally, it is important to note that there are numerous different types of teams—each with their own sses and characteristics:

> *Formal organizational groups.*
>
> *Top management teams.*
>
> *Self-managed work teams.*
>
> *Project teams.*
>
> *Cross-functional teams.*
>
> *Virtual teams.*

20. Control is the fourth (and final) critical function of a manager. It is the integrating function that pulls together the organization's planning, organizing, and leading. Controlling is:

> *The comparison of actual performance to predetermined goals and objectives to see whether the organization is on track and whether changes need to be made.*

Without this control function, organizations cannot take corrective action. There are a wide range of control mechanisms covering:

> *Finance.*
>
> *Production.*
>
> *Human resources (personnel).*

In the finance area, some of the key measurements are:

> *Liquidity ratios ... these focus on how solvent the company is in the short-term (i.e., how able it is to pay its bills).*
>
> *Leverage ratio ... the ratio between the equity that the founders put into the company (equity) and the amount of money they have borrowed (debt).*
>
> *Profitability ratios ... how profitable is the company (i.e., how effectively is it using its assets).*
>
> *Activity ratio ... the turnover of inventory or the efficiency of inventory management.*

And it is important to understand the difference between:

> *Profitability (i.e., the difference between revenue and expenses).*
>
> *Cash flow (i.e., the actual inflow and outflow of funds).*

In the production area, the two key controls are:

> *Quantity ... the number of units produced within a specific period of time.*
>
> *Quality ... the extent to which the units meet pre-determined standards or quality requirements.*

Quality has become a key driving force in business today and it is important to recognize the impact of the Total Quality Management (TQM) movement and the establishment of the ISO standards.

Finally, in the human resource areas, there are two main areas of measurement, namely the determination of the:

> *Productivity and performance of individuals ... as determined by performance appraisals.*
>
> *Effectiveness of the organization as a whole ... utilizing an organizational audit.*

WHERE NEXT?

If you are majoring in a subject other than business ... this is it. Hopefully, however, this broad sweep across the surface of the subject has motivated you to continue to explore your options in this area. It is a fascinating and ever-changing field.

For those of you who are majoring in business, this course has done nothing more than merely touch the surface of the subject. It is like taking a very small taste from dozens of brightly colored dishes. You need to know and appreciate what is in this text because it will provide you with a sense of how the various elements hang together and where more in-depth analysis can be applied.

Each of the four functions of a manager (planning, organizing, leading and controlling) lend themselves to higher level courses where one can dig into specific models and processes. Extensive research has been conducted in each of these fields ... as it has in the intricacies of motivation, teamwork, communications, the use of technology, etc. The range is almost limitless and, hopefully, you can identify courses that focus in greater depth on your areas of interest.

In this text, I have merely introduced some of the basics ideas. The path ahead is an exciting one with growing complexity in a dynamic and changing world.

William E. Matthews